San Diego Architecture

From missions to modern:
a guide to the buildings,
planning, people and spaces
that shape the region

Dirk Sutro, Author

Graphic Design,
Marc Hawkins, viadesign

Published by
San Diego Architectural Foundation
Alison Whitelaw, AIA President

San Diego Chapter
American Institute of Architects
Guidebook Project

Jack Carpenter, FAIA Chair

Neil Larson, AIA Photography Chair

Alison Whitelaw AIA/Gordon Carrier AIA,
Fund Raising Chairs

Robert Noble, AIA Printing and
Publishing Chair

Diane Kane, historian and instructor,
and her students, Newschool of Architecture

Kevin Carpenter, Mapping Chair

Reed Morgan, San Diego AIA Chapter
Executive Officer, Administrative Coordinator

San Diego Chapter
American Institute of Architects,
Michael Stepner, FAIA President

Library of Congress Control Number: 2002115965
ISBN 0-9726020-0-3
Printed and bound in the United States

San Diego

If you are among those who haven't been in San Diego since "the war years," or whose only impressions are what you read in the national press—you are in for some surprises. San Diego is not a "sleepy Navy town" anymore. Several post-war booms have built a colorful modern city with a uniquely region-al flavor. Over the years our best architects have quietly designed some of the most interesting build-ings anywhere, often overlooked by the national media. In barely more than 100 years, we've moved from missions to Irving Gill's primal modernism, to the Balboa Park-inspired Spanish Romance Years,

Irving Gill

followed by decades of fine post-WW II mod-ernism that began with Lloyd Ruocco. Most recently, newer generations led by architects like Rob Wellington Quigley, Ted Smith, Marc Steele, Wallace Cunningham, and Public are redefining notions of regional architecture that began here with Gill.

San Diego hasn't had an official architectural guidebook since 1977. Over the past 25 years the region has come of age: its population exceeds 3 million, plus another 1.3 million in Tijuana. All told, the combined border population is expected to reach 5.7 million by 2010, 7.7 mil-lion by 2020. That constitutes a metropolis by any measure.

One of the more perplexing and engaging pas-times known to man is the analysis, documenta-tion, and interpretation of a place's beginnings, its growth patterns, the look and feel of its neigh-borhoods, public spaces, buildings, and individual works of art. Behind the look and feel of any city or region are the men and women who had a hand in shaping it. This new guidebook morphed to its current size because we decided to present not only the story of our architecture and our buildings, but some of the important stories, institutions, plans, political forces, and people behind those designs. We hope this book is as well planned, designed, and executed as a good building.

Irving Gill's arrival in 1893 marked the beginning of the modern era in San Diego. Gill came from the office of pioneering Chicago modernist Louis Sullivan, where he had worked alongside another young architect named Frank Lloyd Wright. Gill brought a bit of Sullivan west with him. In downtown San Diego, Gill's Pickwick Theatre resembled Sullivan's Transportation Building for the 1893 World's Fair in Chicago. Gill also brought a curiosity that kept him seeking new designs and construction methods.

House by Gill

Ultimately Gill added an ingredient that defined San Diego's best architecture: he took his design cues from the region, not from distant sources. In 1906 and 1907, Gill invented an original regional style. Re-visioning the stark white walls and rhythmic arches of the San Diego mission into a modern approach, Gill designed buildings in harmony with the hot, dry landscape.

In 1916, he published his landmark article in the Craftsman magazine, titled The Home of the Future: The New Architecture of the West.

"If we, the architects of the West, wish to do great and lasting work we must dare to be simple, must have the courage to fling aside every device that distracts the eye from structural beauty, must eak through convention and get down to fundamental truths," Gill wrote. "To eak away from this degradation we must boldly throw aside every accepted structural belief and standard of beauty and get back to the source of all architectural strength—the straight line, the arch, the cube and the circle."

Balboa Park

Gill's prime in San Diego lasted until 1915 and was followed by 30 years of revival styles, beginning with the most romantic revival of all: Bertram Goodhue's

House by Requa

buildings for the 1915 Panama-California Expo in Balboa Park. Gill had been the local favorite for the job. The park—and perhaps the city—would have looked much different had Gill proceeded with his scheme of stark white buildings. Instead San Diegans embarked on a romance with Spanish and Mediterranean revival styles that continues today. Richard Requa and William Templeton Johnson were among architects who designed important buildings in traditional styles, before the re-emergence of modernism after the war.

Apprenticed as a draftsman to Requa, Lloyd Ruocco led San Diego's post-WW II modernist movement. Ruocco's proteges, led by Homer Delawie, produced some of California's finest modern buildings of the 1950s and 1960s. Deems/Lewis, Leonard Voitzer, Tucker-Sadler, and many others carried modernism into the 1960s and 1970s, designing everything from high-rises and steel-frame glass-skinned buildings, to post-Case Study houses.

Inspired by their home region, but in different ways than Gill, a group of young architects in the late 1970s took a new direction. Rob Quigley, Ted Smith, PAPA, and Tom Grondona liked to say that they found inspiration in their own "backyard". They borrowed forms and materials from a building's immediate context, and collaged them together in a style one writer labeled "blendo".

San Diego grew into one of the nation's largest cities in the decades after WW II, with all of the accompanying challenges. Downtown redevelopment began with the creation of Centre City Development Corp. in the mid-1970s. By the mid-1980s, Horton Plaza Shopping Center had opened as the centerpiece of a revitalized downtown, and several new residential projects had been built. Today the redevelopment effort extends into Little Italy and East Village, where a new baseball park designed by Antoine Predock will be the centerpiece.

Over the years, many "vision" plans have been written for the region by respected planners. John Nolen recognized San Diego's natural assets in his regional master plan of 1908, revised in 1926. Among the assets that should be protected, Nolen said, were San Diego's valleys, canyons, mesas; coastline and desert; Mission Valley, and the far reaches of north, south, and east county, where some development had already begun. Nolen seconded Balboa Park as permanent urban open space, connected to the

Horton Plaza

waterfront by a civic mall along Cedar Street (the County Administration Center was the only building realized).

County Administration Building

By the time planners Kevin Lynch and Donald Appleyard re-assessed the region in their 1974 study "Temporary Paradise?," San Diego had added one new "natural" asset: Mission Bay and surrounding tidelands—a manmade recreational mecca, created under the supervision of William Rick and a team of planners, that became home to Sea World amusement park, as well as aquatic diversions and leisure pursuits.

Freeways were added and traffic increased with the population. A new era in regional transit arrived in 1982 with the opening of the first leg of the San Diego Trolley. Expansion continues today, with plans in motion for a new North County line between Oceanside and Escondido.

In recent years San Diego architects have earned national recognition for their solutions to difficult urban problems—especially the design of low-cost housing such as Rob Quigley's single-room-occupancy hotels downtown, and small courtyard apartments by Davids/Killory and Studio E in Escondido.

Single-room occupancy hotel by Quigley

While San Diego has been slow to replace outdated public buildings such as its city hall and main library (although it built outstanding new branch libraries), outlying cities have moved forward. Escondido, Oceanside, and San Marcos developed new civic centers.

If hope for the future resides in a region's spiritual resolve, San Diego has reason to be optimistic. Some of the region's finest newer buildings are sacred: Charles Moore's Church of the Nativity in Fairbanks Ranch, Hyndman and Hyndman's St. Gregory the Great Catholic Church in Scripps Ranch, and Dominy and Associates' St. Elizabeth Seton Church in Carlsbad.

Through decades of growth pains, the San Diego region has done more things right than wrong. Planners and architects come from all over the world to admire a downtown alive with a mix of new buildings and permanent residents, a beach-front that remains accessible, uncommercialized, and relatively uncrowded, and an urban park rivaled only by that other park in a place they call the Big Apple.

But you're Out West now. So. Go through this book page by page, front to back. Or flip through at random. Find whatever catches your eye. Get out there for a look. Welcome, and we think you'll be impressed with this place we fell in love with a long time ago.

Major Milestones in San Diego Architectural History

Mission Colonial Period 1769-1848

Establishment of New Town 1867

Panama California Exposition 1915

World War I 1917

California Pacific International Exposition 1935

World War II 1939-1945

Growth of the Aerospace industry 1945- 1990

Establishment of University of San Diego 1954, University of California San Diego 1964, United States International University and Expansion of San Diego State University. 1954-1964

Mission Valley Development 1961

Mission Bay Development 1964

Downtown Redevelopment- Horton Plaza, Marina District, Gaslamp, East Village/Ballpark, Cortez Hill, and Little Italy. 1975-present

Using this guidebook

This book is geared toward anyone who wants to get out and see San Diego's best buildings. We've organized the contents by neighborhood, and told some of each neighborhood's story. Each neighborhood has its own map. Wherever possible, we've clustered essential buildings within walking distance of each other on one map. In many neighborhoods, you can park your car and explore architectural attractions on foot. By using the regional map we've provided, you can figure out how to get where you want to go. San Diego has a renowned mass transit system. You'll find fast, reliable trolley and light-rail service from Oceanside to the border, through Mission Valley, and between downtown and East County. Dozens of bus routes are run by San Diego's MTDB, and by North County Transit District. If you travel by car, consider car pooling. You'll have a clear eco-conscience, and you'll take advantage of uncrowded car pool lanes on many San Diego freeways.

For more information on San Diego and our evolving downtown, contact Centre City Development Corp. (619-235-2200), or visit their downtown information center (225 Broadway, Suite 160).

For tourist information, contact the San Diego Convention and Visitors Bureau (619-236-1212).

Queries about architecture and buildings should be directed to the American Institute of Architects, San Diego chapter (619-232-0109).

For more information on San Diego's history, visit the San Diego Historical Society (619-232-6203) in Balboa Park.

The San Diego Architectural Foundation (publisher of this guidebook) is a tax-exempt non-profit California corporation whose mission is to encourage, inspire and challenge through education the development of excellent architecture in the San Diego region.

Contents

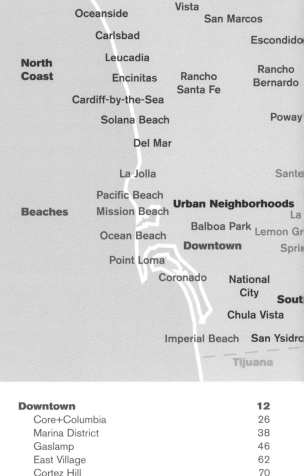

**Inland/
North County**

Oceanside   Vista   San Marcos

Carlsbad   Escondido

Leucadia

**North
Coast**   Encinitas   Rancho
Santa Fe   Rancho
Bernardo

Cardiff-by-the-Sea

Solana Beach   Poway

Del Mar

La Jolla   Sante

Pacific Beach

Beaches   Mission Beach   **Urban Neighborhoods**   La

Balboa Park   Lemon Gr

Ocean Beach   **Downtown**   Sprir

Point Loma

Coronado   National
City

Sout

Chula Vista

Imperial Beach   San Ysidro

Tijuana

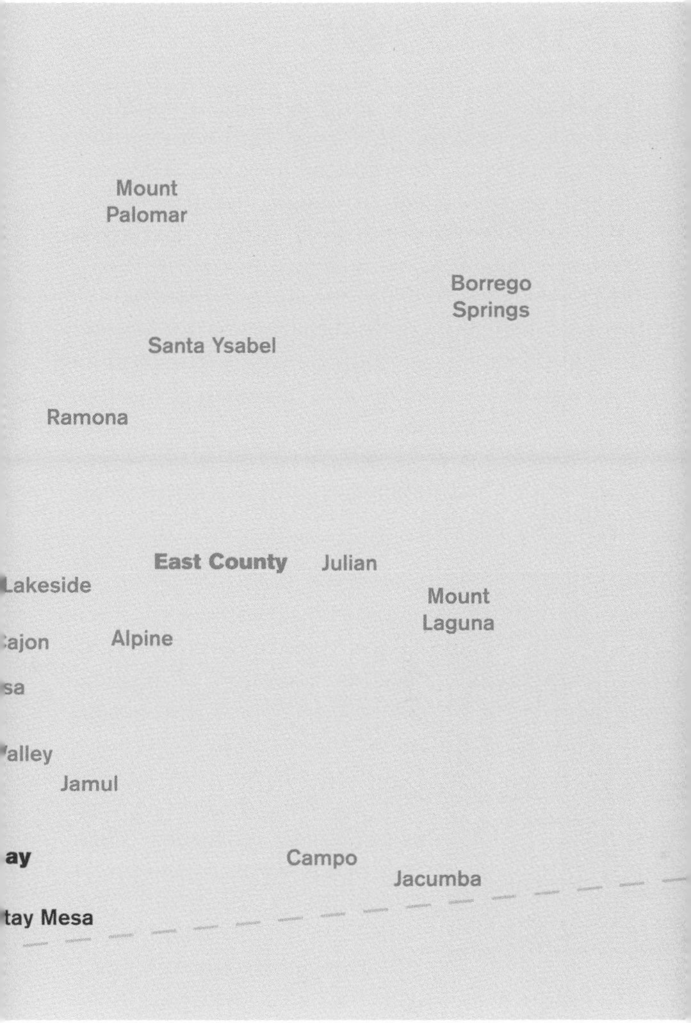

Mount
Palomar

Borrego
Springs

Santa Ysabel

Ramona

East County   Julian

Lakeside

Mount
Laguna

ajon   Alpine

sa

alley
Jamul

ay   Campo

Jacumba

tay Mesa

Downtown

Downtown San Diego at the beginning of the 21st century is coming into its own. The skyline mixes stone-clad Chicago style buildings from the 1920s and 1930s with modern highrises ranging from flat-topped glass boxes from the 1960s to more recent designs with articulated tops. Known mid-century as a military town, the city altered its identity in the 1980s and 1990s. Aircraft carriers became less common and the Naval Training Center closed. Downtown was redeveloped with thousands of new housing units, thousands of square feet of new office space equipped for a new economy built on technology and communications, and public spaces and public art that provide breathing room in an increasingly dense urban center.

Launched in 1975, redevelopment downtown has been largely success-ful, scrutinized as exemplary by politi-cians, developers, and planners from other places. Created to spearhead this effort, Centre City Corp. (CCDC) has been a major force. Other cities envy the delicate blend of old and new: postmodern Horton Plaza next to Victorian Gaslamp Quarter, Mission Revival-style Santa Fe Depot sharing Broadway frontage with a Helmut Jahn high-rise, East Village warehouses next to new urban rowhomes. As an example of urban mass transit, the San Diego Trolley is another success story: soon after it opened in 1982, the red light-rail trains had higher ridership than predicted. They connect downtown with the border, Mission Valley, and East County.

A true urban neighborhood needs permanent residents. Thousands of new homes ranging from affordable rentals to luxurious high-rise condominiums have attracted a downtown population well on its way to redevelopment's target of 50,000 by 2020. Downtown residential develop-ments designed by Rob Wellington Quigley, Jonathan Segal, and others have won international recognition.

The process of planning and approving the new Horton Plaza shopping center gave the first sign that San Diego would have high standards for its redevelopment effort. As originally conceived, the mall was a stock enclosed subur-ban scheme. But before it was approved, CCDC planners had prompted a radical re-design by architect Jon Jerde into a colorful postmodern place bisected diagonally by an multi-tiered open-air promenade modeled on narrow European streets. Jerde's design is much more suited to San Diego's character and climate. In the years since, the architect has become a celebrity for his design of high-profile projects in Las Vegas and Los Angeles, but San

Diego was the first city to take a risk on a new style of retailing that had never been tried before.

Along with Horton Plaza came new high-rise hotels, new office towers, a new water-front convention center with an award-winning design by Canadian architect Arthur Erickson, and revitalization of the Gaslamp Quarter with public improvements and creative re-use of old buildings for new purposes—Italian eateries proved particularly popular. Public art and comfortable public space was also part of the redevelopment

Other cities envy the delicate blend of old and new: postmodern Horton Plaza next to Victorian Gaslamp Quarter, Mission Revival-style Santa Fe Depot sharing Broadway frontage with a Helmut Jahn high-rise, East Village warehouses next to new urban rowhomes.

agenda. In the early years several art pieces were proposed and rejected, but by 20th century's close, many thoughtful pieces had been installed, some of which reflect the region's multi-cultural identity. Perhaps most impressive in the realm of public art was the inclusion of art and artists in the process of creating the Martin Luther King, Jr. Promenade along Harbor Drive. This was an early attempt to make "art" more integral to the built environment, more than just a plopped down steel sculpture.

With the downtown core well on its way as an inviting place to live and work, redevelopment efforts expanded to adjacent neighborhoods during the 1990s. To the north of downtown, Little Italy became a vital mix of residential, retail, and commercial uses, while maintaining and building

on its ethnic history. East Village is destined to become downtown's civic showplace, with plans for a baseball park, a central library, and a new designation as Bandwidth Bay—a place for new buildings equipped with broadband and communications capabilities demanded by technology endeavors. Around the historic El Cortez Hotel, a downtown landmark restored as apartments, a dense residential neighborhood has developed.

Downtown's history began with visionaries such as Alonzo Horton. Before Horton staked his claim in the 1860s, San Diego's center was several miles to the north, in the area known as Old Town, the site of early settlement around the Presidio, and the original site of San Diego's Mission. Down the slope at the edge of the bay, East Coast traders loaded hides onto vessels for shipment back home around the tip of South America. Even then, San Diego was a diverse and wide-open place, a destination for dreamers. Juan Cabrillo sailed into San Diego Bay in 1542. Sixty years later Sebastian Vizcaino named the bay "San Diego". Richard Henry Dana stopped here in the 1830s, during the voyage he documented in his book *Two Years Before the Mast.*

"Everyone was anxious to get a view of the new place," he wrote. "A chain of high hills, beginning at the point (which was on our larboard hand, coming in), protected the harbor on the north and west, and ran off into the interior as far as the eye could reach. On the other sides, the land was low, and green, but without trees. The entrance is so narrow as to admit but one vessel at a time, the current swift, and the channel runs so near to a low stony point that the ship's sides appeared almost to touch it. There was no town in sight, but on the smooth sand beach abreast, and within a cable's length of which three vessels lay moored, were four large houses—built of rough boards and looking like the great barns in which ice is stored on the borders of the large ponds near Boston—with piles of hides standing round them, and men in red shirts and large straw hats walking in and out of the doors…."

Early San Diego looking across the harbor to Point Loma, 1888.

"Our crew fell in with some who belonged to the other vessels and, sailorlike, steered for the first grogshop. This was a small mud building of only one room in which were liquors, dry and West India goods, shoes, bread, fruits, and everything which is vendible in California…. The first place we went to was the old ruinous presidio, which stands on a rising ground near the village, which it over-looks. It is built in the form of an open square, like all the other presidios, and was in a most ruinous state with the exception of one side, in which the commandant lived with his family…The small settlement lay directly below the fort, composed of about forty dark brown-looking huts, or houses, and two larger ones, plastered, which belonged to two of the *gente de razon.* This town is not more than half as large as Monterey or Santa Barbara, and has little or no business."

San Diego's center shifted to its current locale when William Heath Davis and Andrew Gray acquired 160 acres near the waterfront in 1850. They shipped lumber and prefabricated buildings from the East Coast. Remnants of their efforts remain today in the form of Pantoja Park on lower G Street—originally the plaza in what became known as "Davis's Folly".

In 1855, *San Diego Herald* columnist George Horatio Derby took stock of the evolving urb: "The three villages, then, which go to make up the great city of San Diego, are the 'Playa,' 'Old Town,' and 'New Town,' or 'Davis's Folly.'" At the "Playa" there are but few buildings at present, and these not remarkable for size or architectural beauty of design. A long, low, one-storied tenement, near the base of the hills, once occupied by rollicking Captain Magruder and the officers under his command, is now the place where Judge Witherby, like Matthew, patiently "sits at the receipt of customs."

When plans for a transcontinental railroad terminus in San Diego stalled, and epic winter rains in 1861 and 1862 were followed by a drought, Davis and Gray's develop-ment stalled. In 1867 Alonzo Horton bought 800 water-front acres downtown at 33 cents apiece, and two years later added 160 acres for $4,000. He laid out downtown's

grid pattern of streets, with his "Horton's Addition" centered first around Fifth Avenue, later along Broadway near the location marked today by Horton Plaza park and its Irving Gill-designed fountain. Without the alleys typical of other major cities, downtown San Diego as defined by Horton would later be ripe for large redevelopment projects covering whole city blocks.

Horton's real estate ventures boomed with a Gold Rush in Julian east of San Diego between 1870 and 1875. When the transcontinental railroad connected to National City in 1885, "San Diego became real estate mad," according to the Federal Writers' Project book
San Diego: A California City.
"People lived in tents on their lots until they could clear away brush and cactus. More frequently they sold out at fancy prices before they could settle on the land. Buyers bought from maps without inspecting the purchase, and in turn sold to other speculators sight unseen.

"Local people jumped on the bandwagon. Housewives, lawyers, clerks, ministers, maids and businessmen began buying and selling. Some speculators paid as much as $500 for a place in line to buy property. This became the first peak in a real estate rollercoaster ride that first delighted then devastated speculators on at least three occasions between the 1867 birth of the Horton Addition and 1906. Horton counted the greenbacks, then invested in more land or new ventures. He gave lots to the Methodists, Episcopalians, and Baptists for new churches. He donated land to people who pledged to build houses at once. He donated the site for the proposed courthouse. Sometimes he paid his employees with property." By 1869, Horton was grossing $600 to $1,000 per day. Horton House, a grand hotel, once occupied the site across from Horton Plaza now occupied by the U.S. Grant Hotel.

San Diego's military history was a prime contributor to the look and feel of downtown San Diego. The U.S. Navy's Broadway Complex at Pacific Highway is a lowrise supply

Parade passing Horton House.

depot and office building, in a spare, efficient style. Gigantic Navy vessels are the equivalent of moving horizontal buildings that slide by on the bay. Huge hangars once housed aircraft factories north of downtown, next to the airport. Marine helicopters land along Pacific Highway next to Spanish Colonial buildings—many military structures throughout San Diego were designed in the spirit of Balboa Park. The military hired Balboa Park architect Bertram Goodhue to plan and design projects including the Marine Corps Recruit Depot.

DOWNTOWN HIGHLIGHT

San Diego on the Wing

Curtiss Hydroplane   San Diego, Cal.   Arcade View Co.

San Diego's aviation history is commonly thought to have started in 1927, when Ryan Aviation quickly built the *Spirit of St. Louis* for Charles Lindbergh so he could make the first non-stop flight across the Atlantic. But the region had been on the leading edge of aviation innovation long before Lindbergh's plane was built.

On May 21, 1908—his 30th birthday—Glenn Curtiss made his first flight in Hammondsport, New York. In 1911 he opened a flight school on North Island, for training Army and Navy pilots. But his prime inventions in San Diego were designs for amphibious airplanes as well as planes that could utilize the decks of Navy ships as runways. A Curtiss aircraft made the first successful take-off from a Navy carrier in 1910.

In 1911 at North Island, Curtiss made the first successful amphibious takeoff and landing in his Hydro. Curtiss built the first Navy plane—the Triad—and trained the first two Navy pilots. As a result, Curtiss Airplane and Motor Company boomed in San Diego during World War I (1914-1918). In 1919, Curtiss's NC-4 made the first successful flight across the Atlantic.

Curtiss was among the first to establish San Diego as a center of aviation innovation, and his efforts also helped attract the military as a mainstay of the local economy. He launched a string of milestone events that would extend through the 20th century, events that had a significant impact on the look and feel of the urban waterfront and its signature sights and sounds.

Through cycles of boom and bust, the military has been a force almost from the beginning. On July 29, 1846, marines went ashore from the 22-gun *Cyane,* anchored in the bay. *Cyane* was the newest member of America's small Pacific Squadron, charged with securing California's coast from Mexican forces. A small squad rowed ashore, met no opposition as they hiked up a dirt path to the Presidio, and raised the Navy flag "on a small rise overlooking the confluence of the San Diego River into the northern sweep of San Diego Bay".

By the 1890s, military vessels were homeported in San Diego Bay. Piers and waterfront buildings soon followed to serve them. By 1911, San Diego took control of its bayfront tidelands from the state, led by the lobbying of new San Diego Congressman William Kettner, an insurance broker. Bond issues of $1.4 million approved in 1912 and 1913 funded the purchase of 60 acres of bayfront land from Broadway to Date Street, as well as construction of Broadway Pier. Kettner soon found federal funding to dredge San Diego Bay so Navy ships could come through. The Naval Militia's 28th Street Armory opened in 1914, coinciding with World War I. Kettner lobbied San Diego past San Francisco and Los Angeles, and the armored cruiser *California* was renamed *U.S.S. San Diego.*

By 1919, the Navy had a shipyard at 32nd Street downtown, and by 1922 several dozen destroyers anchored at the foot of 32nd. San Diego's military identity was sealed in 1920 when the electorate voted to donate bayfront land and a hospital site in Balboa Park to the Navy. In June

Demolition of old Santa Fe Depot with new depot in background.

1922, the Naval Supply Depot moved from Point Loma to the Fleet Supply Warehouse by the Broadway Pier—where the Navy's Broadway Complex is today. In 1924, the Navy's first aircraft carrier, a behemoth crowned by a broad landing strip, arrived in San Diego. For decades to come, the grey bulk of carriers became as much a part of downtown San Diego's identity as the buildings, and San Diego was the nation's number one carrier port. Decades before Goodyear blimps, the Naval airship *Shenandoah*—buoyed by 150,000 cubic feet of helium—made her first West Coast stop at North Island, where she was visible from miles around. A predecessor of the Navy's airborne Blue Angels flight squad—the Three Seahawks—was assembled in San Diego in 1927 and flew over dedication ceremonies at Lindbergh Field the following year. By the mid-twenties, the Navy transferred its submarine base from Los Angeles to San Diego. Navy Pier downtown was completed in 1929. Through these years, military leaders were often con- scientious about their industry's impact on the form of the city.

"To its undying credit," writes historian Bruce Linder, "the Navy realized early that North Island would form an impor- tant vista from the San Diego bayfront and unusual care was taken in building design to ensure that the base (and thus the Navy) would 'blend into' the community. Key to this masterstroke was the involvement of architect Bertram Goodhue with the North Island designers." Goodhue's low, simple red tile- roofed concrete buildings were good neighbors to Coronado and to other cities ringing the bay—including downtown San Diego.

By the 1930s, San Diego was the dominant West Coast base for both Navy planes and their floating airports. Maj. Reuben H. Fleet developed the Ranger flying boat, and in 1935 moved 400 of his Consolidated Aircraft employees from Buffalo to San Diego. From its 275,000-square-foot sawtooth-roofed plant next to Lindbergh Field, Consolidated launched the region's first major industry. A few years later, World War II sealed downtown's military identity.

"A year ago San Diego was a quiet, slow-moving town," reported *Life* magazine in 1941. "But no longer. The defense boom has hit it…changing the look of the town. With the boom has come housing projects, trailer camps, traffic snarls, bigger red light districts. But it isn't these things so much that worry the old San Diegans. What makes them fret is the change in the tempo of their town. Until a year ago people walked leisurely down Broadway or drove quietly through Balboa Park. Now they stride hur- riedly, drive like mad. Nice old ladies a year ago sat on the waterfront painting pictures of ships coming and going.

Now the ships coming and going are Army and Navy transports and nice old ladies are barred from the docks."

Conflicts in Korea and Vietnam added to the military presence in and around downtown San Diego. "Downsizing" followed in the 1990s, as the Naval Training Center west of Lindbergh Field was decommissioned. For better or worse, writes Linder in *San Diego's Navy,* "an unwritten partnership developed where city fathers generously traded protected anchorages and waterfront installations for protected economic growth and cultural stability…The Navy looked to ceremony and circumstance and played public relations spectacles to the hilt, nearly always well received by appreciative San Diegans." Today, in an era of military base closures, even though more than 100,000 military personnel are based in San Diego, it is difficult to imagine the spectacle of hundreds of sailors marching in formation up Broadway from the pier, past rows of Model A's parked diagonally in front of storefronts shaded by canvas awnings.

Because San Diego was a late bloomer and has never been a corporate headquarters city, the definition of "high-rise" here is more liberal. Combine the lack of capital catalyst with an airport flight path that limits the height of downtown towers, and you get a skyline that reflects San Diego's modest place among American cities. One of Chicago's earliest tall buildings was Jenney's 7-story First Leiter Building in 1879, followed by higher neoclassical structures by architects including Burnham and Sullivan. San Diego's first tower in this spirit didn't come along until the Watts Robinson Building opened at Fifth Avenue and E Street in 1913. At 1,450 feet, Chicago's Sears Tower is three times as tall as any San Diego building. Landmark San Diego "towers" include waterfront Hyatt and Marriott Hotels, and America Plaza and Emerald Plaza on lower Broadway, none of which tops 500 feet.

William Templeton Johnson was San Diego's Louis Sullivan. Like the great Chicago architect, Johnson was a romantic in the Beaux Arts tradition of rusticated stone

DOWNTOWN HIGHLIGHT

Waterfront Plans

A stroke of political and planning diplomacy, the North Embarcadero Alliance Visionary Plan calls for preserving a mile-long stretch of downtown waterfront for pedestrian-friendly uses. Prepared by Sasaki Associates for a consortium of five public agencies (CCDC, city, port, Navy, county) in San Diego, the plan diverts auto traffic inland a block, from Harbor Drive to Pacific Highway. What remains will be a parklike "necklace of activities" between Broadway and Lindbergh Field.

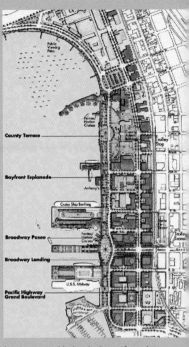

By breaking the area's long blocks into smaller blocks on a par with the rhythms of nearby downtown, the plan emphasizes visual and circulatory connections to the water, including views of Coronado Island and its sky-blue bridge. Central to the plan is a "bayfront esplanade" at water's edge, "animated by public art, urban scale street furnishings, public gathering places, scenic viewing areas, and a garland of pedestrian streetlights." Denser "civic precincts" would develop at Broadway (including a cruiseship terminal and two public piers—one of them probably housing the *U.S.S. Midway* aircraft carrier museum), and a few blocks to the north, where new public parks will surround the WPA-era County Administration Center. San Diego's successful opera company is lobbying for a Sydney-scale opera house near the foot of Broadway.

Implementation of the North Embarcadero plan, with $54 million in public improvements, will partially compensate San Diegans for what happened to the south, where a mammoth convention center and hotels limited visual and pedestrian access to a prime stretch of urban waterfront.

and classical arches and details. Johnson's 13-story San Diego Trust & Savings (1927) is downtown San Diego's finest tall building. Walker and Eisen's El Cortez Hotel (1926) is downtown's most visible tower, with its base of angled wings, square-shouldered shaft, and stepped-back top. In San Diego, there is no early tower as tall or inspiring as New York City's Chrysler Building, Boston's Custom House Tower (1915), or Seattle's 42-story Smith Tower (1914).

More recently, Frank L. Hope and Associates' Home Tower at 7th and Broadway (1962) was among the first modern steel-framed, glass-skinned high-rises—a dozen years after Mies van der Rohe's famous Lakeshore Drive apartments in Chicago. Among early bank towers, Tucker Sadler's First National Bank (later Union Bank) was most graceful and still looks good today. Deems Lewis & Partners' San Diego Financial Center (1974) was the first high-rise that hailed the beginning of redevelopment the following year. The 1980s brought reflective glass high-rises—many of them speculative endeavors that lacked the character of buildings designed for specific clients. The later part of that decade yielded more elegant towers such as First Interstate Plaza at Fifth Avenue and B Street—clad in red granite, with a spare plaza on the corner (due to siting, the plaza is usually in shade). Nineties high-rises by SOM (Hyatt Regency Hotel, Symphony Towers) and Helmut Jahn (America Plaza) are San Diego's best contemporary towers. The Hyatt on Harbor Drive suffers from a blockbuster parking structure. Trolley tracks pass through the base of America Plaza, activating public space between the tower and adjacent modern art museum.

Downtown San Diego has become a role model for redeveloping downtowns across the country. Much urban design credit goes to Max Schmidt, longtime head of urban planning at the Centre City Development Corp.—city government's redevelopment arm. Schmidt insisted on transforming the unsightly railroad easement along Harbor Drive into the imaginative Martin Luther King Promenade. A disciple of Jane Jacobs and William Whyte, Schmidt pushed for inviting public spaces, and was a constant critic of designs that weren't pedestrian-friendly. Schmidt was also instrumental in the transformation of Horton Plaza mall, from early enclosed suburban-style, to the colorful, open-air experience eventually designed by Jon Jerde.

In a new milllenium downtown San Diego is on the brink of two major new projects: an urban baseball park designed by New Mexican Antoine Predock with local architects, and a new central library designed by Rob Quigley. Both Predock and Quigley's designs draw from San Diego past architectural heritage. Predock and his collaborators have obviously taken a long look at the missions and the early 20th century modernism of San Diego architect Irving Gill. Quigley's design, with its signature dome, pays homage to Goodhue's Balboa Park, and to the dome of the old Balboa Theatre downtown.

While a portion of downtown waterfront was blocked off by the new convention center, there is good reason to hope that the North Embarcadero, between Seaport village and the airport, will make pedestrians a higher priority than commerce. Drafted by Sasaki Associates with a consortium of San Diego public agencies including the port and city, the North Embarcadero Alliance Visionary Plan diverts auto traffic a block inland, from Harbor Drive to Pacific Highway—freeing the bayfront for pedestrian-friendly plazas and paths. In the future, planners face many challenges downtown. They must find ways to accommodate and express San Diego's emerging technology-based economy. They must preserve historical buildings (many of which were already lost during redevelopment). They must push for imaginative new housing and high-rises. They must always keep pedestrians in mind as they find fresh transportation solutions to keep downtown San Diego from becoming a car-driven urban core plagued by gridlock.

Downtown Neighborhoods

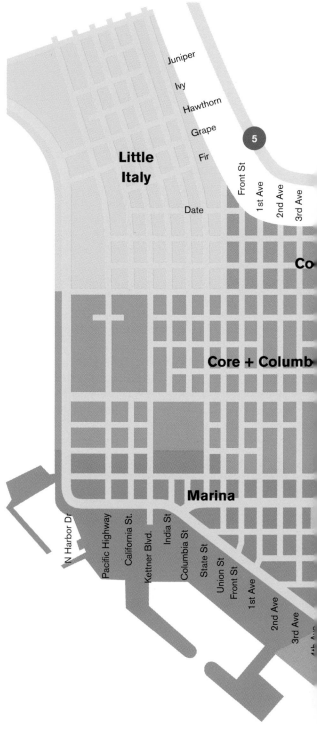

- **Core + Columbia** 26
- **Marina District** 38
- **Gaslamp** 46
- **East Village** 62
- **Cortez Hill** 70
- **Little Italy** 78

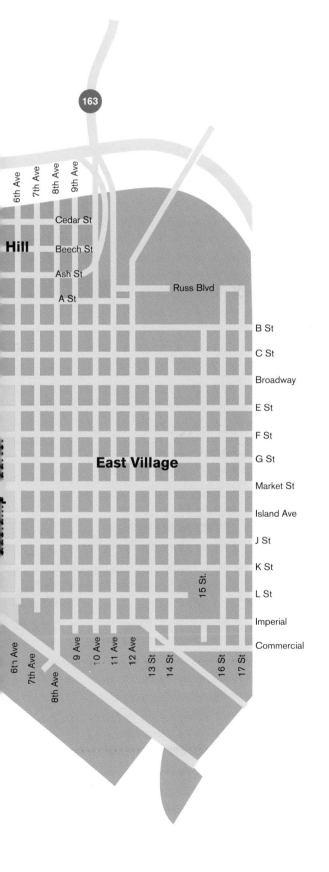

Core + Columbia Locations

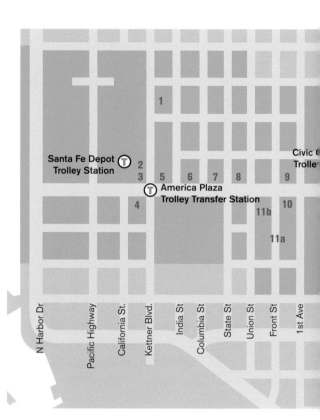

1 **Treo at Kettner**

2 **Santa Fe Depot Baggage Building**

3 **Santa Fe Depot**

4 **SDG&E Station B**

5 **America Plaza**

6 **Armed Services YMCA**

7 **Wyndham Emerald Plaza**

8 **Hall of Justice**

9 **Pickwick Hotel/Greyhound Bus Terminal**

10 **Spreckels Theatre**

11 **Federal Building (a) and U.S. Courthouse (b)**

12 **Horton Plaza Park and Fountain**

13 **U.S. Grant Hotel**

14 **Granger Building**

15 **On Broadway**

16 **First National Bank Building**

17 **San Diego Trust & Savings**

18 **Samuel I. Fox Building**

19 **John D. Spreckels Building**

20 **YWCA**

21 **Imperial Bank**

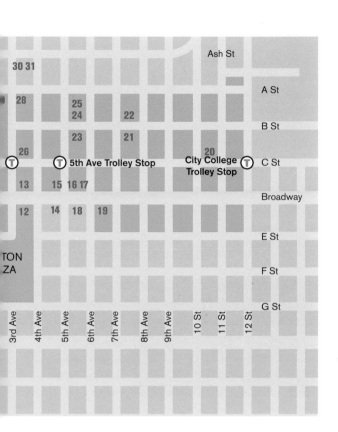

22 **Symphony Towers**

23 **Union Bank**

24 **First National Bank Tower**

25 **San Diego Athletic Club/HBJ Building**
   World Trade Center

26 **California Theatre**

27 **Security Pacific Plaza**

28 **Crabtree Building**

29 **Medical/Dental Building**

30 **Christian Science Church**

31 **SDG&E Substation C/**
   Consolidated Gas & Electric Company

CORE + COLUMBIA

1 / Treo at Kettner (2003)
1240 India & 1277 Kettner
CARRIER JOHNSON

One of San Diego's first new high-rises since the early 1990s, this full-block mixed-use project is a decent neighbor, with a stepped profile that preserves view corridors, and low-rise rowhomes that provide a pedestrian-scale streetwall and feature individual sidewalk entrances.

2 / Santa Fe Depot Baggage Building
(1915 & Planned Renovation)
1050 Kettner Blvd
BAKEWELL & BROWN
GLUCKMAN MAYNER WITH MILFORD WAYNE DONALDSON (RENOVATION)

Expanding its presence across Kettner from its building next to the downtown trolley station, the Museum of Contemporary Art San Diego plans to convert the former baggage building into three galleries and spaces for performance, film/video, and installation art. Gluckman is adding a three-story building of gray corrugated metal, with modern echoes of the historic depot's rhythms.

3 / Santa Fe Depot (1915)
1050 Kettner Blvd
BAKEWELL & BROWN

San Diego's signature Mission Revival building (it replaced the 1887 Victorian-style depot) was one of a string built by the railroad. Arched redwood beam-supported ceilings, bronze-and-glass chandeliers, oak benches, chromatic tiles, and Native American friezes hark back to an era of grand public buildings that resonate with California's history; the forecourt took advantage of San Diego's climate.

4 / SDG&E Station B (1911)
707 W. Broadway
EUGENE HOFFMAN & ANDREW ERVAST (ORIGINAL BOILER ROOM AND TURBINE ROOM)
WILLIAM TEMPLETON JOHNSON (1928 ADDITION AT NORTHEAST CORNER)

San Diego's cool steam plant, which once heated downtown's high-rises, is destined for redevelopment, perhaps as the base of a high-rise hotel and/or condominium tower.

5 / **One America Plaza** (1991)
600 W. Broadway
MURPHY/JAHN

This 34-story tower (sometimes compared to a Philips screwdriver) is a half-pint version of Jahn's 61-story One Liberty Place in Philadelphia; also an example of how hard it is for architects to design spectacular spires within the 400-foot limit imposed by San Diego's airport. At the street level, though, Jahn made urban design magic. A half-vault steel roof covers the s-shaped tracks of the San Diego Trolley station and its shops and restaurants. Across the tracks, a satellite branch of the Museum of Contemporary Art/San Diego adds a splash of activity, including public sculpture at the corner of Broadway and Kettner. Motion, art, public plaza, high-rise bayview offices, and pedestrian-friendly mixed-use—everything a prominent urban corner needs is here.

6 / **Armed Services YMCA** (1924)
500 W. Broadway
LINCOLN ROGERS/F.W. STEVENSON

The 260-room, Spanish Colonial revival and Italian Renaissance Y, which includes an indoor pool with beautiful tilework, was rehabbed as an SRO beginning in 2001.

7 / **Wyndham Emerald Plaza**
(originally Emerald-Shapery Center, 1991)
400-402 W. Broadway
C.W. KIM

This cluster of hexagonal spires is San Diego's most inventive high-rise. Developer Sandor Shapery's inspiration was nature's crystals. Architect C.W. Kim designed office towers up to 30 stories, an adjacent hotel to 28. Green reflective glass and a Donald Trumpish interior amount to sensory overload, but the sidewalk level is engaging, and this signature building looks great from a distance.

8 / **Hall of Justice** (1996)
330 W. Broadway
CARRIER JOHNSON

This new full-block home for the county's Superior Courts and administration utilizes sandstone walls, terrazzo floors, and blue-green glass to echo the primary San Diego elements of sun, sand, and water. A skybridge connects the new building to the earlier courthouse. The building is a bold new presence on lower Broadway.

CORE + COLUMBIA

9 / **Pickwick Hotel/Greyhound Bus Terminal** (1926)
132 & 120 W. Broadway
JAIME TOCHEY

Completed just before cars became dominant transportation, this reinforced concrete brick-faced building is elegantly proportioned and subtly detailed—note plaster rosettes below the roofline.

---

10 / **Spreckels Theatre** (1912)
121 Broadway
HARRISON ALBRIGHT

When it opened Aug. 23, 1912, with George Broadhurst's "Bought and Paid For," this 1,464-seat showplace was touted as the first modern playhouse west of the Mississippi. Albright created a space with no obstructing pillars or columns, a large stage for that era (82-by-58-feet), easy truck access to both sides of the stage, and elaborate Baroque décor that includes murals above the stage and on the ceiling (by Los Angeles artist Emil Mazy), as well as classical statuary in wall niches. Don't miss a chance to experience the tall, narrow interior, which places every seat close to the stage.

---

11 / **Federal Building & U.S. Courthouse** (1976)
880–940 Front St.
HOPE & WHEELER

Completed in the embryonic era of downtown redevelopment, the reinforced concrete courthouse gave government a bold, stark new image with details that include a skybridge and plazas featuring public art.

12 / **Horton Plaza Park and Fountain** (1871 & 1910)
Broadway between Third and Fourth Avenues

IRVING GILL (FOUNTAIN)

Mayors and public figures such as President Benjamin Harrison addressed San Diegans here from a bandstand that also hosted outdoor concerts. Flowing water and electric lights were an innovative and splashy combination when Gill dedicated his fountain on Oct. 15, 1910–the same evening the U.S. Grant Hotel opened across Broadway. Bronze plaques around the fountain's base honor Alonzo Horton, Father Junipero Serra (founder of Mission San Diego de Alcala), and explorer Juan Rodrigues Cabrillo. Horton Plaza Park was once downtown's prime public gathering spot, centrally located for shoppers and for bus and trolley riders. When it became a crashpad for homeless in the 1980s, lawns were replaced with shrubs, eliminating space for civic gatherings.

13 / **U.S. Grant Hotel** (1910)
326 Broadway

HARRISON ALBRIGHT

From his mansion on Cortez Hill (where the El Cortez Hotel is now), U.S. Grant, Jr., son of the 18th U.S. president, could monitor progress on the hotel he built and named in honor of his father. Merging old and new, the Neo-Classical hotel combines historical details outside and Queen Anne furnishings inside with then-modern techniques of concrete construction. FDR and Lindbergh are among celebs who slept here.

14 / **Granger Building** (1904)
964 Fifth Ave.

WILLIAM QUAYLE

Romanesque structure once housed businesses above ground, and zoo founder Dr. Harry Wegeforth's animals, in the basement. Original anchor tenant Merchants National Bank was succeeded in 1924 by Bank of Italy, and later, Bank of America. GASLAMP QUARTER HISTORIC STRUCTURE

CORE + COLUMBIA

15 / **On Broadway** (2003)
Broadway between Fourth and Fifth Avenues
BUNDY/THOMPSON

Re-using the Holzwasser/Walker
Scott Building (1920/John Vawter)
and the Owl Drug Building
(1913/Quayle Brothers & Cressey),
the new development includes 21
residential lofts, retail, restaurant,
and commercial space. Walker Scott
department store, converted now to
a parking garage, was a centerpiece
of mid-20th century downtown,
known for its Spanish Colonial detailing and catchy window displays.

DOWNTOWN HIGHLIGHT

Horton Plaza

(1985)

Bounded by Broadway, G Street, First and Fourth Avenues

ARCHITECT:
JERDE PARTNERSHIP

Conceived as an open-air Euro-style shopping experience, architect Jon Jerde's Horton Plaza mall features a diagonal s-shaped promenade that slices through its center. An earlier design used the enclosed suburban format, but CCDC planners pushed for a re-design that takes advantage of San Diego's climate and

creates a strong sense of place at the city center. As a result, Horton Plaza became Jerde's prototypical shopping-as-entertainment project, one that set the stage for Universal CityWalk in Los Angeles, Fremont Street Experience in Las Vegas, and others. Between the multiplex cinema, food court, department stores, theaters, and boutique shops, you can spend an entire day here—a boon for Horton Plaza but a bane for adjacent businesses who wish the mall connected better with their streets. You may or may not like the sherbet colors, crazy signage, and eclectic historical references (columns, arches, domes, dentil moulding copied from the Knights of Pythias building, demolished during redevelopment), but there's no denying that a walk down any of this mall's serpentine sidewalks is an exhilirating mix of sights, sounds, food smells, and credit card eye candy—-an experience not unlike the compact European streetscapes that Horton Plaza emulates.

16 / **First National Bank Building** (1909)
NE corner Broadway and Fifth Avenue

FRANKLIN P. BURNHAM

San Diego's first high-rise offices, the 11-story Chicago-style building used an innovative reinforced concrete frame with concrete in-fill tile and truss rod supports. A penthouse was added in 1914; original decoration was stripped during a 1940 "modernization". The building was renovated by RTKL Architects to draw "technology-based" tenants in 2002/2003.

CORE + COLUMBIA

17 / **San Diego Trust & Savings** (1928)
530 Broadway
WILLIAM TEMPLETON JOHNSON

San Diego's stateliest 1920s building, designed in the Chicago spirit of Henry Hobson Richardson and Louis Sullivan—pioneering architects of high-rises distinguished by arches, stone, and delicate decoration such as the cherubs, flowers, leaves, and rosettes over the entry. The building was renovated and re-opened in 1999 as a Courtyard by Marriott Hotel.

18 / **Samuel I. Fox Building** (1929)
950 Sixth Avenue
WILLIAM TEMPLETON JOHNSON

A grand four-story showplace of reinforced concrete and steel that once housed Fox's Lion Clothing Co., the building features 16-foot ceilings, walnut window frames, sculptured terra cotta spandrels, and heraldic lion reliefs.

19 / **John D. Spreckels Building** (1927)
625 Broadway
PARKINSON & PARKINSON

Lancashire-born John Parkinson and his son Donald designed some of Southern California's most important buildings of the 1910s and 1920s—including Los Angeles City Hall and Bullocks Wilshire department store. Here, sugar millionaire John D. Spreckels' landmark structure in the heart of downtown echoes the Richardsonian Romanesque Revival style of San Diego Trust & Savings nearby, as well as architect H.H. Richardson's original early century buildings in Chicago.

20 / **YWCA** (1926)
1012 C Street
CLARENCE DECKER/F.W. STEVENSON

This five-story AIA award-winner (in 1933) has Spanish Colonial details including Churrigueresque reliefs surrounding entries; an indoor pool; and interior with Philippine mahogany ceilings and balustrades, decorative stone drinking fountains, tooled fireplace mantels.

21 / **Imperial Bank** (1982)
701 B Street
WARE & MALCOLM

San Diego's unflashy, 24-story "Darth Vader" looks better today than many of its mid-1980s peers.

22 / **Symphony Towers** (1989)
750 B Street
SKIDMORE, OWINGS & MERRILL

One of the best things about this building is hidden within: Symphony Hall, the former Fox Theatre restored in all its gilded glory. Outside, Skidmore Owings & Merrill did a graceful job combining a 34-story office tower and a 27-story hotel on this steep block, with the concert hall in between. Red granite exterior cladding upped the elegance ante in San Diego. Transparent glass at the street level connects interior and exterior space: pedestrians can see the 80-foot Deco-style oil-and-gold leaf lobby mural of an orchestra.

23 / **Union Bank** (1968)
525 B Street
LANGDON & WILSON

Another straightforward modern high-rise from downtown San Diego's first wave.

24 / **First National Bank Tower** (1966)
530 B Street
TUCKER SADLER & BENNETT

One of San Diego's first modern high-rises was also one of its best, with well-defined base, shaft, and top.

25 / **San Diego Athletic Club/HBJ Building/ World Trade Center** (1928)
1250 Sixth Avenue
WILLIAM WHEELER/F.W. STEVENSON/ I.E. LOVELESS

A 13-story Deco extravaganza, made of board-formed reinforced concrete. Ornate friezes and upper-level Gothic window details accent a mostly sleek modern building. Note the blue band of busts over Sixth Avenue—onetime members of the Athletic Club, perhaps?

CORE + COLUMBIA

26 / **California Theatre** (1927)
1122 Fourth Avenue
JOHN PAXTON PERRINE

Once promoted as "the cathedral of the
motion picture," the nine-story reinforced concrete (i.e. quake-proof) Spanish Colonial
revival building combined a theater with
offices and shops. Parapets have red tile trim
and dentils or arched corbeling. Plaster urns
are among decorative details. The interior
emulates a Spanish church. The Beatles' "A Hard Day's Night" played in
this 2,200-seat venue, as did several rock bands. It was the last of West
Coast Theaters' moviehouses designed by a regional architect–
Pasadena's Perrine, the chain's most prolific architect.

27 / **Security Pacific Plaza** (1972)
1200 Third Avenue
TUCKER SADLER & BENNETT

More monolithic than Tucker Sadler's First
National Bank Tower, this 19-story uses a zig-
zag window pattern to stress its vertical thrust
and bring natural light to offices.

28 / **Crabtree Building** (1962)
303 A Street
DEEMS-MARTIN & ASSOCIATES

A floating modern marvel of prestressed concrete slab floors cantilevered from four central
columns, later victimized by renovation.

29 / **Medical/Dental Building** (1927)
233 A St.
FRANK STEVENSON

One of San Diego's early, elegant high-rises is
this 14-story reinforced concrete structure, with
granite cladding and interior marble. A fine example of its era's classical revival style, it exemplifies
the notion among early high-rise designers that
these buildings should have a clearly defined
base, middle, and top.

30 / **Christian Science Church** (1904)
317 Ash Street
HEBBARD & GILL

Humble vine-covered brick building (formerly Goodbody's
Mortuary, now occupied by attor-
neys) that shows Gill's fascination with landscape/architecture connections, with arched windows reminiscent of buildings by San Francisco Bay
Area architect Bernard Maybeck.

31 / SDG&E Substation C/
Consolidated Gas & Electric Company (1923)
SW corner Fourth Avenue & Ash Street
REQUA & JACKSON

Combining the rich stone appearance of Chicago's H.H. Richardson and his Romanesque designs, with delicate Spanish Revival detailing, the building reminds us of a time when public utilities took pride in their buildings.

DOWNTOWN HIGHLIGHT

Coronado Bridge
(1969)

DESIGN CONSULTANT FOR THE BRIDGE:
ROBERT MOSHER, FAIA

ARCHITECT FOR THE TOLL PLAZA:
STEPHEN ALLEN, FAIA OF ANSHEN AND ALLEN

This 2.23-mile-long blue arc is San Diego's grandest piece of public art. The bridge employs the world's longest continuous orthotropic spans, utilizing a structural system, developed in Europe, which conceals struts and braces within a box girder to preserve the sleek, sinuous profile. The design of its supporting pylons was, according to architect Robert Mosher, inspired by the Laurel Street Bridge leading into Balboa Park, and makes a gesture to local history. The gradual arc of the roadbed maintains highway speed standards, and meets the Navy's clearance require-

ments for aircraft carriers at high tide. The color was chosen to blend the blue of the bay and the sky.

Marina Locations

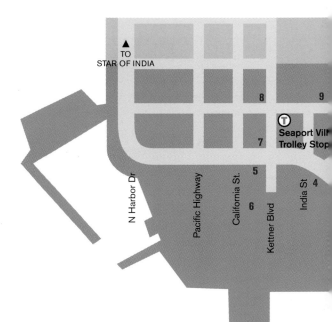

1 **San Diego Convention Center**

2 **San Diego Marriott Hotel**

3 **City Front Terrace**

4 **Hyatt Regency San Diego**

5 **San Diego Police Headquarters**

6 **Seaport Village**

7 **Park Place**

8 **Seven on Kettner**

9 **Pantoja Park**

10 **Metropolitan Correctional Center**

11 **U.S. Custom and Courthouse**

12 **The Meridian**

13 **City Walk**

14 **600 Front**

15 **Renaissance**

16 **Horizons**

17 **101 Market**

18 **235 on Market**

19 **202 Island Inn**

20 **J Street Inn**

21 **Pacific Terrace**

22 **Crown Bay**

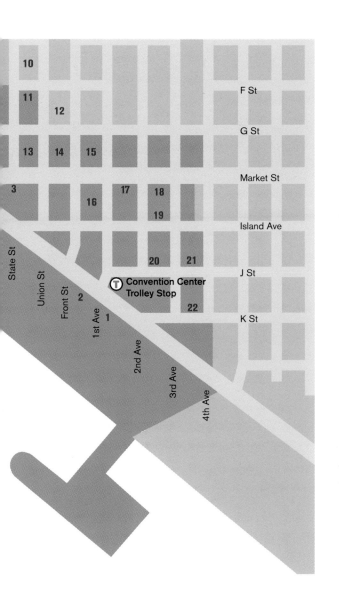

10

11

12

F St

G St

13   14   15

Market St

3

17   18

16   19

Island Ave

20   21

J St

State St

Union St

Front St

2

1st Ave

1

(T) **Convention Center**
Trolley Stop

22

K St

2nd Ave

3rd Ave

4th Ave

MARINA DISTRICT

1 / **San Diego Convention Center** (1989 and 2002)
111 W. Harbor Drive

ARTHUR ERICKSON/DEEMS-LEWIS (PHASE I)
TUCKER SADLER (PHASE II)

This 1.1-million-square-foot leviathan has been a boon to the downtown economy. From a pedestrian point of view it is imposing, and it cuts off waterfront views and access. But from automobiles, airplanes, and boats on the bay it's an epic piece of waterfront sculpture. Canadian architect Arthur Erickson's Phase I design, with its flying buttresses, rooftop sails, and greenish skylight tubes, is visually poetic.

2 / **San Diego Marriott Hotel** (1984, 1987)
333 W. Harbor Drive

F.L. HOPE (#1) AND WELTON BECKETT (#2)

These 25-story towers may look like twins, but they are really only cousins. Kim's original east tower cut a more graceful profile inspired by spinnakers. The second, thicker tower accommodates more guest rooms—but took the wind out of Kim's "twin sails" concept.

3 / **City Front Terrace** (1993)
500 W. Harbor Drive

SOLOMON CORDWELL & BUENZ

Chicago-style elegance came to San Diego with this jumbo brick-and-limestone-clad 13-story residential mid-rise, set in Martin Luther King Promenade—the innovative linear park. One planning drawback: the building's bulk casts a chilling afternoon shadow along Market Street in a neighborhood where more modest residential redevelopment came first. San Diego architect Milford Wayne Donaldson designed the renovation of the historic 4-story brick soap factory building here, as the loft portion of City Front Terrace.

4 / **Hyatt Regency San Diego** (1992)
One Market Place

SKIDMORE OWINGS & MERRILL

Skidmore Owings & Merrill is world-famous for modern high-rises such as New York City's Lever House (1952) and Chicago's John Hancock Center (1970), but SOM's more recent San Diego skyscrapers don't embody that spare, singular vision. The Hyatt's tapered top is one of downtown's better crowns, but the street level's main feature is a blockbuster parking garage that belongs at a 1960s shopping mall—not along a prime stretch of waterfront that should be pedestrian-friendly. A second tower was under construction in 2002.

5 / **San Diego Police Headquarters** (1939)
801 W. Market Street
QUAYLE BROTHERS & A.O. TREGANZA

In the Spanish Colonial tradition of towers, courtyards, tile roofs, and deepset arched openings, this romantic structure stood vacant for several years as preservationists battled development interests. As one of the few fine downtown buildings from its era, the headquarters could be put to new use and/or a portion preserved as part of some new project.

6 / **Seaport Village** (1980)
849 W. Harbor Drive
HOPE ARCHITECTS

A theme-parkish mix of Mexico, Old Monterey, and Victorian San Francisco, aimed more at visitors than locals; but compared with the convention center and high-rise hotels next door, 14-acre Seaport Village is a pedestrian paradise. Even today, it stands as San Diego's most effective waterfront development, emphasizing public plazas over buildings. The waterfront boardwalk offers an intimate connection to sights and and sounds of the waterfront. Best of all, though, is an 1890s Looff carousel from Coney Island, restored to its original glory.

7 / **Park Place** (2002)
700 W. Harbor Drive
DIKEAKOS AND COTTER

Canadian architects add their 30-story impression of San Diego to the downtown skyline—bland, generic, with a swatch of tile roof that presumably adds a regional flavor.

8 / **Seven on Kettner** (1988)
702, 704, 706, 708, 710, 712 Kettner Boulevard
JONATHAN SEGAL

These New York-inspired rowhomes stand on an orphan wedge of land by the trolley tracks. Balconies, street-facing windows, and front stoops provide a Jane Jacobs/William Whyte sense of security. Segal's small-scale development set the stage for other small- and medium-size downtown housing projects that provide a richer fabric than old-school full-block redevelopment.

9 / **Pantoja Park** (1850)
G Street between India and Columbia

Originally the heart of William Heath Davis's 160-acre New Town, this area would have been a busy public plaza, but Davis's plan never panned out. In 1871, Alonzo Horton established a new central plaza on Broadway at Fourth Avenue. Today Pantoja Park is a public park next to condominiums built in the early 1980s.

MARINA DISTRICT

10 / **Metropolitan Correctional Center** (1975)

808 Union Street

TUCKER SADLER

Not often mentioned as one of downtown's land-mark buildings, this well-proportioned high-rise prison utilizes vertical strip windows to provide natural light while maintaining security.

11 / **U.S. Custom and Courthouse** (1913)

325 W. F Street

JAMES KNOX TAYLOR

Italian Renaissance reinforced concrete structure—which looks particularly striking when compared with some of the public buildings added downtown during the 1960s and 1970s.

12 / **The Meridian** (1985)

700 Front Street

MAXWELL STARKMAN

San Diego's first residential high-rise cuts a 24-story profile with its zig-zag view-grabbing southwest facade. A base of bulky horizontals looms over sidewalks like Fallingwater on steroids.

13 / **City Walk** (2002)

Bounded by State, G, Union, and Market Streets

NESTOR AND GAFFNEY

Elegant street-level stone and imaginative Craftsman-inspired eaves are eye-grabbers, but the building lacks pedestrian-friendly details such as stoops—or, better yet, retail spaces. The mix of townhomes, condominiums, and lofts, plus the variety of forms and materials, equals a refreshingly rich collection of homes.

14 / 600 Front Street (1988)
ROB WELLINGTON QUIGLEY

Mysterious clues let you make up your own story about this innovative apartment complex—a stairway-to-nowhere at the southeast corner. Unlike other low-rise urban apartments of this era, Quigley's is truly inspired by San Diego, with a central courtyard and outdoor corridors that take advantage of the weather. Quigley wanted ground floor retail to liven up sidewalks, but he was ahead of the downtown redevelopment curve.

15 / Renaissance (2002)
Bounded by First, Front, Market, and G
CARRIER JOHNSON

San Diego architects boldly abandon the faux-historical in favor of a sleek modern approach that makes its statement with large architectural volumes. Street-level retail grounds twin 22-story towers.

DOWNTOWN HIGHLIGHT
Martin Luther King Jr. Promenade
(1993)

Harbor Drive from Eighth Avenue to Broadway
PETER WALKER/MARTHA SCHWARTZ
WITH AUSTIN HANSEN FEHLMAN

Conceived by redevelopment urban planner Max Schmidt, this 1/4-mile linear park is a "serape" of colors, textures, water features, and public art in keeping with San Diego's cross-cultural heritage. The park is a pedestrian/bicycle/trolley thoroughfare connected to major projects such as CityFront Terrace and the Bridgeworks, with their adjacent plazas. The art includes bronze plaques bearing quotes from Dr. King; Roberto Salas's "Dream" near the Children's Museum; and

"Shedding the Cloak" by Jerry and Tama Dumlao and Mary Lynn Dominguez near Market and Columbia.

MARINA DISTRICT

16 / **Horizons** (2001)
510 First Avenue
ARC DESIGN INTERNATIONAL

Thoughtfully detailed mixed-use project that hailed a new generation of residential high-rises downtown. Ample, pedestrian-friendly first-floor retail space synergizes with 211 condominiums. An interior courtyard is an outdoor "living room" for residents.

---

17 / **101 Market Street** (2002)
101 Market Street Street
ROB WELLINGTON QUIGLEY

The Quigley firm refines the urban residential approach it pioneered in the 1980s: outdoor hallways, inviting corner entries, street-level commercial uses, thoughtfully concealed parking, and an interior courtyard that brings natural light into these homes.

---

18 / **235 on Market** (2001)
235 Market Street
WITHEE MALCOLM

Solid if somewhat generic low-rise condominium project that illustrates progress of CCDC planners in their push for articulated, pedestrian-friendly facades. Intense colors go a bit overboard—but beat the stock beige and tan of earlier redevelopment housing.

---

19 / **202 Island Inn** (1992)
202 Island Avenue
ROB WELLINGTON QUIGLEY

The architect's refined design for a "single-room occupancy" hotel (see his Baltic Inn) of stucco with aluminum windows, but at a larger scale and with concrete walls that reference parapets of California missions, well-disguised underground parking, a central courtyard for natural light (with a trickling water sculpture by landscape architects Spurlock-Poirier), and a cafe that animates this downtown corner. Raspberry and grape stucco sweeten interesting volumes along Second Street.

20 / **J Street Inn** (1990)
222 J Street
ROB WELLINGTON QUIGLEY

Smart angles and recesses that
scoop natural light into rooms are
hallmarks of another SRO ("single
room occupancy") hotel designed
by architect Rob Quigley.
Fractured chromatic tiles and
diagonal aluminum window frames
energize the entry. Awnings add scale to facades and control summer sun,
vertical slots in exterior walls admit natural light.

21 / **Pacific Terrace** (2003)
J Street between Third and Fourth Avenues
FEHLMAN LABARRE

Another new-millenium urban
residential development that
realizes many planning ideals:
mixed-use (including street-
level retail), intricately detailed
facades, and imaginative (i.e.
not all flat) rooflines.

22 / **Crown Bay** (2001)
350 K Street
WITHEE MALCOLM

A stylistic cousin of
these architects' 235
On Market condomini-
ums, this condo block's
arches and vaulted
roofs are stultifyingly
familiar. The inclusion of
ground-floor retail
spaces marks a step in the right direction for creating a lively urban sidewalk scene that brings built-in security (William Whyte's "eyes on the
street") to the downtown neighborhood.

DOWNTOWN HIGHLIGHT

Star of India
(1863)

1306 N. Harbor Dr.
Ramsey Shipyard,
Isle of Man.

A monument to San Diego's
maritime heritage, this globe-
traveling square-rigged tall ship—
originally named *Euterpe*—was
restored and resumed sailing for
educational purposes in 1976.

Gaslamp Quarter

Downtown's first business and night life district spent roughly half a century as San Diego's prime place for lascivious adventures. Between 1885 and 1910, the city matured from a wild western town into an urban center. Between Market Street and Broadway, luxurious Gaslamp buildings such as the Backesto Block, Louis Bank of Commerce, Nesmith-Greeley, and Keating became centerpieces of San Diego's commercial core. Beginning with the Stingaree red light district of the 1870s, the southern end of the Gaslamp had a reputation; for several mid-century decades, into the 1970s, these 16 blocks flanking Fifth Avenue between Broadway and the Bay were known more for dive bars, X-rated moviehouses, and ladies of the night, than for legitimate businesses.

Architecturally, Victorian-era Gaslamp buildings were very much in keeping with the Queen Anne, Eastlake, and Italianate styles popular across America. Comstock & Trotsche, who also designed the Villa Montezuma, were responsible for the Gaslamp's Nesmith-Greeley and Grand Hotel buildings. Other important architects in the Gaslamp of the 1890s included Burkett & Osgood, John B. Stannard, Levi Goodrich, Charles Delaval, the Reid Brothers, and the Stewart Brothers. Merchants behind the Gaslamp's early growth were a multi-cultural mix: Asian-American, Mexican-American, African-American, Euro-American. The Chinese contribution is commemorated in the district by a small group of historic buildings.

Modernism came to the Gaslamp in the form of the Watts-Robinson Building (1911), one of downtown's first tall buildings, and the Golden West Hotel (1913), designed by Harrison Albright with an assist from Frank Lloyd Wright's son John Lloyd. As the business district shifted north toward Broadway, other "entrepreneurs" previously confined south of Market followed behind. Luckily the Quarter was spared from the variety of cold and uninviting structures built in San Diego and in many other American downtowns during the late 1950s and 1960s. In that era, new office space was built north of Broadway, while retailing shifted to Mission Valley and other outlying areas.

In 1974, with the assistance of the city, gaslamp merchants and property owners began dusting off and reviving their neighborhood as a destination for mainstream San Diegans. Following a survey of buildings by historian Ray Brandes, with the initiative of city planner Michael J. Stepner, the entire district received National Register of Historic Places status in 1980, triggering tax incentives that helped restore centerpiece buildings.

Sidewalks were widened and paved with brick, street trees and period street lamps were added. Porno palaces and liquor stores catering to transients were squeezed out. The opening of the San Diego Trolley along Harbor Drive lined with new high-rise hotels and condominiums and a new waterfront Convention Center brought a new concentration of residents and visitors to the the Gaslamp southern end, feeding the revitalization.

Skeptics predicted the opening of the nearby Horton Plaza mall in 1984 might take away the Gaslamp's momentum, but the district made the most of its gorgeous Queen Anne buildings, many of which were adapted for use as restaurants, fashion boutiques, live-work lofts, night clubs, and upscale shops aimed at both locals and tourists. With few exceptions, planners and architects maintained scale and historic character as new projects such as Bridgeworks (re-designed several times), a multiplex cinema, and tasteful small office buildings were added. Even the new Park-It-On-Market structure just east of the Quarter has architectural character.

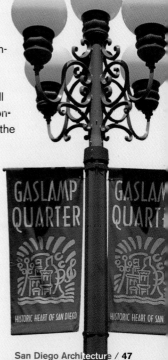

By the beginning of the 21st century, the Gaslamp Quarter had become downtown San Diego's most magnetic neighborhood. All day and into the night, conventioneers, tourists, and locals take in the sights and sounds on foot—the Gaslamp has become a pedestrian-friendly entertainment and shopping mecca rivaled locally only by downtown La Jolla. Downtown's original urban center, now adapting to its third century, has become a model for mixing preservation with new development.

Gaslamp Locations

1 **Lawyer's Block Building**

2 **Balboa Theatre**

3 **Ingle Building/Golden Lion**

4 **Horton on Fourth Apartments**

5 **Golden West Hotel**

6 **Lester Hotel**

7 **Royal Pie Bakery**

8 **Horton Grand/Kahle Saddlery Hotels**

9 **Grand Pacific Hotel**

10 **Pioneer Warehouse Lofts**

11 **Bridgeworks**

12 **Gaslamp Quarter Park**

13 **Brunswig Drug Company**

14 **East West Building**

15 **William Heath Davis House**

16 **Wimmer-Yamada Building**

17 **The Baltic Inn**

18 **Backesto Building**

19 **McGurck Building/Z Gallerie**

20 **I.O.O.F. Building**

21 **Yuma Building**

22 **Aztec Theatre/Urban Outfitters**

23 **Old City Hall**

24 **Cole Block Building**

25 **Gaslamp Pacific Stadium 15**

26 **Llewelyn Building**

27 **Loring Building/Fritz Building**

28 **Spencer Ogden/DeLaval Building**

29 **George Hill Building**

30 **St. James Hotel**

31 **Marston Building**

32 **Nesmith-Greeley Building**

33 **Louis Bank of Commerce**

34 **Keating Building**

35 **Ingersoll Tutton Building**

36 **San Diego Hardware**

37 **Onyx Building**

38 **Watts-Robinson Building/
Jewelers Exchange**

39 **Dalton Building**

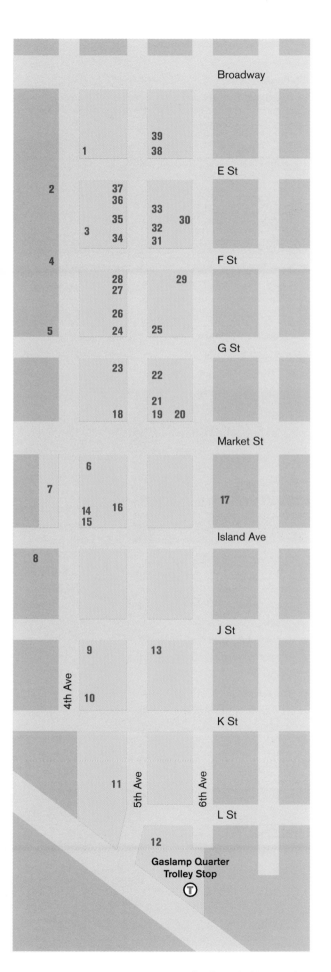

Broadway

39
38
1

E St

2
37
36
33
35   30
3   34
32
31

4

F St

28   29
27
26
5   24   25

G St

23
22
21
18   19   20

Market St

6
7
17
14   16
15

Island Ave

8

J St

9   13

4th Ave

10

K St

11

5th Ave

6th Ave

L St

12

Gaslamp Quarter
Trolley Stop
Ⓣ

GASLAMP QUARTER

1 / **Lawyer's Block Building** (1889)
919 Fourth Ave.
MCDOUGALL AND SONS

Longtime home to San Diego barristers, this structure mixes Italian
Renaissance and Victorian details with Roman arches and pilasters.

GASLAMP QUARTER HISTORIC STRUCTURE

---

2 / **Balboa Theatre** (1924)
Fourth and E St.
WILLIAM WHEELER

Downtown's landmark the-
ater had been mostly dor-
mant since the mid-1980s,
until renewed renovation
efforts began in 2001. This
1,500-seat playhouse
showcased both movies
and stage dramas, with its
sizeable orchestra pit,
stage, and overhead "fly
space" for scenery. Waterfalls flanking the stage gushed during intermis-
sions. The tiled dome is a cousin of domes on the Santa Fe Depot downtown, and on the California Tower in Balboa Park. Visionary planners
included the Balboa in the Horton Plaza mall redevelopment scheme.

GASLAMP QUARTER HISTORIC STRUCTURE

---

3 / **Ingle Building/Golden Lion** (1906)
424 F St.
EDWARD QUAYLE

A prototypical renovation that hailed the beginning of the Gaslamp's
rebirth in 1982, this building had its stained glass windows restored, and
a 25-foot stained-glass dome from the Stockton Elks Club, circa 1906,
was added, along with the mural along F Street.

4 / **Horton on Fourth Apartments** (1994)
808 Fourth Ave.
CARRIER JOHNSON

After a decade of look-
ing at the exposed steel-
and-concrete edge of
Horton Plaza's parking
structure, this inventive
project filled the long
narrow strip between the garage and the sidewalk with 66 residential
units above street-level restaurant and retail spaces. The architecture combines modern details and uptempo colors with a scale that suits the
neighborhood.

5 / **Golden West Hotel** (1913)
720 Fourth Ave.
HARRISON ALBRIGHT WITH JOHN LLOYD WRIGHT

Frank Lloyd Wright
designed unbuilt proj-
ects for San Diego;
his son John realized
a handful of designs
here. He collaborated
on the Golden West as a 19-year-old in the office of San Diego architect
Harrison Albright. Originally a blue collar hotel, this reinforced concrete
block structure features corner sculptures by Alfonzo Ianelli, hired in 1914
by FLW to create sculpture for Midway Gardens in Chicago.

GASLAMP QUARTER HISTORIC STRUCTURE

6 / **Lester Hotel** (1906)
417 Market St.
WILLIAM QUAYLE

A cornerstone of early San Diego
night life, this building housed the
Goodwill Bar from 1906 to
1945, a pool hall beginning in
1923, and downtown's famed McDini's Corned Beef beginning in 1945.
The Lester Hotel opened here in 1915. Note the decorative brick at the
roofline and the diagonal corner entry. GASLAMP QUARTER HISTORIC STRUCTURE

7 / **Royal Pie Bakery** (1884)
554, 558, 560 Fourth Ave.

In the early 1980s, you could
still smell sweet potato pies
baking here, before the space
became an Irish pub. Upstairs,
the Anchor Hotel was a turn-
of-the-century favorite spot for
hookers and their clients; citing
"rampant immorality," building
owner Martha Kuhnel closed the hotel in the 1920s. Now occupied by
contemporary restaurants.

GASLAMP QUARTER

8 / Horton Grand/Kahle Saddlery Hotels
(1886-8/1980s)

311 Island Ave.

M.W. DONALDSON
(RECONSTRUCTION)

San Diego's oldest Victorian hotel, the Grand was renamed the Hotel Horton in 1907. In 1981 the Horton and the downtown Kahle Saddlery were taken apart and re-assembled here as a single hotel joined by a new atrium, with the Horton on the left and the Saddlery on the right.

GASLAMP QUARTER HISTORIC STRUCTURE

9 / Grand Pacific Hotel (1887)
437 J St.

CLEMENT & STANNARD

The Gaslamp's only Victorian hotel still in its original location, the Grand Pacific was home to Children's Hospital and various children's agencies. Brick veneer facings, iron cornices and columns, and plate-glass windows make this one of the most distinctive Victorian-style buildings in the Gaslamp.

GASLAMP QUARTER HISTORIC STRUCTURE

10 / Pioneer Warehouse Lofts (1919/1991)
311 Fourth Ave.

EUGENE HOFFMAN

A smart conversion (by Bundy & Thompson) of a cast concrete and brick warehouse building into 85 live-work lofts paved the way for many other adaptations of nearby period buildings for contemporary uses.

11 / Bridgeworks (2000)
Fifth Avenue between K Street and Harbor Drive

CARRIER JOHNSON

Originally presented as a blockbuster project including a highrise tower that would have dwarfed adjacent historical buildings, Bridgeworks is the positive result of several years of haggling between the developer, architect, and city planners. A reduced hotel tower was built behind a lowrise retail strip that suits the scale of Fifth Avenue and incorporates bricks and design details from the T.M. Cobb warehouse that formerly stood here.

DOWNTOWN HIGHLIGHT

Asian-Pacific Historic District

Since the turn of the 20th century, Chinese-Americans have been a force in the Gaslamp Quarter. Recognition of their impact came with the creation in 1987 of this Gaslamp adjunct district, bounded by Second, Sixth, Market, and J streets, and  including more than a dozen historic structures. Some of the architecture exhibits Asian roots. Buildings here include: Chinese Laundry (1923), 527 Fourth Ave, occupied most recently by an art gallery; Casa de Tomas Addition/Sewing Factory (1930), 520 Fourth Ave.; Tai Sing building (1923), 539 Fourth Ave; Quin Building (1930), 500 Fourth  Ave.; the red-tile-roofed Lincoln Hotel (1913), 536 Fifth Ave.; and the Pacifica Hotel (1910), 547 Fourth Ave., once a Chinese-owned warehouse, a dance hall, and, most recently, a restaurant with a flamenco club in the basement. Also note the Manila Cafe (1930), 515 Fifth Avenue, where former San Diego Mayor Maureen O'Connor's father, once a popular local boxer known as Kid O'Connor, ran a billiard hall on the ground floor from 1939 to 1943; the Nanking Cafe (1912), 467 Fifth Ave., with details including a cast-iron column decorated with 3/4-inch tiles; the Chinese Mission Building (1927), 400 Third Avenue—designed by Irving Gill's nephew Louis Gill—one of the Gaslamp's few Mission Revival style, featuring a clay tile roof and bell tower; the Chinese Consolidated Benevolent Association (1911), 428 Third Avenue, where original  tenants the Gee Goon Tong helped plot the 1912 revolution that made China a republic; and the Ying-On Merchants & Labor Benevolent Association (1925), 500 3rd Avenue.

12 / Gaslamp Quarter Park (1994)

Foot of Fifth Avenue

In Martin Luther King Promenade, by trolley tracks

AUSTIN HANSEN DESIGN GROUP

A fountain of unpredictable water spouts designed by L.A.'s Wet Design makes this Parterre-designed plaza an entertaining place for tourists and locals, children and adults who still know fun when they see it.

GASLAMP QUARTER

13 / **Brunswig Drug Company** (1900)
363 Fifth Ave.

This brick building, with its cast-iron columns and big windows, was home to the Brunswig store and pharmacy until 1960. San Diego artist David Robinson added a mural on the south wall.

GASLAMP QUARTER HISTORIC STRUCTURE

14 / **East West Building** (1990)
517 Fourth Ave.
RNP

Contemporizing the traditional brick warehouse, the architects created a sculptural mix of simple geometric forms energized by a curving upper facade that "floats" above the rectilinear ground level—the curve softens the appearance from the street, and the visual impact of this new structure on the historic William Heath Davis House next door. The building is skinned in brick veneer—the thinness revealed to signal that the material is a wrapper, not a structural element. A Japanese courtyard garden in back adds natural light.

15 / **William Heath Davis House** (1850)
410 Island Ave.

Shipped around Cape Horn, this was one of a handful of prefab kit "saltbox" houses that were New Town's earliest structures when the center of the city shifted away from Old Town—developer Alonzo Horton occupied the home in 1867. Originally at State and Market Streets, it was restored and moved by the City of San Diego to its current location in 1984 to house Gaslamp Quarter information offices and museum.

GASLAMP QUARTER HISTORIC STRUCTURE

16 / **Wimmer-Yamada Building** (1982)
516 Fifth Ave.
BRUCE DAMMANN

A simple facade framed in teak respects the district's scale and adds a fresh modern face to a historic block.

17 / **The Baltic Inn** (1987)
521 Sixth Ave.
ROB WELLINGTON QUIGLEY

For some 50 years, down-
town San Diego saw no new
affordable rental-room hotels,
known as SROs. Quigley's
204-room Baltic, with its
smart forms and affordable graphic pizazz, proved that "inexpensive" does-
n't have to mean "boring".

---

18 / **Backesto Building** (1873)
614 Fifth Ave.
BURKETT & OSGOOD

The Gaslamp's stateliest retail/commercial building steadies the
streetscape with its long, low, horizontal profile and elegant classical
detailing. In the early 1980s, the Backesto was among the first buildings
restored as the Gaslamp came back to life. GASLAMP QUARTER HISTORIC STRUCTURE

---

19 / **McGurck Building/Z Gallerie** (1887/1995)
611 Fifth Ave.

When this home fur-
nishings store moved
from Horton Plaza to
the Gaslamp (into this
space designed by
Bundy & Thompson), it
legitimized mainstream
retailing in the historic

district. From 1903 to 1984, the space was occupied by Ferris + Ferris
drugstore, where Gregory Peck's father worked as night pharmacist.

---

20 / **I.O.O.F. Building** (1882)
526 Market St.
LEVI GOODRICH

Masons and Odd
Fellows shared this
two-story Italian
Renaissance revival
building.

GASLAMP QUARTER
HISTORIC STRUCTURE

GASLAMP QUARTER

21 / **Yuma Building** (1888)
633 Fifth Ave.

ARMITAGE & WILSON

Restored as a live/work loft by interior designer Marsha Sewell (with architects Macy Henderson Cole), the Yuma became a pioneering example of adaptive re-use in the early 1990s; projects like this revived the notion of living downtown. The building was originally owned by a Captain Wilcox, who arrived here in 1849 as skipper of the *U.S. Invincible.*

GASLAMP QUARTER HISTORIC STRUCTURE

---

22 / **Aztec Theatre/Urban Outfitters** (1905)
665 Fifth Ave.

CLINTON DAY

Originally a meat market (in the old sense), this building became the California Theatre in 1919, and the Aztec in 1930, before becoming a fashion outlet (designed by Pompei) in the 1990s.

---

23 / **Old City Hall** (1874)
433 G St.

WILLIAM LACY

Italianate details include classical columns and brick arches. Two floors added in 1887 by architects Comstock & Trotsche housed the San Diego Public Library. City government moved here in 1890, with the Police Department on the first floor and council chamber on the fourth. Covered with stucco in the 1950s, Old City Hall was restored during the Gaslamp's renaissance to its original brick and stone (including El Cajon granite).

GASLAMP QUARTER HISTORIC STRUCTURE

24 / **Cole Block Building** (1890)
444 G St.

Albert Cole committed suicide soon after his commercial building was completed. Theopile Verlaque, a pioneering vintner, once ran a liquor store on the corner. GASLAMP QUARTER HISTORIC STRUCTURE

25 / **Gaslamp Pacific Stadium 15** (1997)
701 Fifth Ave.
BENSON & BOHL (EXTERIOR) AND KMA (INTERIOR)

Earlier attempts to in-fill new buildings within this historical district failed, often because of inadequate budgets or poor design. The Cineplex succeeds, with a scale suited to the neighborhood and uplifting Deco-inspired details.

26 / **Llewelyn Building** (1887)
726 Fifth Ave.

Ladies of the night were home-ported here during the building's early-20th-century decades, following its early years as the Llewelyn family's shoe store.

27 / **Loring Building** (1873)/**Fritz Building** (1908)
764 and 760 Fifth Ave.

The Renaissance Revival Loring is sibling to the adjacent Fritz. Two facades blend together as one building. The Fritz's lobby features onyx and Tennessee marble. GASLAMP QUARTER HISTORIC STRUCTURE

GASLAMP QUARTER

28 / Spencer Ogden/DeLaval Building (1874)
770 Fifth Ave.
WILLIAM LACY

One of the Gaslamp's oldest structures, this French Renaissance tribute features ironwork forged at San Diego Foundry, as well as locally quarried Cajon granite detailing. Realtors, drug stores, a home furnishings outlet, and dentists including "Painless Parker" were among early tenants. GASLAMP QUARTER HISTORIC STRUCTURE

29 / George Hill Building (1897)
533 F St.
ZIMMER & REAMER

Built after fire destroyed Horton's Hall, the three-story stone-and-pressed-brick building housed five storerooms and 30 offices. The San Diego State Normal School (now SDSU) had space on the upper floors in 1898; the Isaac Ratner Cap Manufacturing Company, later Ratner's Clothing, once manufactured here. GASLAMP QUARTER HISTORIC STRUCTURE

30 / St. James Hotel (1912)
830 Sixth Ave.

When it opened, this was San Diego's tallest building, housing a barber shop, Turkish bath, billiard parlor, and observation room with a prime view of the city. Modern conveniences included hot and cold running water and two high-speed elevators.

31 / **Marston Building** (1881)

801 Fifth Ave.

STEWART BROTHERS

San Diego's first department store was opened in this Italianate Victorian in 1881 by civic father George Marston, who later commissioned planner John Nolen's prescient plans for the San Diego region. The YMCA board (chaired by Marston) and the Prohibition Temperance Union met here in the 1880s. San Diego Federal Savings and the San Diego Building and Loan Association (the first S.D. bank to offer home loans) opened offices here in 1885; after a 1903 fire, the building was remodeled. The city's first gaslamp was installed on this corner in 1885, its first electric arc lamp illuminated here in 1886.

GASLAMP QUARTER HISTORIC STRUCTURE

32 / **Nesmith-Greeley Building** (1888)

825 Fifth Ave.

COMSTOCK & TROTSCHE

This four-story brick-and-granite Romanesque Revival gem features cast-iron pillars that support brick piers. In 1889 and 1890, Mrs. Clara Shortridge Foltz, the first woman admitted to the California State Bar, had her law office here. In the 1910s and 1920s, Asian merchants occupied space here.

GASLAMP QUARTER HISTORIC STRUCTURE

33 / **Louis Bank of Commerce** (1888)

835 Fifth Ave.

CLEMENT & STANNARD

Built by the same siblings as the Hotel Del Coronado, this twin-towered, four-story brick-and-granite Grande Dame is the Gaslamp's most stately Victorian. The ground floor housed a bank, and later an oyster bar frequented by Wyatt Earp. Upstairs was the Golden Poppy Hotel, a brothel run by a fortune teller.

GASLAMP QUARTER HISTORIC STRUCTURE

GASLAMP QUARTER

34 / **Keating Building** (1890)
432 F St.
REID BROTHERS

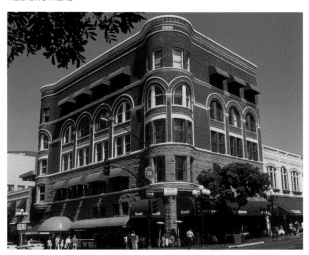

Cornice bears the name of the original owner's husband George. Steam heat and a wire cage elevator made this a state-of-the-art Victorian office building.

GASLAMP QUARTER HISTORIC STRUCTURE

---

35 / **Ingersoll Tutton Building** (1894)
832 Fifth Ave.

Corbelled brickwork and Palladian windows contribute to the Romanesque theme here. With its 16-foot ceilings and picture windows, this was the most expensive San Diego building the year it opened: it cost $20,000.

GASLAMP QUARTER HISTORIC STRUCTURE

---

36 / **San Diego Hardware** (1910)
846 Fifth Ave.

A dance hall and a Woolworth's once operated here; San Diego Hardware is one of the region's few remaining independent home improvement centers, not squeezed out by warehouse chains.

GASLAMP QUARTER HISTORIC STRUCTURE

37 / **Onyx Building** (1910)
852 Fifth Ave.

Modeled after the Fritz building on Fifth near F, this three-story pressed-brick structure housed offices and apartments upstairs, and retail at the street level, including Cleator's shoestore. Stained glass and green-and-white tiled sign are original. GASLAMP QUARTER HISTORIC STRUCTURE

38 / **Watts-Robinson Building/ Jewelers Exchange**
(1913)
520 E St.
BRISTOW AND LYMAN

This concrete Chicago-style high-rise was one of San Diego's first towers. It housed jewelers amid marble wainscoting, tile floors, and brass fixtures; in the 1980s and 1990s, it was renovated as a restaurant and hotel.

GASLAMP QUARTER HISTORIC STRUCTURE

39 / **Dalton Building** (1894)
939 Fifth Ave.
F.W. STEVENSON

Manhattan Restaurant and Hotel (a hookers' haven) once operated here; the basement was a Prohibition-era speakeasy. In 1930, the building received an Art Deco facelift.

GASLAMP QUARTER HISTORIC STRUCTURE

East Village

Downtown's newest redeveloped neighborhood, East Village is also its most diverse. Originally a Victorian mixed-use neighborhood, later a warehouse district conveniently situated near railroad freight and shipping lines, today East Village is a collection of artists' lofts, new hotels, and new apartments where a new baseball park and central library will be situated. San Diego City College provides an academic anchor for a growing number of technology and communications companies in new offices wired for the future. The New School of Architecture and Woodbury University add two strong design institutions.

Long, low utilitarian warehouse buildings define the rhythms of East Village's streets. Some of the new loft-style residential projects capture the scale and feel of old warehouses, which range from basic boxes to more stylish buildings designed by some of San Diego's most prominent architects: William S. Hebbard, John B. Stannard, Louis Gill, Harrison Albright, Charles and Edward Quayle, Eugene Hoffman, Gustav Hanssen, and William Templeton Johnson.

Although many of its original buildings have been torn down, East Village still has a few fine homes from the Victorian era, when SDG&E built an oil gas manufacturing plant south of Imperial between 8th and 9th Avenues, as well as a forge and blacksmith shop. Original hotels serving visiting businessmen included the Orford, the Lee, and the Clermont. Lawton's Car Hop Restaurant (now a liquor store) on Market Street was San Diego's prototypical drive-in fast food outlet—years before Jack-In-The-Box was born here.

During the 1960s and 1970s, East Village—then known as Centre City East—suffered the same neglect as the rest of downtown, as new development and business interests gravitated to other areas in the region. When redevelopment began in 1975, efforts focused on downtown's core, but later expanded to include East Village.

East Village is well connected to the region at large, with the San Diego Police Headquarters situated here, and the San Diego Trolley cutting through on 12th Avenue. As part of the revitalization effort, this street was designated as an urban boulevard that connects Balboa Park with the waterfront. As such, it was the focus of an urban design effort that added street trees, new landscaping, and public art.

In the past decade East Village has become a vital 24-hour-a-day neighborhood of diverse uses; with its overall density still low, and with much land still eligible for new projects, this area will continue to transform.

East Village Locations

1 **Riviera Apartments**

2 **Timken Building**

3 **Old Main Post Office**

4 **Fletcher-Lovett Building**

5 **Pierrot Theatre/First Baptist Church**

6 **Hotel Mediterranean**

7 **Coliseum Athletic Club/ Jerome's Furniture Warehouse**

8 **Broadway Manor**

9 **The Buckner**

10 **Maryland Hotel**

11 **Arlington Hotel**

12 **Eagles Hall**

13 **Gaslamp Liquor/Lawton's Car Hop Restaurant**

14 **Coast Hotel/Occidental Hotel**

15 **Klauber-Wangenheim Building**

16 **Fire Station #4**

17 **T.R. Produce Warehouse/ Wellman Peck and Company**

18 **Palms Hotel**

19 **Roberto Martinez/ Sheldon Residence**

20 **Mills Building**

E St

F St

G St

Market St

Island Ave

J St

K St

L St

6th Ave

7th Ave

8th Ave

Im

2

10

11

12

14

15

16

1

A St

1

B St

City College
Trolley Stop

C St

8

Broadway

5

6   7

9

12th & Market
Trolley Stop

18

19

20 12th & Imperial
Trolley Transfer Station

10th Ave
11th Ave
12th Ave
13th St
14th St
15th St
16th St
17th St

Commercial

EAST VILLAGE

1 / **Riviera Apartments** (1928)
1312 12th Ave.

Stepping from five to four stories due to its sloped site, this brick building features horizontal tan brick bands at the roofline and top floor, and raised brick quoins at corners.

2 / **Timken Building**
(1908-1910)
861 Sixth Ave.
HARRISON ALBRIGHT

One of San Diego's early Chicago-style buildings, this eight-story reinforced concrete structure was stripped of Albright's original classical exterior details during a 1950s makeover.

3 / **Old Main Post Office** (1936)
815 E St.
WILLIAM TEMPLETON JOHNSON

A grand reinforced concrete public building in the WPA Moderne style of the day, with fluted travertine pilasters and terra cotta reliefs above nine entrances depicting various modes of transport.

4 / **Fletcher-Lovett Building** (1910/1932)
920 E St.

Moved to this location and remodeled in 1932, this three-story brick and steel structure has tall Corinthian pilasters set off by commercial steel windows: ancient meets modern.

5 / **Pierrot Theatre/First Baptist Church** (1912)
906 Tenth Ave.
NORMAN MARSH

This three-story Mission Revival structure has been altered from the original, but this twin-towered building remains (along with downtown's Santa Fe Depot) as a rare San Diego example of that romantic style. It has recently been converted for residential lofts.

6 / **Hotel Mediterranean** (1915)
1327-1331 E St.

Fine and simply detailed box of a neoclassical structure, with clapboard siding and decorative wood bands around the base. Window placement is meticulously ordered; each triple window has a leaded glass transom and a double-hung window on each side of a large fixed window.

7 / **Coliseum Athletic Club/Jerome's Furniture Warehouse** (1926)
1485 E St.
JOHN S. SIEBERT

Before use by San Diego's large discount furniture chain, this was a popular spectator sports venue, with vaulted roofs adding extra space for lighting and seating. Arched doorways and decorative grates are part of the simple Spanish Revival design scheme.

8 / **Broadway Manor** (1912)
1640 Broadway

A three-story Italian Renaissance Revival apartment building is classical in the symmetry of its facade and plan including the centered entrance.

9 / **The Buckner** (1906)
765 Tenth Ave.
S.G. KENNEDY

Combining Craftsman (leaded windows), Italianate (rooftop balustrade), and Victorian (bay windows) elements, this 27-unit apartment building is an example of early-century transitional architecture.

10 / **Maryland Hotel** (1914)
612-650 F St.
W.S. HEBBARD AND FRANK P. ALLEN.

A six-story brick beauty with Italian Renaissance Revival details including corner quoins, and a belt course and cornice lining the top floor, and with steam heat, a central vacuum system, and marble tile floors.

EAST VILLAGE

11 / Arlington Hotel (1928)
701 Seventh Ave.
LOUIS GILL

Originally used as a hospital, this three-
story flat-roofed brick building designed
by Irving Gill's nephew stood out as a spare, modernist design, at a time
when neoclassical and Mediterranean influences predominated.

12 / Eagles Hall
(1917 & 1934)
733 Eighth Ave.
WILLIAM WHEELER AND
JOHN SELMAR SIEBERT

Three-story stucco-covered brick build-
ing combines Greek-spirited Colonial Revival (instead of the Spanish
mode common to San Diego) and Egyptian Deco elements.

13 / Gaslamp Liquor/Lawton's Car Hop
Restaurant (1949)
837 Market St.

Before Jack-in-the-Box was
born in San Diego, Lawton's
was one of the first Southern
California drive-ins, an early
sign of the coming culture of the car.

14 / Coast Hotel/Occidental Hotel (1887)
501 Seventh Ave.

This wood-frame stucco building
was unusually free of ornamentation for its time.

15 / Klauber-Wangenheim Building (1929)
611 Island Ave.
WILLIAM WHEELER

Named for two prominent entrepreneurs and city fathers, the structure is
important as one of San Diego's early International-style warehouses,
sparingly decorated with small reliefs.

16 / **Fire Station #4** (1936-1938)

400 Eighth Ave.

GUSTAV A. HANSSEN

Sleek, WPA-funded modern structure of poured reinforced concrete, with a land-mark corner tower that serves as a hanging/ drying space for hoses. Dentilated freeze and parapet are Deco details.

17 / **T.R. Produce Warehouse/ Wellman Peck and Company** (1933)

808 J St.

JULIUS KRAFT & SONS

A block-size brick warehouse with Chicago-style steel windows and a rooftop clerestory spine to admit natural light.

18 / **Palms Hotel** (1889)

509 12th Ave.

Three-story brick-and-wood structure features rectangular, angular, and octagonal bay windows, with Italianate cornices, brackets, friezes, and window mouldings. French Second Empire (think mansard roofs) rooftop towers were removed in the 1920s.

19 / **Roberto Martinez/Sheldon Residence** (1886)

1245 Island Ave.

COMSTOCK AND TROTSCHE

Quirky Queen Anne by San Diego's leading Victorian-era residential architects, this home is a kaleidoscope of details: fish-scale shingles, angled and square bay windows topped by pediments, and a wraparound porch with turned posts, pediments, and spindlework. The house was moved from 11th and Broadway to this site in 1913; a tower was replaced with a dormer in the 1940s.

20 / **Mills Building** (1988)

1255 Imperial Ave.

DELAWIE BRETTON WILKES

With its clean lines, this significant transit hub in a revitalizing neighborhood was something of an anomaly when it opened, at a time when frillier postmodernism was still kicking. The Mills Building—which combines offices and retail space with a light rail trolley station and a land-mark clock tower—proves once again that form and function can co-exist.

Cortez Hill

Hilltop views drew prominent San Diegans such as Andrew Johnston, John Ginty, Rev. E.S. Chase, Dr. Sarah Winn, and others to build homes here during the 1870s, 1880s, and 1890s—subdividing land once set aside as part of Balboa Park. As plans for the 1915 Panama-California Exposition in the park progressed, apartments and hotels were added: the Sandford, the Arno, the Wilsonia, the Hotel Reiss.

Planner John Nolen's 1926 update of his 1908 regional plan emphasized development of downtown along the waterfront, including a civic mall at the foot of Cedar Street, connecting the seat of government with Balboa Park. With civic attentions turned to Cortez Hill, the El Cortez Hotel and Convention Center, designed by Los Angeles architects Walker & Eisen, was built in 1926—a modern structure with ornate Spanish Colonial details in the spirit of Balboa Park's buildings.

With the addition of the Sky Room and glass elevator in the 1950s, the El Cortez became even more of a land-mark: not only a visible urban icon, but a place where San Diegans dined and shared drinks on special occasions such as marriage proposals, anniver-saries, and graduations, while watching the spectacle of air-planes touching down at Lindbergh Field, and ships pass-ing in and out of San Diego Bay.

By the 1970s, however, other hotels and convention centers were taking business away from the El Cortez, and the once-vital and upscale residen-tial neighborhood had become an affordable rental zone. At various times in the next two decades the hotel was deserted; it was also used by the military and charitable organizations to provide inexpensive lodging. In the early 1980s, the El Cortez was owned and occupied by Morris Cerrullo and his World Evangelism. Several plans for reno-vation and re-use followed, but none materialized until Peter Janopaul and Anthony Block bought the building, renovated it as apartments (removing the 1950s additions to meet historic guidelines), and re-opened it in 1999.

Revival of the Cortez spurred neighborhood revitalization through a combination of historic preservation and major new residential development.

Today, Cortez Hill is a legitimate urban neighborhood again, with homes ranging from rentals to upscale condo-miniums, and architecture spanning 100 years, from turn-of-the-century homes such as the Ginty residence (moved

to its current location in 2001) and the Mills residence sharing the hill with newer developments such as architect/developer Ted Smith's modest mixed residential project to the 22-story Discovery at Cortez Hill condominium tower–which overshadows the El Cortez as the highest building on the hill. Pedestrian-friendly planning elements include the new Tweet

Street neighborhood park featuring colorful birdhouses designed by San Diego artists and children.

Cortez Hill is a legitimate urban neighborhood again, with homes ranging from rentals to upscale condominiums, and architecture spanning 100 years.

Cortez Hill Locations

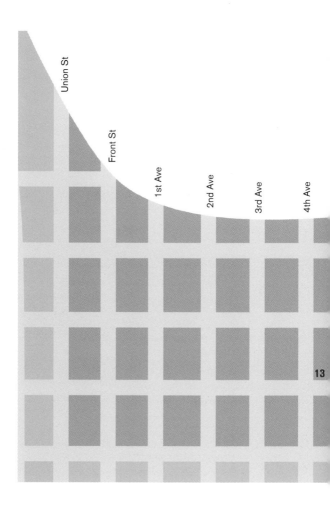

1 **Cortez Hill Transitional Housing**

2 **Ninth and Beech**

3 **CityMark on Cortez Hill**

4 **Soleil Court**

5 **Cortez Hill Park/Tweet Street**

6 **Discovery at Cortez Hill**

7 **Heritage Apartments**

8 **El Cortez Hotel**

9 **Mills Residence**

10 **The Mills at Cortez Hill**

11 **St. Cecilia Chapel**

12 **Dr. W. Peper Residence**

13 **Hearne Surgical Hospital**

14 **Sandford Hotel**

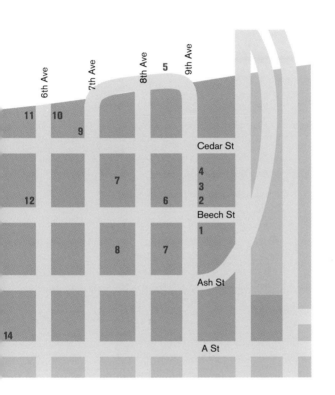

CORTEZ HILL

1 / Cortez Hill Transitional Housing (2003)
Ninth Avenue and Beech Street
GOLBA ARCHITECTURE

Here is an imaginative conversion of the old Days Inn Motel, into light-filled modern housing for homeless families.

2 / Ninth and Beech (1991)
1515 Ninth Avenue
SMITH AND OTHERS

Ranging from small apartments near the corner to spacious townhomes up Ninth, this is another of developer/architect Ted Smith's scrappy infills, with an exterior that utilizes common materials in uncommon ways.

3 / CityMark on Cortez Hill (2002)
1523 Ninth Avenue
MCKINLEY & ASSOCIATES

Sixteen townhomes inspired by East Coast brownstones, the project features pedestrian-friendly stoops and street trees, and, for residents, backyards and roof decks. These "walkups" have underground parking.

Other units are accessible on 10th avenue.

4 / Soleil Court (2002)
1539-1545 Ninth Ave.
JIM KELLEY-MARKHAM

Mixing Californian and Parisian traditions, these eight townhomes are arranged in a courtyard plan, and feature details such as balconies, recessed windows, and french doors.

5 / **Cortez Hill Park/Tweet Street** (2003)
North of Date Street between Eighth and Ninth Avenues

Artist Candace Lopez conceived the "Tweet Street" public art installation: pole-mounted birdhouses designed by artists and students. On the seam between the dense urb and nearby Balboa Park, this gesture toward Mother Nature is much appreciated.

6 / **Discovery at Cortez Hill** (2002)
850 Beech Street
JOHN PERKINS & CO.

At 22 stories, it's bigger than the historic El Cortez Hotel a block away—but makes a neighborly gesture by stepping back from surrounding streets. Horizontal window bays maximize views, and they are spectacular from this high point in downtown San Diego. A rooftop pool and deck help residents enjoy their panoramic perspective.

7 / **Heritage Apartments** (2002)
750 & 855 Beech Street
TOGAWA & SMITH

Covering two blocks adjacent to the historic El Cortez tower, the Heritage is more noteworthy design-wise for preserving two Victorian houses, than for its 230 new apartments in 4-story structures. Formerly at 1543 Seventh Ave., the Ginty Residence (1886) was relocated to the corner of Cedar and Ninth, renovated, and used by an interior designer as live-work space. The Kroenert Residence (1899), 1471 Eighth Ave., is a prime pre-modernist design by Irving Gill with William Hebbard.

8 / **El Cortez Hotel** (1927)
702 Ash Street
WALKER & EISEN

San Diegans spent many romantic evenings in the Sky Room lounge, added in the 1950s to this 14-story tower. The modern reinforced concrete building has a Spanish Churrigueresque entry featuring pilasters, ornate capitals, and decorative urns, crests, foliage, and ribbons. In the late 1990s, the Sky Room was removed when the tower was renovated as apartments, with its original red neon sign restored.

CORTEZ HILL

9 / **Mills Residence** (1901)
1604 Seventh Ave.
HEBBARD AND GILL

Another example of pre-modern Gill, here combining Craftsman and Prairie influences. The sideways gabled roof has a steeper-than-Prairie pitch. Craftsman details include exposed, carved rafter tails and a Granite chimney.

10 / **The Mills at Cortez Hill** (2003)
Cedar Street between Sixth and Seventh Avenues
M.W. STEELE GROUP

New apartments built around the historic Mills residence (1901), a grand Craftsman mansion on a raised granite foundation, with clapboard siding and a granite chimney.

11 / **St. Cecilia Chapel** (1928)
1620 Sixth Ave.

An extreme example of adaptive re-use: this former funeral chapel has been used in recent years as a theatrical playhouse.

12 / **Dr. W. Peper Residence** (1894)
1502 Sixth Ave.

Intriguing asymmetrical design features cross-gabled roof and diagonal corner entrance. Decorative details include turned porch posts, fish-scale shingles—it's a quirky variation of Queen Anne.

13 / **Hearne Surgical Hospital** (1906)
400-420 Ash St.
QUAYLE BROTHERS

Three eyebrow arches crown this eclectic Edwardian-style building, with its base of brick and artificial stone inspired by Chicago's Richardsonian era. Originally a private hospital, the building was renovated in 1973, and has been adapted for office use.

14 / **Sanford Hotel** (1913)
1301 Fifth Ave.
HENRY LORD GAY

Built to house visitors to the 1915 Panama-California Exposition, this u-shaped four-story hotel has decorative cornices and friezes; an arcade that ran along A and Fifth has been partially enclosed. Originally this was an early example of mixed-use development, with three floors of hotel rooms, above ground-level retail/commercial uses.

Little Italy

In 1850, speculators bought 800 acres between Old Town and the New Town being promoted miles to the south by William Heath Davis. Investors including Tennessean Cave Couts, Peruvian Juan Bandini, and Mexican Jose Maria Estudillo, foreshadowing the cross-cultural mix of sights, sounds, cuisines, and architectural details that became Little Italy's calling card. Being speculators, though, the investors held their land for several decades without building.

Lusardi, Piazza, Mosto, Remondino, and Raffin were among the earliest Italian families who came to San Diego during the 1860s and 1870s. By the first decade of a new century the area known as Middletown was populated with Portuguese and Genoese fishing families who founded San Diego's tuna industry. By the late 1930s, the waterfront strip south of Washington Street had a business district, fish canneries, and a residential neighborhood supported by the nearby fishing and aircraft industries. Eventually the concentration of homes and businesses became known as Little Italy.

Italian residents were forced from waterfront homes during the fear of foreigners induced by World War II. The area's original distinguishing architecture consists mainly of residences in late Victorian and early 20th century Craftsman styles. Some of the newer buildings reference the district's heritage, others make no attempt to encompass history.

More than 6,000 families once lived in Little Italy. Construction of Interstate 5 during the 1960s ripped through the neighborhood's heart, destroying an estimated 35% of homes and businesses, prompting 30 years of decline. Through economic ups and downs, including the collapse of the tuna industry, and urbanization, though, the authentic core of Little Italy survived along India between Cedar and Grape, centered around Assenti Pasta, Filippi's Pizza Grotto (formerly a stable and blacksmith shop), Solunto's Bakery, Mimmo's café, and Café Zucchero; Our Lady of the Rosary remains as a symbol of the community's faith.

Despite Little Italy's will to survive, recognition of the district's significance was slow to come. By 1980, when 30 or so buildings were designated as historic, protecting such essential details as facades and tow-

ers, some of the best buildings had already been torn down. Other buildings that give Little Italy its character remain at risk; the area has become a hot spot for downtown housing ranging from small apartments to high-rise condominiums that threaten not only the architectural character of the neighborhood, but its scenic views of San Diego Bay and the shoreline.

Architects including Rob Wellington Quigley (whose La Pensione Hotel replaced the old Bernardino's Dry Good Store and Tait's Market), Ted Smith, Jonathan Segal, and Public designed new residential projects beginning in the late 1980s that proved new buildings, whether contemporary or historical in character, can fit well with the scale and character of this colorful early San Diego neighborhood. To Little Italy's credit, a strong local merchants association has emphasized locally owned businesses and insisted on advising the planning and design of new developments, in order to avoid the kinds of generic chains that have turned other areas of San Diego into theme parkish zones that feel like nowhere or everywhere.

Through economic ups and downs and urbanization, the authentic core of Little Italy survived

Little Italy Locations

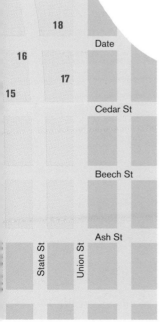

LITTLE ITALY

1 / McDonough Cleaners/City Dye Works (1930)
2400-2404 India St.

An arrow sign signals the corner entry tower (minus its original clock), flanked by tile-roofed wings. Rounded pilasters divide display windows of this commercial Spanish Revival structure.

2 / San Diego Macaroni Manufacturing Co. (1924)
2308 Kettner Blvd.

Reminiscent of other waterfront warehouses and aeronautical buildings, this two-story brick warehouse, with its vaulted roof, is the essence of 1920s San Diego.

3 / Waterfront Apartments (2001)
Kettner Blvd.
JONATHAN SEGAL

You can't tear down the most popular neighborhood watering hole, so Segal saved the circa-1927 bar, with its glass block Deco entry, and named his 42-loft development after it.

4 / Doma Lofts and Townhomes (2003)/California Stamp Building (1930)
Kettner Boulevard between Date and Fir Streets
MARTINEZ & CUTRI

Natural light and open plans make these 124 lofts and townhomes flexible and inviting; retail spaces lining Kettner add to the neighborhood's pedestrian appeal. The new project preserved the original California Stamp Company's cool zigzag Moderne tower.

5 / Camden Tuscany (2003)
West side of Kettner Boulevard, between Cedar and Date Streets
ARK ARCHITECTS

Mixing 163 apartments with retail space and parking, the building incorporates neighborhood forms and Tuscan colors into a modern scheme that transcends the kitschy norm.

6 / **Lusso Lofts** (2001)
1601 Kettner Blvd.
JONATHAN SEGAL

Next generation urban housing from downtown rowhome pioneer architect/developer Jonathan Segal, this 31-unit project extends his legacy of pedestrian-friendly modernism.

---

7 / **Bella Via** (2003)
1608 India St.
CARRIER JOHNSON

Mixed-use residential-retail-commercial creates lively pedestrian activity. Courtyards help this building of 41 flats and town-homes maintain some of the neighborhoods intimate, friendly scale.

---

8 / **LIND** (1999-2001)

Block bordered by Kettner Boulevard; India, Cedar, and Beech Streets

ROB QUIGLEY ARCHITECTS; SMITH AND OTHERS; JONATHAN SEGAL; PUBLIC; ROBIN BRISEBOIS; LLOYD RUSSELL

Redevelopment officials vowed "never again" when they reached the end of this harrowing project (LIND stands for

Little Italy Neighborhood Development), which coordinated six design /development teams on one site to create healthy variety with 16 row homes (Segal), 12 affordable rental lofts (Smith and Public), and 37 low- and moderate-income apartments (Quigley). Yet, when the building began picking up awards, officials were the first to claim credit for this vital project, which maintains the scale and urban character of the neighborhood without resorting to Mediterranean cliches.

LITTLE ITALY

9 / Standard Sanitary Manufacturing Company (1911)

726-734 W. Beech St.

Edwardian details such as dentil moldings decorate this three-story building of concrete cast to resemble quarried stone.

10 / Hampton Inn (2001)

1531 Pacific Highway

JOSEPH WONG

This homage to the circa-1936 County Administration Center at the foot of Cedar Street is a thoughtful alternative to blockbuster hotels that dominate other downtown locales.

11 / San Diego Globe Grain & Milling Co./ Parron-Hall (1909)

820 W. Ash St.

One of the tallest buildings of its day, this concrete, brick, and steel structure is crowned with a gabled ventilating skylight, where dust escaped during production of 20,000 barrels of flour a year.

12 / Village Walk (2001)

1501 India St.

MARTINEZ AND CUTRI

An explosion of colors and geometric forms that bypasses the scale and historic character of the old Little Italy. This project's prime asset is a public plaza lined with cypress trees.

13 / Fire Station/Museum (1915)

1572 Columbia St.

One of Little Italy's few remaining historic public buildings, this utilitarian structure has spare Mission detailing. Today it's a museum for early firefighting memorabilia.

14 / **Porto Siena** (2002)
1601 India St.
WITHEE MALCOLM

Tuscan colors, tile roofs, and wrought iron railings come together in this eclectic attempt at infusing this 88-condominium project with authentic Italian flavor.

15 / **Beaumont Building** (1985)
434 W. Cedar
ROB WELLINGTON QUIGLEY

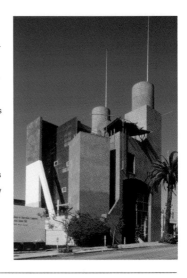

A pale gray presence that echoes twin towers on a nearby Catholic Church, architect Rob Quigley's live-work building contains a top-level penthouse (what views!), Quigley's fourth-floor offices, and leasable space below. It also has the distinction of winning both an Honor Award from his peers and an Onion from a lay public that didn't look at it long enough to see connections to both fine abstract art and the surrounding city.

16 / **Our Lady of the Rosary Church and Parish Hall** (1923)
1654-1668 State St.
GIANNINNI & FERGUSON

This twin-towered community centerpiece has Mediterranean details including tiled roof, arched openings, and ornamental moldings, murals, frescas, panels, and recesses. Ionic columns support statuary flanking the gabled entry—echoes of Italian hilltowns.

17 / **Victorian House Condominiums** (2003)
1632 Union St.
SFERRA-CARNINI

What do genuine Italian architects do in San Diego's Little Italy? They opt for a touch of 19th century Americana—a thoughtful homage to the circa-1887 Oscar Millard Queen Anne Victorian, with its steep roofs and fish-scale shingles.

LITTLE ITALY

18 / **Amici Park** (2001)
State and Date Streets
LANDSCAPE DESIGN: MARIAN MARUM
PUBLIC ART: NINA KARAVASILES

A sort of "town square" created for families, workers, and students from nearby Washington Elementary School, the park celebrates the neighborhood's heritage with a bocci

ball court, and with Karavasiles' sidewalk plaques and café tables, which emphasize the fine Italian cuisine that ties the neighborhood together. Her tables carry recipes in relief on bronze place settings, from which visitors can rub off copies of favorite local recipes using paper and pencil.

19 / **DeFalco's Grocery/San Diego Reader**
1703 India St.

Formerly a neigh-borhood grocery, now home to San Diego's independ-ent alternative weekly, the building is a humble box-like Italianate affair with

clay tile roof trim, and pilasters crowned with bulb-shaped capitals.

20 / **La Pensione** (1991)
600 and 606 W. Date Street
ROB WELLINGTON QUIGLEY

Rather than saving the worn-out Tait's Meat Market building that had been a neighborhood social hub, Quigley recreated the facade along India Street as part of a new four-story building that combines an 80-room sin-gle-room-occupancy hotel and two street-level restaurants that have side-walk tables. Bernardini building also replaced.

21 / Mimmo's Italian Village/Auto Body Company (1927)

1743 India St.

Three arched bays pierce the parapet front facade, which hides a flat roof. The building housed an auto body shop, an aircraft parts warehouse, and a washing machine parts company, before becoming an Italian deli famous for its epic "grab-n-go" submarine sandwiches served amid murals of Italian villages.

DOWNTOWN HIGHLIGHT

County Administration Center

(1936)

1600 Pacific Highway

ARCHITECT:
LOUIS GILL, SAM HAMILL, RICHARD REQUA, WILLIAM TEMPLETON JOHNSON

San Diego's finest civic architecture (not counting Balboa Park) is a WPA-era classic designed by a team of four top architects. Conceived as a Spanish Revival design in the spirit of Balboa Park, the center evolved into a simpler, beautifully proportioned building in the popular 1930s "moderne" style also used for Los Angeles Public Library and Nebraska's state capital building in Lincoln (both by Bertram Goodhue, chief architect for Balboa Park). The landmark tower was scaled back from 225 to 150 feet, due to air traffic and budget concerns. Get out of your car to view exquisite details: Spanish tiles designed by Chicago architect Jess Stanton, fluted plaster mouldings that emphasize the tower's verticality, and, on the west side, sculptor Donal Hord's "Guardian of Water" fountain. John Nolen's urban master plan (1908, 1926) envisioned this building as the seat of a government mall along Cedar Street, but other public buildings never materialized here.

LITTLE ITALY

22 / Filippi's Pizza Grotto/ Albert Muller Grocery (1914/1939)
1747-1753 India St.

Nothing fancy here, but plain white stucco walls, a colorful awning, simple signage, a tiled parapet evoke the humble architecture of Italian villages.

23 / Essex Lofts (2002)
NW corner of State and Fir Streets
SMITH AND OTHERS

With this 36-unit project, architect/developer Ted Smith continues the style-on-a-budget aesthetic he pioneered with the Merrimack Building on nearby Beech Street, and in Del Mar in North County. His neighborly "blendo" approach borrows forms and materials from adjacent buildings.

24 / Milton E. Fintzelberg Commercial Building (1928)

1917-1921 India St.
Concrete-and-brick structure once housed the Avalon movie theater, but the original marquee is long gone. Unadorned pilasters symmetrically divide the front wall, along with four evenly spaced arched windows.

25 / Vue de L'Eau Apartments (1913)
550 W. Grape St.
Craftsman and Mission Revival elements merge in this four-story stucco apartment complex.

26 / India Street Design Center/ San Diego Coffee Co. (1926)

2141-2165 India St.

Two-story brick building combines a warehouse scale and appearance typical of this neighborhood, with more intimate details such as storefront bays defined by brick pilasters and shaded by canvas awnings, and smaller second-floor windows.

Balboa Park

San Diego's greatest triumph of urban planning came in 1868, when the city set aside 1,400 acres as permanent open space just north of downtown. At the time, the context was suburban—more "country" than "city". Today, however, Balboa Park is the cultural and recreational centerpiece of the sixth largest American city—an urban open space and greenbelt as significant to San Diego as Central Park is to New York.

The need for open space was recognized at the outset of downtown development. In 1868, a year after Alonzo Horton acquired 168 downtown acres where he hoped to build a new town, city fathers set aside 1,400 raw, native acres as park land.

"Canyons and mesas were covered by dense chaparral and after winter rains the arid land bloomed in large patch-

es of yellow, white and blue with the many small flowers of wild adenostema, sage brush, 'Spanish' violets, shooting stars, mimulas and white popcorn," wrote Gregory Montes in the *Journal of San Diego History*. "The low-lying vegetation was home to coyotes, wildcats, rabbits, squirrels, quail and lizards."

In 1890, more than 10,000 trees (blue and sugar gums, acacias, pepper trees, fan palms, cypresses) were planted on the 100-acre Howard Tract between Cabrillo and Florida Canyons, and the Ladies Annex of the San Diego Chamber of Commerce planted 700 additional trees and shrubs including eucalyptus, Monterey cypress, acacias, pines, flame trees, and poinsettias along the park's western edge. In 1892, Kate Sessions was granted a free 10-year lease for 32 acres and free water in exchange for creating a public nursery, and planting and maintaining 100 trees in the park each year.

Sessions knew Frederick Law Olmsted's pastoral landscapes in Central Park and elsewhere, and hoped to combine her horticultural ideas with a park plan by a leading landscape architect. She knew that with it's temperate climate, San Diego would support palms, bamboos, cacti, bougainvillea, eucalyptus, pepper trees, poinsettias, and other plants from around the world.

In 1902, the city retained Samuel Parsons, Jr., a protégé of Olmsted and believer in naturalistic planning and landscape design, in letting terrain dictate development. Parsons "warned that when landscape architects created streams and lakes where there was no natural flow of water or when they filled in valleys and canyons formed by nature the results would be disastrous," according to histo-

rian Richard Amero. "Parsons proposed that peripheral roads and bands of trees should define the park's borders. In contrast to straight peripheral roads that would carry through traffic, paths and roads within the park would wind around natural contours, would open surprise views, and would pass along highlands at the edges of canyons. Recognizing that rainfall was scant in Southern California, Parsons advised planting water-consuming grasses in small plots at park entrances. He suggested naming these entrances after trees grouped there, such as Pepper Tree, Blackwood Acacia, Monterey Pine, and Torrey Pine.

"To accentuate wild flowers and to dramatize vistas, he proposed keeping trees on mesas low. Nevertheless, to provide enclosure and to frame views, he would allow eucalyptuses at strategic points on the mesas. Because cuts and fills would mar the contrast between mesas and canyons, he cautioned against them. To intensify the sense of depth in the canyons, he would plant trees in the canyons rather than on the mesas. These trees would become taller as they approached the canyons' rims…he advocated preserving native plants where 'they made the best display,' and…emphasized that flower beds and build-ings should be few and that they should be located in the southern portion of the park." According to historian Montes, Balboa Park's "design and uses," at this point, "were linked more closely than ever to an unbroken chain of 19th- and 18th-century Anglo-American public parks and landscaping tradition from Frederick Law Olmsted to Andrew Jackson Downing, Sir Joseph Paxton, John Nash, Humphrey Repton, William Kent, and Lancelot Brown."

San Diego's population was 39,000 in 1909, when Chamber of

Commerce President G. Aubrey Davidson proposed an internationl expo to celebrate the 1915 christening of the Panama Canal. When San Francisco announced its own expo, San Diego decided on a fair with a regional flavor. "City Park" was renamed "Balboa Park" in 1910, in honor of the explorer who crossed Panama in 1513 and reached the Pacific Ocean.

Despite the significant amount of planning already accomplished by Parsons, the expo committee first choice as master planner for the new expo grounds was Daniel Burnham, founder of the City Beautiful movement and planner for the 1893 World's Columbian Exposition in Chicago. But Burnham was too busy, so San Diego instead retained the Olmsted Brothers—Massachusetts planners and landscape designers, sons of John Olmsted, the patriarch of modern landscape planning who was responsible (with Calvert Vaux) for Central Park in New York. Frank P. Allen, known for his orderly management of an earlier Seattle fair, became director of works for San Diego's expo.

In choosing a lead architect for the expo, the Olmsteds vetoed local favorite Irving Gill, whose spare Mission modernist style was, along with Berkeley architect Bernard Maybeck's designs, one of the earliest examples of regional modernism in California. Instead, the position of fair architect was awarded to New Yorker Bertram Goodhue, who had lobbied hard for the commission.

"I suppose…they have got some incapable local talent for the job, which was, I suppose, no more than could be expected, since human nature in California is very much like human nature everywhere, only perhaps more so," Goodhue wrote, prior to his selection. "I am sorry too for the San Diegans because I consider myself quite a shark on the sort of stuff (Spanish Colonial style) they ought to have and am pretty familiar with California conditions." After prominent architects helped Goodhue with letters of support, San Diego hired him in 1911.

Goodhue discards Olmsted plan

The Olmsted plan concentrated buildings and activities north of San Diego High School.

"A 250 foot wide formal avenue, the 'Plaza Larga' (Long Plaza), extending for almost a quarter mile, was to have been flanked by twenty-five foot wide, arcaded sidewalks and behind them, as this was still pre-Goodhue, several 'Spanish Mission' style exhibition buildings," according to a historical account. "The Plaza Larga ended in a three-acre square, the 'Plaza de Musical' also arcaded and surrounded by several major buildings in the Mexican colonial and Spanish style of a 'Plaza Mayor' (Main Plaza). North and

east of the formal Plaza de Musical the Olmsted plan adapted to a small canyon with informal, curving, 'Picturesque' paths leading to foreign government buildings and a terraced, formal Hispano-Moorish garden with cascades and fountains, modelled somewhat on the Alhambra's Generalife Garden at Granada. The extensive waterworks were to be fed by a fifty million gallon reservoir at the top of the hill near the present Naval Hospital parking lot."

Olmsted and Goodhue made several revisions to this plan. They changed building locations and landscape details to cut costs, enhance views, accommodate a changing list of exhibitors, and incorporate the switch in architectural style from Gill's spare approach to Goodhue's Spanish Colonial.

But Goodhue's ultimate vision was for a more elaborate, higher-profile expo. He decided to concentrate on the site's central mesa, instead of the canyon to the south. Ultimately, the Olmsted notion of a pastoral escape from the city lost out to Goodhue's more formal collection of buildings, exhibits, and gardens. Goodhue and Frank P. Allen then developed the park layout that survives today, organized around the east-west promenade known as the Prado.

Goodhue's Spanish "dream city"

Watercolor renderings of the 1915 expo depict

Goodhue's dreamy vision for the park, and show how San Diego began to be romanticized for marketing purposes, along the same lines as Los Angeles was sold with pastoral images of orange groves on packing crate labels and real estate brochures.

Goodhue felt that the blockbuster scale of international expos in

America overshadowed any sense of place or local character—he believed San Diego to be among the world's most inviting regions:

"The Riviera, the bays of Naples and Salerno, some of the Greek Islands, certain mountain valleys in India, the Vega of Granada, the parallel one of Shiraz….(but) in Southern California may be found every attraction possessed by those cited—the tenderest of skies, the bluest of seas, mountains of perfect outline, the richest of sub-tropical foliage, the soft speech and unfailing courtesy of the half-Spanish, half-Indian peasantry." During the 1915 expo, Goodhue recalled in a memoir, "everything that met the eye and ear of the visitor were meant to recall to mind the glamour and mystery and poetry of the old Spanish days…

"Between the site and that boundary of Balboa Park from which it is most effectively and readily reached, runs a great cleft in the earth, the Canon Cabrillo. Any approach from the west must cross this canon, so, quite as a matter of course, we all visualized a bridge whose eastern end should terminate in a great pile of buildings that should be at once the crux of the whole composition and, with the bridge, should ever remain the focal and dominant point of the city when the Fair, and even the memory of the Fair, had passed utterly."

As a fantasy, the expo was intended as a temporary installation, "for it must be remembered," Goodhue wrote, "that Exposition Architecture differs from that of our everyday world in being essentially of the fabric of a dream—not to endure but to produce a merely temporary effect." Yet several generations of San Diegans successfully fought to preserve the original buildings and gardens—perhaps their efforts have been symptomatic of a region more comfortable with a romanticized past than a modern present and future.

Today, when one walks or drives into Balboa Park over the bridge described by Goodhue, the experience is dramatic transition from the urban realm to a pastel-hued dreamscape.

Beyond the bridge are the California Building's brightly tiled dome and ornately decorated tower—the tower was the first of many towers that would become the region's defining icons and landmarks. The bridge marks the entry to a pedestrian promenade—the Prado—that anchors a Beaux Arts-style axial site plan. Hundreds of yards down this mall to the east, the axis culminates in a fountain with a spire of water that serves as the California Tower's counterpoint.

In most accounts of Southern California's architectural history, it is usually the Los Angeles modernists who are credited for exploiting the intimate connections between indoor and outdoor spaces, between rooms and gardens or courtyards or patios, made possible by temperate weather. But while Goodhue's architectural leanings were traditional, his ideas about responding to climate laid the foundation for generations of regional modernism.

"Only in such a climate and amid such surroundings are open-air concerts possible, therefore, the Great Organ, that was the gift of one of San Diego's most munificent citizens, would remain, faced by its auditorium surrounded by trees and open to the stars. And so, too, would the Botanical Building, under whose protecting treillage grow in rank luxuriance the plants of other and hotter countries.

"In the introduction to a book dealing with the buildings of an exposition," Goodhue concluded, in the years before the second Balboa Park expo, "it is perhaps strange to say quite flatly that so many buildings that have given pleasure to so many should be destroyed; but, after all, this was the paramount idea in the minds of the fair's designers, and only by thus razing all of the temporary buildings will San Diego enter upon the heritage that is rightfully hers."

1935: Richard Requa amends the dream

Twenty years after the first expo established Balboa Park, San Diego presented a more extravagent reprise, with San Diego architect Richard Requa assuming the supervisorial role occupied by Bertram Goodhue for the first expo.

"The Exposition of 1935 represents the full flowering of the ideals which motivated our earlier effort, said G. Aubrey Davidson, president of the first expo, chairman of the board for the second. "In the building of this exposition Mr. Richard Requa figured as the presiding architectural genius. The manner in which he interpreted Mr. Goodhue's architecture scheme in terms of a series of buildings representing a complete history of the Southwest, presents an eloquent testimonial to his great ability and artistry."

According to Requa, "I turned, for ideas and inspiration, to the perhistoric and native architecture of the Southwest, studying the Indian Pueblos and the architecture developed to such a wonderful state of perfection in Mexico and Yucatan by those mysterious early inhabitants, the Aztecs and the Mayas."

Relying on his travels through Morocco, Algeria, and other Mediterranean places, Requa added authentic architectural and landscape details, including the House of Hospitality's new courtyard and Casa del Rey Moro Garden (both of which required significant alterations to Winslow's original design, including removal of a south wing(both of which required significant alterations to Winslow's original design, including removal of a south wing). Also new in 1935 was the Alcazar Garden.

Requa's plan for the 1935 expo expanded the park's building program onto a mesa southwest of the Organ Pavilion. The new area was named "the Palisades" and included the Palisades Building, the New Mexico Building, the House of Pacific Relations, the Ford Building, the Municipal Gymnasium, and the Federal Building.

Requa's own designs of regional-flavored buildings included Spanish Village, intended to replicate real everyday buildings and spaces, and the Pueblo-style Palisades Building. Requa also designed the Moderne Conference Building and Municipal Gymnasium.

Whatever has been said of Requa's eclectic approach, he brought thorough historical knowledge and a commitment to authenticity to his job as director of expo architecture.

To see the evidence, visit the San Diego Historical Society in the park and ask for Requa's oversize limited edition leather-bound travel journals, which include his own photos, sketches, and diary entries from his visits to foreign lands.

Also to his credit, Requa recognized—perhaps to a greater extent than his predecessor Goodhue—that outdoor spaces are as important, maybe more important, than the park's buildings. At the outset, Requa acknowledged the thoughtful plant selections and public spaces made in 1915.

"Indeed, the landscaping had become the outstanding feature of the whole harmonious ensemble," he wrote in his account of the 1935 expo. "This made apparent the fact that the planting of the trees, shrubs, and vines for the first exposition had been carefully planned for the future and not just for the duration of the fair. This consideration of ultimate results influenced me in the planning of garden features for the new exposition. Not only must they harmonzie with the present planting but they should also be permanent additions to the park enhancing the charm of the whole, through the years to come."

"In my travels about the world, I had found three gardens of outstanding interest and beauty. They are all what I call architectural gardens. Gardens that were designed and built, not just graded and planted; gardens that were intimately associated with and really an integral part of the buildings that adjoined them; gardens that were really planned to be furnished and lived in, as an outdoor addition to the building—not merely an improvement of the plot surrounding the structure."

In the future

In the decades since the 1935 expo, several controversies have come to Balboa Park. As recently as the 1970s, it seemed significant original buildings could be lost to neglect. But the 1990s reconstruction of the House of Hospitality and House of Charm sealed the city's commitment to preservation in the park. Meanwhile, landscapes that dated from both expos had been altered with careless or inappropriate plantings, and original plantings had been neglected to an extent that they obscured the buildings. As part of architect Milford Wayne Donaldson's House of Hospitality restoration, landscape architects Garbini & Garbini restored the building's gardens. The Botanical Building has also been restored with all new redwood lath. Over the years, Highway 163 through the park has been preserved as a greenbelt.

San Diego has employed some of the region's most capable planners to map out the park's future—there is still much vacant land that could be developed, especially the expansive East Mesa across Park Boulevard from the park proper. The intrusion of autos has sparked much debate.

Auto traffic has been excluded from some areas, while debate continues as to how or where new parking might be added. Planners have also addressed various proposals to expand the adjacent San Diego Zoo.

Smitten with Goodhue's Spanish Colonial dream, San Diego has occasionally gone overboard in its attempts to hue to and even expand the original themes. In the 1990s, a particularly questionable addition was made to the park: a freestanding arcade in front of the modernist Timken Museum that preservationists claimed was true to 1915 (the Timken's predecessor included an arcade). Rather than enhancing the park's historical aura, the arcade seems more like an attempt by old-school purists to make the Timken invisible with a faux flourish that skeptics refer to as "facade-omy". At the same time, the park (perhaps reflecting the attitudes of the city at large) has not evolved with the times. Architect Rob Quigley's new Activity Center (across Park Boulevard from the rest of the park) is the only truly contemporary design.

If Balboa Park is considered the region's prime cultural respository, then it ought to include some evidence that creativity is alive and well. But it is difficult to imagine Balboa Park ever gaining the equivalent of I.M. Pei's pyramid at the Louvre in Paris – San Diego has never been very comfortable with the notion that the past and present can peacefully co-exist. Balboa Park, and to a large extent the art presented there, reveals a region that has always been most at home with the status quo.

Balboa Park Locations

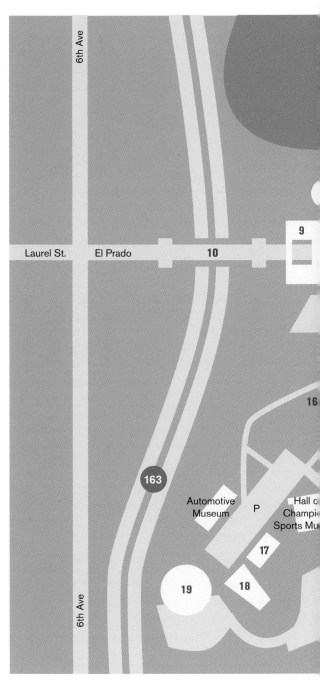

1 **Spanish Village**

2 **Natural History Museum**

3 **Casa Del Prado**

4 **Casa de Balboa**

5 **Botanical Building + Lily Pond**

6 **Timken Museum**

7 **San Diego Museum of Art**

8 **Old Globe Theatre**

9 **California Building/Museum of Man**

10 **Cabrillo Bridge**

11 **Alcazar Garden**

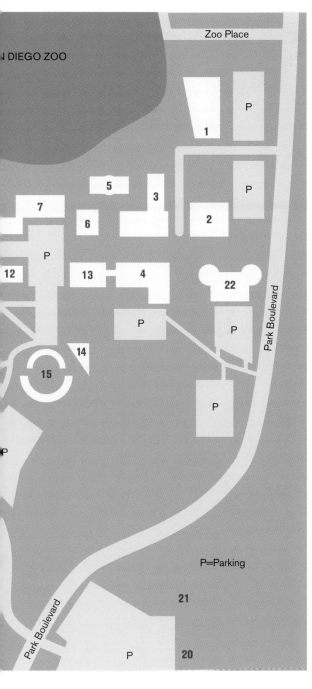

P=Parking

12 House of Charm/Mingei Museum

13 House of Hospitality

14 Japanese Friendship Garden

15 Spreckels Organ Pavilion

16 House of Pacific Relations

17 Municipal Gym

18 Ford/Starlight Bowl

19 Ford Building/Aerospace Museum

20 Naval Hospital

21 Balboa Park Activity Center

22 Reuben H. Fleet Science Center

1 / **Spanish Village** (1935)

RICHARD REQUA

Monumental public buildings inspired by the Spanish Colonial era are well represented along the park's Prado—but Requa also wanted the second expo to offer glimpses of the simpler architecture of everyday life. "Such were the shops, and dwellings of the humbler citizens, not ostentatious but none the less interesting in the naïve expression of native art," Requa wrote in his personal account of planning the expo. "We therefore provided examples of this more intimate phase of the picture of the times in the Spanish Village and in the group of cottages forming the House of Pacific Relations." Situated at the northern edge of the park, near San Diego Zoo, Spanish Village has been the subject of much debate as to whether it should be redeveloped—but changing the look and character of the Village would deprive the park of a folk-art enclave representative of California and Baja's simpler times.

2 / **Natural History Museum** (1933 + 2000)

WILLIAM TEMPLETON JOHNSON/BUNDY & THOMPSON

Only one wing of Johnson's original two-sided design was built, causing a space crunch that persisted until a millenial expansion doubled the museum's size. Johnson's museum is an oddity among park buildings designed by Goodhue—consistently praised for their historical detail and pedestrian-friendly planning. Johnson's museum, by contrast, has a second-story entry that forces visitors to scale a grand staircase. Between its awkward access and monumental scale, the Natural History Museum makes no connections to Goodhue's carefully crafted system of arcades, gardens, and public spaces (nearby is the Plaza de Balboa Fountain designed by Delawie, Macy & Henderson with Wimmer Yamada in 1972). According to historian Richard Amero, "the main facade of the Natural History Museum is a hodgepodge of inharmoniously related trivia [ranging from bison heads to Egyptian cats and sea horses] that does nothing to dramatize the contents inside the building." At the new millenium, Bundy + Thompson designed a major addition.

BALBOA PARK HIGHLIGHT

San Diego Zoo
(1916)
2900 Zoo Dr.

Launched as a rambling series of cages along Park Boulevard that provided a sideshow to the 1915 expo in Balboa Park, the zoo eventually grew into one of the world's largest, with buildings designed by a variety of leading architects. Louis Gill (Irving's nephew) designed the first aviary. Lloyd Ruocco added a building in the Children's Zoo. Tucker Sadler Bennett designed the Otto Center, and several exhibits were designed by Delawie Macy Henderson. Contemporary exhibits (designed under the direction of Zoo Architect David Rice) include Larson Carpenter's Panda Research Station and Dale Jenkins' Heart of the Zoo.

3 / Casa Del Prado (1971)
WHEELER WIMER

Known originally as the Varied Industries and Food Products Building (designed by Carleton Winslow in 1915), this L-shaped Spanish Colonial structure featuring a church-like entrance marked by twin towers crowned by blue-and-yellow tiled domes was the largest of the "temporary" expo buildings. Slated for destruction following the fair, the building was spared during World War I, when it became a military barracks and post office. For the 1935 expo, this became the Food and Beverage building. With reliefs commemorating Father Junipero Serra, the north wing was known as "the church". The south wing includes decoration made from the same molds as on the north, with the addition of seeds, fruits, vegetables, and other agrarian/fertility myth imagery. The east facade served as a surrogate San Simeon in Orson Welles's "Citizen Kane". Campaniles that originally distinguished each wing were not replicated in a 1970-1971 reconstruction that added a second floor and patio within the south building, as well as an open-air patio between the wings.

4 / Casa de Balboa (1915)
WHEELER WIMER

Architect Carleton Winslow's Spanish Renaissance proposal lost out to an eclectic scheme from architect Frank Allen that combined Venetian elements with corner pavilions (dramatically crowned by finials) modeled after a 17th century mansion in Queretaro, Mexico. Despite its haphazard borrowing, the building makes high romance: along the Prado, first-floor arches make this building a part of the arcade through the park's center, beneath second-story balconies with wrought-iron railings and richly detailed mouldings. The tiled roof floats fantastically above it all, supported by kneeling nudes. Although modern architecture wasn't big in 1930s San Diego, L.A. modernist Richard Neutra designed a prefab 20-by-60-foot steel structure erected for the 1935 expo behind the then-Palace of Better Housing. Following destruction by a fire in 1978, the building was reconstructed and renamed "Casa de Balboa." It now houses The San Diego Historical Society, the Model Railroad Museum, and the Museum of Photographic Arts.

5 / **Botanical Building + Lily Pond** (1915)
CARLETON WINSLOW

When it opened, this steel-framed, bent-redwood enclosure was the largest wood lath building in the world—250 feet long, 75 feet wide, 60 feet tall. The steel frame was originally intended for a railroad station; expo planners got it at a bargain price. Renovated at the turn of the new millenium, the building contains more than 2,100 permanent plants as well as changing displays; the adjacent 250,000-gallon lily pond is decorated with dozens of floating water lilies and lotus plants.

6 / **Timken Museum** (1965)
FRANK L. HOPE

When the art collections of the Timken and Putnam families were home-less in the 1950s, the only modern building along the Prado was built—against protests from purists who favored consistency with the architec-ture of the expos in 1915 and 1935. City leaders initially seemed to favor a historical design, but approved the modern proposal, afraid that the col-lections would end up elsewhere. Although controversial, the building is a solid example of spare modernism and contains excellent, well-lit galleries. To make way for it, the once-grand Home Economy Building by architects Carleton Winslow and Bertram Goodhue was demolished—a loss that tra-

ditionalists tried to partially recoup in the 1990s by reconstructing an arcade along the Prado (in front of the Timken) where the Home Economy Building's arcade once con-nected it to the rest of the park.

7 / **San Diego Museum of Art** (1926)
WILLIAM TEMPLETON JOHNSON

One of San Diego's most prolific architects (from San Diego Trust & Savings downtown to Serra Museum in Presidio Park and several houses), Johnson had never before designed a museum when he was awarded this job. Enclosing the north end of the park's Plaza de Panama, this is one of the most prominent sites within the park's axial Beaux Arts plan. Johnson trained at the Ecole des Beaux Arts in Paris from 1908 to 1911, and became one of San Diego's major proponents of Spanish Revival-style architecture during the 1920s and 1930s. His Fine Arts Gallery, as it was called initially, is more restrained in its detailing than other park buildings. It features tile roofs, windows surrounded with cast stone moldings, and a main entry ornamented with busts of Spanish painters Ribera and El Greco, miniature statues of Donatello's "St. George" and Michelangelo's

"David," and reliefs of galleons and shields of Spain, the United States, and California, plus a city seal above the U.S. shield. Statues of painters Murillo, Zurbaran, and Velazquez are mounted in niches above the entry. The west wing (designed by Mosher & Drew) was added in 1966; and an east wing including 25,000 square feet of exhibit space, in 1970.

8 / Old Globe Theatre (1982)
LIEBHARDT & WESTON

Modeled on Shakespeare's London Globe, Balboa Park's Globe (1935) was destroyed by an arson fire in 1978, rebuilt, and re-opened in 1982. Originally an open-air venue intended as tempo-rary, the Globe was upgraded to meet building and fire codes, and received a roof, in 1936.

9 / California Building/Museum of Man (1915)
BERTRAM GOODHUE

No other structure has defined San Diego's identity as much as this build-ing's romantic tower, often pictured on postcards and in travel articles. Visible from within the park as well as out in the surrounding city, the tower provides a comforting sense of place and serves as an orienting landmark. Up closer, the tower's companion dome, covered with chromatic tiles, resonates with the power of Renaissance-era duomos that anchor many a town square in Latin locales. According to historian Richard Amero, "Goodhue's design amounts to a twentieth century recapitulation of Plateresque, Baroque, Churrigueresque, and Rococo details. It is impure historically and odd in its imposition of a secular window and balustrade on an ecclesiastical frontispiece." Ornamental details include masks, cupids, candelabra, garlands, and fruit—fine, flat ornamentation in the Spanish Plateresque style that originated with silver flatware. Baroque twisted columns and curved mouldings mingle with Rococo scrolls and myriad other details derived from various periods and styles. Prominent fig-ures from San Diego's history are depicted in the decoration, including Father Luis Jayme, a Francisco missionary murdered by Native Americans in 1774; Gaspar de Portola, California's first Spanish governor; and explor-

ers Juan Rodriguez Cabrillo and Sebastian Viscaino, who rediscov-ered the harbor decades after Cabrillo, and named it "San Diego". Although Goodhue beat out native Irving Gill for the job of expo architect, the late historian David Gebhard surmised that the simpler look of Goodhue's subse-quent building's may reflect Gill's influence.

10 / **Cabrillo Bridge** (1914)

FRANK P. ALLEN, JR.
THOMAS B. HUNTER, ENGINEER

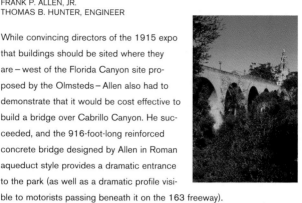

While convincing directors of the 1915 expo that buildings should be sited where they are – west of the Florida Canyon site proposed by the Olmsteds – Allen also had to demonstrate that it would be cost effective to build a bridge over Cabrillo Canyon. He succeeded, and the 916-foot-long reinforced concrete bridge designed by Allen in Roman aqueduct style provides a dramatic entrance to the park (as well as a dramatic profile visible to motorists passing beneath it on the 163 freeway).

11 / **Alcazar Garden (next to House of Charm)**

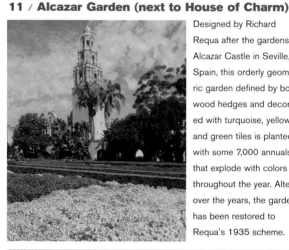

Designed by Richard Requa after the gardens of Alcazar Castle in Seville, Spain, this orderly geometric garden defined by boxwood hedges and decorated with turquoise, yellow, and green tiles is planted with some 7,000 annuals that explode with colors throughout the year. Altered over the years, the garden has been restored to Requa's 1935 scheme.

12 / **House of Charm / Mingei Museum** (2000)

Originally the Indian Arts Building (1915)
BSHA WITH M.W. DONALDSON (RECONSTRUCTION)

Designed by Carleton Winslow, the building replicated the Sanctuary of Guadalupe in Guadalajara. Winslow modeled the tower after the Church of Santa Catarina in Puebla, Mexico. Compared with other park buildings, according to historian Richard Amero, the facade "has a grim aspect reminiscent of fortress churches in sixteenth century Mexico," and is not consistent with the "exuberant Baroque and Churrigueresque detail elsewhere on the grounds". A 1990s ground-up reconstruction replicated the exterior, but reconfigured the interior as modern multi-floor office and museum space including new underground levels – instead of the original high-ceilinged exhibition hall. Original elements including doors, window frames, railings, and cobblestones were re-used, while plaster details were replicated in fiberglass-reinforced plastic. Some feel the renovated landscape should have included original Blackwood acacias (circa 1915) instead of replacement cedars (circa 1935). The fear is that the new cedars will eventually obscure the building.

13 / **House of Hospitality** (1915 and 1935)
CARLETON WINSLOW + RICHARD REQUA
M.W. DONALDSON (RECONSTRUCTION)

Designed, like other park buildings, as temporary scenery more than a permanent building, the House of Hospitality has become a romantic darling
of the park that merges Winslow's ornate Plateresque details (including
coats of arms) with a courtyard garden and landscape inspired by Requa's
travels through Morocco and Algeria. Winslow modeled the main facade
after the Hospital of Santa Cruz in Toledo, Spain, according to historian
Richard Amero. Plantings in 1915 included rows of Blackwood acacias
"groomed to look like candles that were interrupted at strategic points by
Italian cypresses. Grass and flowers grew in front of the trees. Behind
them a hedge of Coprosma covered the railing between the posts of the
arcades and Bignonia and Bougainvillea hung down from the pergolas or
clamored up the walls of the arcades. Unlike monochrome palaces in
Spain and Mexico, color from the plants gave the building a sprightly air."
Between expos, the building was nearly demolished many times. Its sur-
vival is partly due to the preservation efforts of city father and downtown
department store owner George Marston. In 1935, Requa oversaw
remodeling and new "architectural gardens," as he called them. He credited Mexican artist Juan Larrinaga, trained in Hollywood film studios, with
color renderings and models that gave form to numerous design details,
including "ingenious lighting fixtures". Requa created a new
Mediterranean courtyard by opening an enclosed hall. Requa and his staff
architect Sam Hamill (who also collaborated on the
County Administration Center) used the State
Museum in Guadalajara as inspiration. At the patio's
center is artist Donal Hord's "Woman of
Tehuantepec" fountain, surrounded by tropical plants
including banana. H.O. Davis's lighting scheme was
inspired by Maxfield Parrish. Color-tinted lights
played on landscape details, instead of building

facades, adding mystery. Ground-level spaces include a ballrooom and a
restaurant space where David and Leslie Cohen opened the Prado on
New Year's Eve 1999. After decades of neglect that included voter rejec-
tion of a park-renovation bond issue in 1987, the city retained preservation
architect Milford Wayne Donaldson in 1993. He reconstructed the House
of Hospitality from scratch (to 1935 status) around a steel frame (instead
of the original wood), and recast original plaster mouldings in durable
fiberglass-reinforced concrete. A new basement houses mechanical functions; the makeover included modern elevators, heating, ventilating, fire
sprinklers, and air conditioning. As part of the renovation, non-authentic
landscaping was removed, and the plant palette was restored to authentic
status, with guidance from Garbini and Garbini landscape architects.

14 / **Japanese Friendship Garden** (1999)
UESUGI TAKEO, NAKAJIMA KEN, HIROO KURANO

Symbolizing connections between San Diego and sister-city Yokohama, Japan, the garden's history in Balboa Park dates back to the Japanese Pavilion built for the 1915 expo. The new garden combines Japanese design and craftsmanship (such as the shoji-screened Exhibit House), with ancient landscape principles evident in features including a traditional sand-and-stone garden, a wisteria arbor overlooking the canyon, and a koi pond.

15 / **Spreckels Organ Pavilion** (1915)
HARRISON ALBRIGHT

Amid the Spanish-Colonial romance that predominates in Balboa Park, the 2,000-seat pavilion is a fantasy flight back to ancient times, with a grand arch at centerstage flanked by curved arcades. Rosettes, stars, satyr heads, floral sprays, and musical motifs are among decorative details. But the real centerpiece here is the pipe organ, built by Austin Organ Co. in Hartford, CT, equipped with 4,445 pipes, and said to be the largest outdoor pipe organ in the world.

16 / **House of Pacific Relations** (1935)
RICHARD REQUA

During the '35 expo, these cottages represented houses from colonial phases of Mexico's history, each one furnished with the flavor of the country represented.

17 / **Municipal Gym** (1935)
RICHARD REQUA

The architect's design was intended to reflect a merger of modern and Mayan sensibilities, reflective of the San Diego region's history. Known as the Palace of Electricity and Varied Industries, the building was converted to a gym with hardwood-floored basketball courts, volleyball courts, table-tennis tables, and re-opened in 1939.

18 / **Ford/Starlight Bowl** (1935)
VERN KNUDSEN

Earfuls of irony here—Knudsen, an acoustical engineer and co-founder of the Acoustical Society of America, designed the 4,000-seat outdoor venue for good live sound, but air traffic at nearby Lindbergh Field today makes live performances a test of audience patience.

19 / Ford Building/Aerospace Museum (1935)
WALTER TEAGUE

Balboa Park's sole Streamline Moderne building was donated by Ford to house the '35 expo's transportation exhibits, including the major display by Ford. Similar structures were built at the same time for fairs in New York and San Francisco, but this is the only one remaining. Previously located in the park's Electrical Building, the Aerospace Museum re-opened (after a 1978 fire destroyed much of its collection) in 1980 in the Ford Building.

20 / Naval Hospital (1922)
2125 Park Blvd.
BERTRAM GOODHUE

After a prolonged battle that lasted through the 1970s, the city and Navy agreed on a land swap. The Navy received city land in order to build a new hospital to the east, in Balboa Park's Florida Canyon. In exchange, the city acquired the original Naval Hospital. Eventually all buildings were demolished except for three: the twin-towered administration building (now occupied by the city's Parks and Recreation department), the chapel (1944, now home to the Veterans Memorial Center & Museum), and a modernist medical library designed by Delawie & Macy, completed in 1968 (now the Native American Cultural Center).

21 / Balboa Park Activity Center (1999)
ROB QUIGLEY/WHEELER WIMER BLACKMAN

The park's first new building in 30 years is also its only example of contemporary architecture. Quigley, who has often experimented with concrete a material also used often by Irving Gill—utilized tilt-up concrete slabs, crowned by a bowed roof that echoes the rooflines of earlier San Diego buildings including aviation hangars dating from World War II.

22 / Reuben H. Fleet Science Center (1972/1996)
LOUIS BODMER/DELAWIE WILKES RODRIGUES BARKER

To Bodmer's original Omnimax theater and entry, Delawie Wilkes added a grand rotunda, exhibit halls, and meeting rooms, all in keeping with the styles and scale of historical park buildings.

Old Town

Native Americans had occupied the San Diego region for centuries before the area known today as Old Town became its first European-style city, a Spanish-influenced collection of buildings around a plaza. Early buildings include both adobe structures and wood-frame houses—some of them shipped from the East Coast (similar to the Heath-Davis house at Fourth and Island downtown).

According to the "Ordinances of Discovery, New Population, and the Pacification of the Indies" issued by Spanish King Philip II, the site of a new settlement should be "one that is vacant and that can be occupied without doing harm to the Indians and natives or with their free

consent—a plan for the site is to be made, dividing it into squares, streets, and building lots, using cord and ruler, beginning with the main square…

"The main plaza is to be the starting point for the town; if it is situated on the sea coast, it should be placed at the landing place of the port, but inland it should be at the center of the town. The plaza should be square or rectangular, in which case it should have at least one and a half its width for length (in San Diego's case, 130-by-280 feet) in as much as this shape is best for fiestas in which horses are used and for any other fiestas that should be held."

Clearly these new towns placed a high priority on the social life of their citizens. In fact, San Diego's initial town center fared better than its first seat of government; while the Presidio declined, the new town grew steadily, until by 1829 there were more than 600 residents and 30 houses in Old Town, loosely arranged around the plaza. But in 1872 a fire destroyed most of the buildings.

Old Town's basic street plan today also reflects the Spanish mandate for town planning, according to Mexican architect and historian Antonio Padilla-Corona's article in the *Journal of San Diego History:* "From the Plaza shall begin four principal streets: One from the middle of each side, and two streets from each corner of the Plaza." Old Town has only five streets—not eight—from each corner.

In early San Diego, however, two usual Spanish institutions were missing: the church and the monarchy. Churches are generally the central feature of Spanish Colonial towns, typically sited at the edge of a plaza in a way that one's attention is directed there. San Diego, by contrast, was a less civilized place: Duhaut-Cilly described Old Town in 1823 as "thirty to forty houses of poor appearance and some badly cultivated gardens." A few years later in *Two Years Before the Mast,* Richard Henry Dana recalled a "small settlement…directly below the fort, composed of about forty dark-brown-looking huts, or houses, and three or four larger ones, whitewashed, which belong to the gente de razon."

Secrets of those early years continue to be uncovered during periodic archaeological digs on the former site of the presidio, below the Serra Museum designed by architect William Templeton Johnson in 1929. In the blocks surrounding the original Old Town, many period buildings have been restored for use as shops, offices, and restaurants. Visiting the old adobes, one can experience some of the inspiration behind the work of 20th-century San Diego architects including Richard Requa, Irving Gill, and Frank Mead, all of whom helped develop a regional style of design.

Old Town Locations

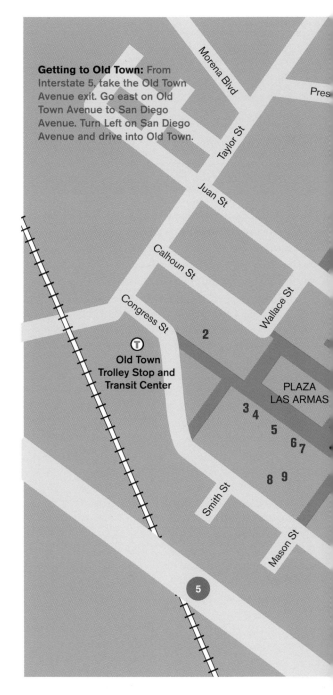

Getting to Old Town: From Interstate 5, take the Old Town Avenue exit. Go east on Old Town Avenue to San Diego Avenue. Turn Left on San Diego Avenue and drive into Old Town.

Old Town Trolley Stop and Transit Center

PLAZA LAS ARMAS

1 **Serra Museum**
2 **Silvas-McCoy House**
3 **Wrightington House**
4 **Light-Freeman House**
5 **Casa de Machado y Silva**
6 **Colorado House/Wells Fargo History Museum**
7 **First San Diego Courthouse**
8 **Casa de Machado y Stewart**
9 **Mason Street School**

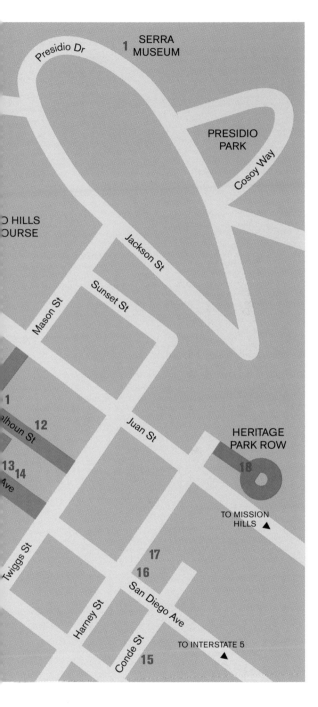

10 **Casa de Estudillo**

11 **Casa de Bandini**

12 **Seely Stables**

13 **Altamirano-Pedrorena House**

14 **San Diego Union Museum**

15 **Old Adobe Chapel**

16 **Whaley House Museum**

17 **Derby-Pendleton House**

18 **Heritage Park Victorian Village**

OLD TOWN

1 / **Serra Museum** (1929)
2727 Presidio Dr.
WILLIAM TEMPLETON JOHNSON

Designed by San Diego's master of Mediterranean Revival styles, the mission-like museum is situated near where the original mission (moved several miles up Mission Valley) was established. Johnson's design is a masterful composition of view-framing arches, a sanctuary with a high timbered roof, and a tower visible from miles around.

2 / **Silvas-McCoy House** (1869)
Between Congress St. and Calhoun St.

Restored in the 1990s after archaeologists excavated remains of the original two-story wood-frame residence.

3 / **Wrightington House** (early 19th century)
2769 San Diego Ave.
Adobe structure built under Mexican rule, with a wing added in 1852.

When he arrived in San Diego on the ship *Ayucucho* in 1833, Thomas Wrightington became San Diego's first American settler (with the possible exception of Henry D. Fitch).

4 / **Light-Freeman House** (1830)
2767 San Diego Ave.
Adobe saloon and store owned by black pioneers Richard Freeman and Allen Light.

5 / **Casa de Machado y Silva** (1832)

Southwest side of Old Town Plaza facing San Diego Avenue

Spanish Corporal Jose Manuel Machado came to San Diego's presidio in 1782 and built this home in 1832 for his daughter Maria Antonia and her husband Manuel de Silvas. It later served as a boarding house, saloon, restaurant, art studio, souvenir shop, museum and church.

6 / **Colorado House/ Wells Fargo History Museum** (1851)

2733 San Diego Ave.

Formerly a hotel, saloon, and gaming parlor, built by San Diego forefather Cave Couts.

7 / **First San Diego Courthouse** (1847)

San Diego Ave.

Built by the Mormon Battalion that arrived in 1847 to assist the American military effort against Mexico, this was Old Town's first fired-brick structure and served as a townhall, schoolroom, and central government offices.

8 / **Casa de Machado y Stewart** (1830s)

Near northwest corner of Congress and Mason

Mud-brick adobe built by Jose Manuel Machado for his daughter Rosa and her husband Jack Stewart–a shipmate of Richard Henry Dana Jr., whose voyage along California's coast is recounted in his book *Two Years Before the Mast.*

9 / **Mason Street School** (1865)

3966 Mason St.

San Diego's first public school house.

OLD TOWN

10 / **Casa de Estudillo** (1829)
Between Calhoun and Mason

San Diego's grandest period adobe, featuring 3-foot-thick walls surrounding a courtyard, was restored in 1910 under supervision of Irving Gill's protégé Hazel Waterman. Jose Maria de Estudillo commanded San Diego's presidio, his son Jose Antonio served as tax collector, treasurer, alcalde, and judge under American rule. For many years it was mistakenly identified as "Ramona's Wedding Place" made famous by Helen Hunt Jackson's novel *Ramona*.

11 / **Casa de Bandini** (1829)
Corner of Mason and Calhoun

Bandini sailed from his native Peru to California in 1819; he became a Mexican citizen, and later an official in California under Mexican rule. His adobe home was the socio-political hub of Old Town. Later a store, a pickle factory, and motel annex, the Casa is today a popular Mexican restaurant.

12 / **Seely Stables** (1869/RESTORED 1970s)
Calhoun St.

Stable and barns housings buggies, wagons, and carriages typical of the time when Albert Seeley ran the San Diego-Los Angeles Stage Line.

13 / **Altamirano-Pedrorena House** (1869)
2616 San Diego Ave.

Miguel de Pedrorena came to San Diego in 1842 and married into the Estudillo family. His son Miguel, Jr., built this adobe home (now a bakery) in 1869, and left it to his son-in-law Jose Antonio Altamirano.

14 / **San Diego Union Museum** (1851)
San Diego Ave.

Wood-frame structure shipped to San Diego from the East Coast, became the San Diego Union newspaper's first office. Restored to its 1868 condition, including original printroom.

15 / **Old Adobe Chapel** (1850)
3950 Conde St.

This building became San Diego's first parochial church in a new parish in 1858, following secularization of the missions in 1832. It was covered with wood siding in 1889 and restored in 1937.

16 / **Whaley House Museum** (1857)
2482 San Diego Ave.

San Diego's oldest brick structure, now is home to Save Our Heritage Organization.

17 / **Derby-Pendleton House** (1851)
4015 Harney St.

When it was moved next door to the Whaley House, this place is said to have provoked the spirit of Thomas Whaley, which by some accounts still haunts Old Town. George Horatio Derby was a *San Diego Herald* columnist also known as Squibob or John Phoenix.

18 / **Heritage Park Victorian Village**
(1880s and 1890s)

Heritage Park Row

This village is made up of several historic victorians and San Diego's first synagogue. Many of the structures have been moved here from various locations. Buildings include the Senlis Cottage (1896), Sherman-Gilbert house (1887), and Temple Beth Israel (1889).

Mission Hills

Once a wild place where Kumeyaay hunted small game with bows and arrows, nets and snares, Mission Hills entered a new era in 1869 when Captain Henry Johnston paid $16.25 for 65 acres of public land at Sunset and Witherby Streets. That same year, the Arnold & Choate Addition became the neighborhood's first subdivision, bounded by University, Randolph, Curlew, and Arbor, now the site of the Goldfinch business district. In 1887, Johnston's daughter, Sarah Johnston Miller, subdivided the property and named it Johnston Heights. She built her own home (still standing) at the highest point, incorporating pieces of the dismantled ship *S.S. Orizaba,* which had brought many new San Diegans (including horticulturist Kate Sessions) down the coast from San Francisco.

Since then, Mission Hills has grown into San Diego's most romantic neighborhood, where tree-lined streets run past the city's highest concentration of architecturally significant homes. These range from dozens of vintage Craftsman places, to period masterpieces by prominent architects such as Richard Requa, Cliff May, and William Templeton Johnson, to modern and contemporary designs by Irving Gill, Randy Dalrymple, and Steve Adams.

The marriage of landscape design with architecture has been an ongoing Southern California experiment, one that had roots in Mission Hills. In 1903, after she lost her lease in Balboa Park, Sessions began buying land in Mission Hills. Eventually she owned several blocks. She opened a new nursery, operated into the 1990s by Frank Antonicelli, son of one of Sessions' gardeners. At the time, few people lived in the area, and the "landscape" consisted primarily of a citrus grove near Trias Street and an olive grove on

the present site of Mission Hills First Congregational Church. Sessions supervised the scrubby area's first plantings: a row of eucalyptus in Calvary Cemetery (later Pioneer Park), and "an ocean of poinsettias in the fall and sea lavender in the spring," according to historian Mike McLaughlin.

Sessions helped lobby J.D. Spreckels to extend his electric rail line; by 1909 the trolley ran from Market Street downtown to Lewis and Stephens in Mission Hills. Speculators saw the coming boom, and investor and city benefactor George Marston christened the development Mission Hills (the original San Diego mission was temporarily located below Mission Hills in what is now Presidio Park before it was moved to its current location near Qualcomm Stadium in Mission Valley).

In order to make the new development exclusive, single-family homes had to cost at least $3,500, there could be "no male poultry or farm animal of any kind," and property could only be sold or leased to those "belonging to the Caucasian race." Commercial development was also restricted from Mission Hills; just over the property line, Nathan Rigdon and Morris Irving developed two commercial buildings that became the heart of a small shopping district that still thrives today on West Lewis Street.

Architect William Templeton Johnson, designer of landmark buildings in Balboa Park and Presidio Park, also designed Francis Parker School, which opened in Mission Hills in 1913. The first home on Sunset—the main through-street—was built in 1912, and by 1922, 10 homes lined this inviting Craftsman-era avenue, with its lush front gardens, deep front porches, and river-rock garden walls.

Marston added new Mission Hills developments in the 1920s. Presidio Ridge and Presidio Hills overlooked the

MISSION HILLS

land he envisioned for Presidio Park, where Johnson eventually designed the Mission-style Serra Museum (where the author married Sally Van Haitsma in 2002). World War II brought a boom to San Diego's military industrial complex, and housing prices spiked. In 1953, author Oakley Hall set his murder mystery, *The Corpus of Joe Bailey,* in Mission Hills, stirring a controversy by undermining the community's peaceful and stately image.

Beginning in the 1960s and 1970s, many Mission Hills retailers and restaurateurs (including Piggly Wiggly and Richard Brewer's Variety Store) closed as residents shopped and dined in Mission Valley and various suburban centers. The neighborhood's lone high-rise—Green Manor senior apartments—opened in 1970.

In 2002, Mission Hills is one of San Diego's most magnificent and most exclusive neighborhoods. As recently as the 1990s, middle-class San Diegans could afford one of the smaller homes in Mission Hills. Today, it is rare to find anything under $500,000, and two-bedroom bungalows fetch as much as $900,000. But even if you can't afford to live here, it's worth spending an afternoon seeing some of San Diego's finest residential designs, in a neighborhood that has nary an architectural clinker.

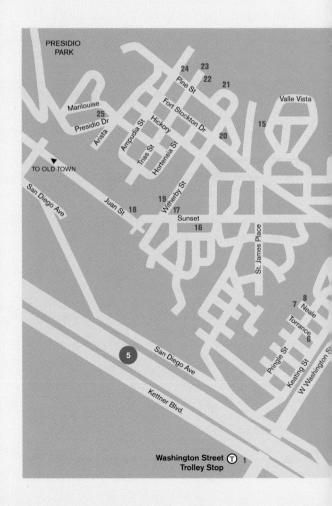

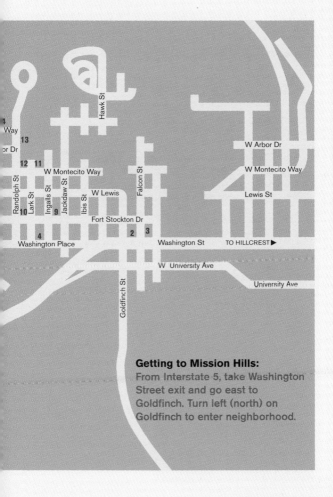

Getting to Mission Hills:
From Interstate 5, take Washington Street exit and go east to Goldfinch. Turn left (north) on Goldfinch to enter neighborhood.

MISSION HILLS

1 / **Mission Brewery** (1913)
1751 Hancock St.

RICHARD GRIESSER

Near Mission Hills and west of I-5, this was the first Mission style brewery in the U.S. Although clad in non-Mission-style brick masonry, the brewery features several key traits of the genre: rhythmic series of arches, a terraced bell tower, and unadorned stucco surfaces that emulate plastered adobe brick.

---

2 / **Mission Hills Shopping Center** (1950s)
Washington and Goldfinch Streets

Commercial buildings were not a part of original early-20th-century plans for Mission Hills, but necessity prompted their arrival decades later. This center, with its simple, clean lines, awnings, and big curvy neon beaming out its name, is the coolest old building along this stretch of Washington.

---

3 / **Mission Hills Commons** (2002)
4021 Falcon St.

CARRIER JOHNSON/BRUCE DAMMANN

This pedestrian-friendly mixed-use infill, features retail space as well as residences ranging from lofts to apartments, with East Coast-style stoops connecting some homes to surrounding sidewalks.

---

4 / **King Residence** (1913)
1302 Washington Pl.

Well-preserved middle-class Craftsman bungalow, with a double gable roof, exposed trusses, and river-rock details. This home proves that ele-

gant Craftsman dwellings could be done on a scale much more modest than Pasadena's Gamble House (Greene & Greene), or San Diego's own Marston residence.

5 / **Paul McKim Residence** (1965)
3911 Portola Place
PAUL MCKIM

Ingenious simplicity marks this tall, contemporary home, with its H-shaped plan enclosing gardens. Balconies and lofts double as sleeping spaces while maintaining the open feel.

6 / **Homer Delawie Residence** (1958)
1773 Torrance St.
HOMER DELAWIE

The "boxcar" shows the architect's genius for finding the simple, elegant solutions to challenging issues such as this hillside site. Formerly one story, it later received an unfortunate addition.

7 / **Homer Delawie Residence** (1963)
1833 Neale St.
HOMER DELAWIE

A disciple of Lloyd Ruocco, Delawie was the most prolific and proficient of the post-war modernists who followed Ruocco. Here, his minimalist L-shaped scheme makes maximum use of a hillside location, with a California pepper tree incorporated as a central design feature.

8 / **Mooney Residence** (1940)
1820 Neale St.
JOHN LLOYD WRIGHT

Showing the influence of his father's horizontal, deep-eaved Prairie style, this home is also FLW-like in its use of natural materials for elegant impact.

MISSION HILLS

9 / Mission Hills First Congregational Church (1921)

4070 Jackdaw St.
LOUIS GILL

Irving Gill's nephew designed as many important civic buildings around town as his more famous uncle did. This Spanish Colonial/Mission-style building features a walled garden and a sloped floor of terra-cotta cement in the sanctuary that affords good views for all members of the congregation.

---

10 / Dalrymple Residence (1988)
4061 Randolph St.
RANDY DALRYMPLE

One of the few San Diego projects ever to grace the cover of *Progressive Architecture* magazine, Dalrymple's own residence features a master bed that slides out over the rear garden, and giant window flaps that open the interior to fresh air and light. Take a look at nearby buildings to see how the architect borrowed from the neighborhood to make his own far-out house fit in surprisingly well.

---

11 / Kate Sessions Residence (1912)
4159 W. Montecito
ATTRIBUTED TO WILLIAM
TEMPLETON JOHNSON

It's fitting that the matriarch of San Diego horticulture lived in a house as eclectic as the array of plants she brought to San Diego neighborhoods. Its bold cubic massing is Gill-like, but the ziggurat brick corners, perforated parapet, and two-tone color scheme are a lot more exuberant that most of Gill's designs.

---

12 / Rental Residence (1912)
4154 Lark St.
ATTRIBUTED TO WILLIAM TEMPLETON JOHNSON

Nestled among San Diego's predominant Mediterranean revival-style buildings are a few classical revival designs, such as this columned, symmetri-

cal home that may have been a speculative development or rental property.

13 / Francis Parker School (1913)
4201 Randolph St.
WILLIAM TEMPLETON JOHNSON

This pioneering example of a California-style "open-air" school was founded by Johnson and wife Clara, and is a fine early example of the architect's Spanish Colonial revival mode.

14 / Three Houses (c. 1915)
4239-1610-1625 Plumosa
MEAD & REQUA

Mission Revival dwellings designed by two early San Diego architectural legends—Requa, the historicist, and Mead, the modernist who (like his mentor Irving Gill) stripped Mission style to bare essentials.

15 / Richard Requa Residence (1903)
4346 Valle Vista St.
RICHARD REQUA

Requa's commissioned homes were often magnificent estates, but his own place is a small symmetrical gem with an arched entry, stucco walls, and deep eaves. It is set in a garden with multiple patios connected to various rooms. View from over low fence in front yard.

16 / Edward Tindall Guymon Residence (1921)
2055 Sunset Blvd.
ROBERT RAYMOND

A signature manse on a prime thoroughfare, this Italianate showplace recalls country estates in Italy.

MISSION HILLS

17 / Jarboe Residence (1925)
2150 Sunset Blvd.

Designed and built by contractor Fred Jarboe (builder of the Spreckels Building at 121 Broadway downtown), this majestic brick showplace is one of the city's finest examples of Tudor Revival, from its steep gable roofs to its leaded-glass Gothic windows and half-timbering.

18 / Soldiers in Argyle (1984)
2282 Juan St.
RANDY DALRYMPLE/PAPA

With its movie-set facade of gabled soldiers marching down Juan Street, "Soldiers" is one of Dalrymple's early experiments with collaging elements from other buildings found in the neighborhood.

19 / Wita Gardiner Residence (1995)
4222 Witherby St.
STEVE ADAMS

The client, a gallery owner, went through several prominent architects before Adams saw the project through to completion. One of Mission Hills few modern homes, it has a zen-like simplicity, and makes ingenious use of windows, skylights, and planning to rake every room with natural light.

20 / Lenahan Residence (1916)
2154 Ft. Stockton Dr.

How much progress has really been made in the realm of tract housing? This inviting Craftsman/Prairie-style place is one of more than 125 homes built in San Diego by developer Morris B. Irvin, who led the spread

of the city outward from downtown along streetcar lines.

21 / **Percy Whitehead Residence** (1917)
4474 Hortensia St.
CRESSY & QUAYLE

This shingled English country cottage, featuring leaded-glass windows, concealed gutters, and large fireplace, shows the versatility of the Quayle father and sons, who also designed the old Spanish Revival police headquarters on Market Street downtown.

22 / **Asian-style Residence**
4479 Trias St.

This Japonesque Craftsman house—with its curved teahouse beams and eaves—is an extreme example of the Oriental roots of the Arts and Crafts movement.

23 / **Crabtree Residence** (1962)
4522 Trias St.
LIEBHARDT & WESTON

Modernism in wood from San Diego's leading proponents of post-and-beam/Case Study-style. Multiple levels make good use of the site, maintaining privacy while providing views. Interior gardens play up the California ideal of indoor/outdoor living.

24 / **Moritz Trepte Residence** (1928)
4467 Ampudia St.
WILLIAM TEMPLETON JOHNSON

This finely detailed Moorish home is by one of San Diego's most prolific 20th-century architects.

25 / **Highland Residence** (1934)
2400 Presidio Dr.
CLIFF MAY

Prime specimen from the creator of the modern California ranch house, this Spanish Colonial hacienda romanticizes Old California, with a U-shaped courtyard plan, low-profile, red tile roofs, and white stucco walls. According to historian Alexander Bevil, this home "combines elements of the rustic medieval Andalusian farmhouse with the spacious 19th century

Spanish California hacienda style ranch house." Check out May's signature chromatic tile door-bell surround.

Hillcrest

Hillcrest began with a touch of Wild West: in the 1880s Wyatt Earp owned a block here. He sold out in 1887, when San Diego's boom economy fizzled. Hillcrest was a scrubby, boulder-strewn expanse split by a gully. At the turn of the century, it became known as "pill hill"—Mercy Hospital opened at Eighth and University in 1891, followed in 1903 by County Hospital (later UCSD Medical Center).

In 1907, William Whitson (who later claimed he had been the first San Diegan to own an automobile) bought and subdivided 40 acres between First and Sixth Avenues. His real estate company sold property from an office at Fifth and University. Other early suburbs began modestly, but Hillcrest's early buildings were substantial and neoclassical: Florence Elementary School opened in 1908,

 University Avenue Bank in 1910. Mercy Hospital moved in 1924 to a substantial new building.

Fifth and University was the heart of the community's commercial district, as development spread from early bank buildings, to the north, south, east, and west. University Avenue became Hillcrest's first paved street in 1912. The Hillcrest Theater—later the Guild—opened in 1913.

Hillcrest offered housing to attract a diverse population, ranging from single-family homes to bungalow court apartments. In the 1920s and 1930s Hillcrest included singles and young couples, many of them drawn by reasonably priced housing close to downtown.

Sears opened a Hillcrest store in the 1950s. By the 1960s, the new Mission Valley Shopping Center had drawn customers away from many older San Diego retail districts, and Hillcrest's population had become elderly. With its local economy faltering, Hillcrest became a neighborhood of neglected buildings. In the 1970s, as gays came out across the country, Hillcrest became known as San Diego's gay community. Today, its annual Gay & Lesbian Pride Parade attracts celebrities such as Margaret Cho and Cyndi Lauper.

A changed population served as a catalyst for the innovative Uptown District mixed-use redevelopment, opened in 1990 on the former Sears site along University, east of Sixth. Townhomes are situated adjacent to retail spaces, with additional residential units above shops. Planners convinced Ralphs supermarket to design a new urban prototype—the store is set back from the street, with underground parking, so the impact of cars on pedestrians is minimized.

Village Hillcrest, another mixed-use development, opened in 1991, combining offices, retail, and residential uses with a multiplex cinema. BSHA's design called for the kinds of vibrant colors found south of the border; developers chickened out and went with beige, only to bring back the color a few years later, after numerous complaints about the complex's drab appearance.

Today the intersection of Fifth and University is the hub of San Diego's most diverse neighborhood: historic architecture and contemporary storefronts, people of all ages and orientations, and street scenes along both Fifth and University characterized by vibrant collages of buildings and Venturi-worthy signage.

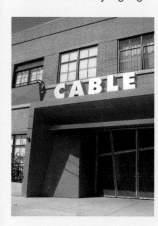

Hillcrest Locations

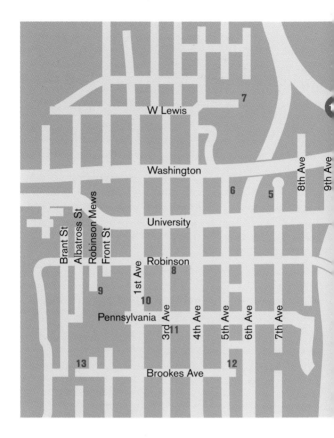

1 **Georgia Street Bridge**

2 **Park Theatre**

3 **House**

4 **Uptown District**

5 **Cable Lofts**

6 **Village Hillcrest**

7 **Mercy Hospital and Convent Building**

8 **First Church of the United Brethren in Christ/Thackeray Gallery**

9 **Sunnyslope Lodge**

10 **Hall-Sherman House**

11 **Hardesty House**

12 **Design Center**

13 **Louis Gill Residence**

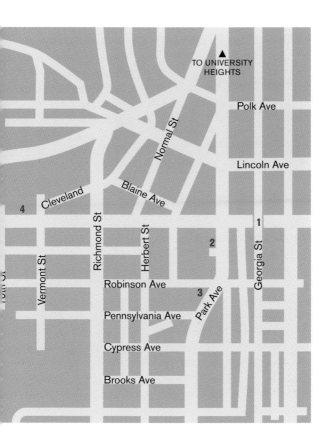

Getting to Hillcrest:
From 163 south take University
Avenue exit, and drive into the
heart of Hillcrest.

HILLCREST

1 / **Georgia Street Bridge** (1914)
Georgia Street and University Avenue
JAMES COMLY, ENGINEER

Threatened with demolition at the time of this publication, this magnificent bridge—supported by three parabolic hinged-rib arches, and featuring cantilevered sidewalks—is an early San Diego example of the emergence of reinforced concrete as a prime material for bridges and public works projects.

2 / **Park Theatre** (1926)
3812 Park Blvd.
F.W. STEVENSON

Originally known as the Bush Egyptian Theatre, later as the Fox Egyptian Theatre and the Capri Theater, this Egyptian Revival building reflected enthusiasm for the style sparked by discovery of King Tutankhamen's tomb in Egypt in 1922. Originally the front included a forecourt flanked by wings housing retail space, but the building was remodeled in the 1950s. The theater was part of a miniature Egyptian Revival district that also included the courtyard apartments and automotive garage to the west. Take a good look at the garage and you can still spy Funky Tut detailing.

3 / **House** (1924)
1735 Robinson Ave.

Single story bungalow blends Mission Revival and Spanish Colonial elements.

4 / **Uptown District** (1990)
1000 block of University Ave.
SGPA (COMMERCIAL)/LORIMER-CASE (TOWNHOMES)

On a 14-acre site formerly occupied by Sears, Uptown District mixes commercial and retail with residential including townhomes and lofts. Along University, new facades reflect the architects' concerted effort to incorporate design details from decades worth of nearby buildings. City planners hold this project up as an example of how San Diego should grow: by adding density in existing urban neighborhoods, rather than sprawling farther into suburbia.

5 / **Cable Lofts** (1997)
3940 Seventh Ave.

Developers Jeremy Cohen and Ronny Werbeloff converted this bunker-like former phone company switching center into spacious lofts. It took longer than expected, but after cutting through brick and concrete to add windows, and outfit-

ting lofts with plenty of storage and outdoor decks, they succeeded in creating one of San Diego's more impressive adaptive re-uses. These 16 freeway-close homes in a neighborhood with entertainment and shopping within walking distance sold out at original prices ranging from $200,000 to $500,000."

---

6 / **Village Hillcrest** (1991)
Fifth and Washington
BSHA

Mixed-use infill of the kind planners promote, combining medical, office, and retail uses, with urban lofts and a multiplex cinema, and 800 parking spaces tucked underneath.

---

7 / **Mercy Hospital and Convent Building** (1926)
4077 Fifth Ave.
ILTON LOVELESS

On a promontory overlooking Mission Valley, the hospital complex was one of the area's earliest commercial developments. Together, the convent and nearby nursing college (below, also by Loveless) and chapel represent the prime of Mediterranean Revival in San Diego, as well as being early religious and medical landmarks.

HILLCREST

8 / First Church of the United Brethren in Christ/Thackeray Gallery (1912)

321 Robinson Ave.

One of the neighborhood's earliest buildings is still one of its landmarks, built of granite blocks when the material and labor were still affordable, in the neoclassical style.

9 / Sunnyslope Lodge (1921)

3733 Robinson Mews

IRVING GILL

Gill's experiments in low-cost, rustic construction included this building of thin walls incorporating 1-by-4 studs covered with diagonal lath and plaster; brick and tongue-and-groove fir floors; and baseboards flush with walls. Three-part windows are reminiscent of the sort popularized in Chicago by Louis Sullivan—whom Gill worked for before coming to San Diego.

10 / Hall-Sherman House (1891)

3720 First Ave.

Following the 1970s and 1980s boom in dingbat stucco apartment buildings, this Queen Anne (hipped and gabled roofs, lath work, turned porch posts, patterned masonry chimney, tongue-and-groove redwood siding) remains as an example of a style that is nearly extinct in this neighborhood.

11 / **Hardesty House** (1905)
3695 Third Ave.

This quirky Queen Anne features elements from many other styles, and represents the end of an era in a neighborhood where architect Irving Gill's first modern designs began emerging a few blocks away. Look at the cast stone veneer exterior wainscoting, corner turret, and perpendicular yin-yang gables.

12 / **Design Center** (1950)
3611 Fifth Ave.

LLOYD RUOCCO

Mentor to San Diego modernists including Homer Delawie, Ruocco himself was an intriguing mix of modernist and naturalist. Stepped gracefully into its urban canyon, the design center (where Ruocco had his offices) uses no-nonsense post-and-beam construction, with an open plan and glass walls connecting indoor spaces to outdoors, merging the building with the eucalyptus- and jacaranda-shaded site.

13 / **Louis Gill Residence** (1921)
244 W. Brookes Ave.

LOUIS GILL

Prior to designing this redwood Craftsman bungalow for himself, Gill and his family lived with his uncle Irving—San Diego's most famous architect. Louis worked with his uncle, but also designed a number of significant buildings on his own, also including the Wegeforth house at 210 Maple St., and St. James by the Sea church in La Jolla.

Bankers Hill

Some of San Diego's architectural masterpieces can be found in the urban neighborhood between downtown San Diego and Hillcrest, west of Balboa Park and east of I-5. Some of San Diego's most prominent citizens lived here beginning early in the 20th century. It is a showplace for styles ranging from Queen Anne Victorian to post-WWII modern to contemporary.

Cross-cut by canyons and steep hillsides that provide panoramic views of downtown, the bay, Coronado, and the airport, Bankers Hill has historically offered architects some of the city's most challenging sites. Exploring the neighborhood, one can see how difficult sites often provoke extremely creative designs.

Irving Gill, Louis Gill, Richard Requa, Emmor Brooke Weaver, Hazel Waterman, Carleton Winslow, William Templeton Johnson are among important San Diego architects whose designs can be seen here. So are onetime Irving Gill associates William Hebbard and Frank Mead.

Early development of Bankers Hill north of downtown paralleled development of Golden Hill east of downtown. In the 1890s, both places had some of San Diego's grandest Queen Anne Victorians. In recent years, however, Bankers Hill has kept its status as a pricey, pristine neighborhood, while Golden Hill went through decades of neglect. Many Bankers Hill Victorians have been preserved and converted to offices.

For a short time in the early 1890s, electric cable cars with names like Montezuma, El Escondido, La Jolla, and Tia Juana ran from downtown to University Heights—along Fourth Avenue through the heart of Bankers Hill. Although the cable line shut down in 1893, those few years of steady traffic helped establish business and residential districts north of downtown.

Bankers Hill has San Diego's highest concentration of Irving Gill houses—several are situated next to Balboa Park on a short strip of Seventh Avenue; to the west many more Gill designs can be found, including several spare, boxy canyon houses on Albatross.

Mead & Requa's Sweet residence is one of the region's grandest surviving masterpieces—a 1913 Spanish Colonial Revival showplace with modern touches including a dining room ringed by french doors that look out on a garden and

on the city. Winslow's 1916 Coulter residence on Second Avenue is a Spanish Mission Revival mansion that served as the Designers Showcase house in 1985.

Louis Gill's Wegeforth House (Harry Wegeforth founded the San Diego Zoo) and his medical complex that now houses Rees Steely medical center are both in this area. Apartment buildings range from converted Victorians to 1950s modern, offering homes here for those who can't afford to buy.

Some of the region's earliest urban mid-rises built outside of downtown are also in Bankers Hill: the Fifth Avenue Financial Center (and its legendary rooftop restaurant Mr. A's), and several condominium towers including a new generation under construction in 2002 and 2003 across from Balboa Park

In addition to well-designed buildings, Bankers Hill also has some masterful bridges: Spruce Street Footbridge (a suspension bridge from 1912) at Front and Spruce; Quince Street Bridge (1905) at Quince and First, a 236-foot span across a canyon; and the steel-truss First Avenue Bridge (1931) over a canyon between Nutmeg and Quince.

Driving some of San Diego's less pedestrian-friendly neighborhoods, one wishes their planners had modeled them more after Bankers Hill, where the architecture is first-rate and walking is still a viable option.

Bankers Hill Locations

1 **Wednesday Club**

2 **Marston Garden**

3 **George White and Anna Gunn Marston Residence**

4 **Mary J. Cossitt Residence**

5 **Katherine Teats Residence #1**

6 **Frederick R. Burnham Residence**

7 **Arthur H. Marston Residence**

8 **Alice Lee Residence #1**

9 **Alice Lee Residence #2**

10 **Solomon Apartments**

11 **Lightner & Hilmen**

12 **LKR-Medical Building**

13 **Gallagher Residence**

14 **A.F. Hunt Residence**

15 **Wood/Forney Residence**

16 **Louis M. Arey Residence**

17 **Charles Martin Residence**

18 **Bishop's Day School**

19 **Rebecca Schiller Residence**

20 **White Residence**

21 **Hortense Coulter Residence**

22 **Quince Street Bridge**

23 **Palomar Apartments**

24 **Park Laurel**

25 **Clayton Residence**

26 **E.F. Chase Residence**

27 **First Church of Christ Scientist**

28 **Tucker-Sadler-Noble-Castro Offices**

29 **George Keating Residence**

30 **Barcelona Apartments**

31 **Laurel Bay Apartments**

32 **The Rees-Stealy Clinic**

33 **H.E. Watts Residence**

34 **Sherman-Doig Residence**

35 **Joseph Mumford Residence**

36 **Redwood Cottages**

37 **Major Miles Moylan House**

38 **Grove Residence**

39 **Elisha Swift Torrance Residence**

40 **Long-Waterman Residence**

41 **Campbell Residence/Elnisa Tea Room**

42 **Henry H. Timken Residence**

43 **Wegeforth Residence**

44 **First Avenue Bridge**

45 **Spruce Street Bridge**

46 **Charles W. Fox Residence**

47 **Low Residence**

48 **Lacoe/Gist Residence**

49 **Sweet Residence**

50 **Ackerman Residence**

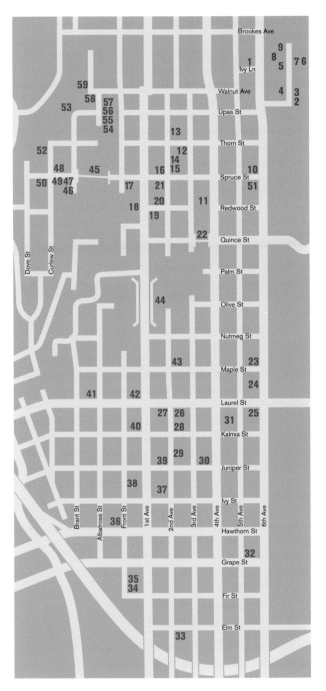

Getting to Bankers Hill:
From 5 north, take 6th Avenue exit.
From 5 south, take Laurel Street exit,
turn left on Laurel, drive up hill.

51 **Park Manor Apartment Hotel**

52 **Churchill Residence**

53 **Evangeline Caven Bungalow**

54 **Alice Lee Residence #4**

55 **Alice Lee Residence #3**

56 **Katherine Teats Residence #3**

57 **Katherine Teats Residence #2**

58 **Letitia Lovett Residence**

59 **Rental Cottage**

BANKERS HILL

1 / **Wednesday Club** (1913)
540 Ivy Lane
HAZEL WATERMAN

Mentored by Irving Gill, Waterman also designed several innovative buildings inspired by indigenous architecture and climate—she learned a lot as restoration architect for the Casa Estudillo in Old Town. Vine-covered pergolas merge the building with the landscape, creating outdoor "rooms" for social occasions. Simple, orderly window placement and the idea of plant materials entwined with the building are elements straight from Gill.

---

2 / **Marston Garden** (1930)
3525 Seventh Ave.

Situated at Balboa Park's edge, this garden was designed by several of the same people who landscaped the park: George Cooke's preliminary English Romantic scheme featured a rolling lawn, a mix of eastern ivy and evergreens with the eucalyptus and bougainvillea more commonly associated with San Diego. After Cooke's accidental death, George Marston and his wife Anna continued developing the garden with the help of pioneering horticulturist Kate Sessions, who introduced dozens of plant species to San Diego. In the 1920s, while planner John Nolen was updating his master plan for the city, he also updated the Marstons' garden with help from younger assistants including Thomas Church (later a prominent California landscape designer) and Hale Walker. The Marstons' eldest daughter Mary also became involved. Under Walker's supervision, a tea house, garden walls, gates, a pergola, and a fountain were added, as well as metal candelabras and iron-trimmed hanging pots that Mary brought back from Spain. But with Nolen & Co. often advising from the East Coast, many of the plant materials added during the 1920s were favorites of Sessions: creeping fig, false acacia, jacaranda, cup of gold vine, bignonia, as well as a Moreton Bay Chestnut brought from Australia by Marston's son-in-law. Over the years the Marstons accumulated a first-class botanical collection. Today, the garden contains dozens of plant species including seven varieties of eucalyptus and an assortment of shrubs and creeping vines. It's a gardener's paradise in a land where almost anything will grow, a physical manifestation of the California Dreaming that has gone on since Gold Rush times.

3 / George White and Anna Gunn Marston Residence (1904)

3525 Seventh Ave.
HEBBARD & GILL

This is the grandest and best-known surviving house by Gill—the closest San Diego comes to Pasadena's Gamble House by Greene &

Greene. With its shingle roof and interior wood detailing, this home is more Prairie and Craftsman than it is modern. But Gill's manipulation of interior volumes with vertical spaces, and clerestories that wash walls and ceilings with natural light, show his advancement beyond Victorian thinking. Situated at the edge of Balboa Park, the home is also a monument to Marston, who was instrumental in the development of Balboa Park, and who personally paid visionary planner John Nolen on two occasions (in 1907 and in 1926) to prepare and update master plans for the San Diego region that remain relevant today.

4 / Mary J. Cossitt Residence (1905)

3526 Seventh Ave.
HEBBARD & GILL

Considering it came at the same time as more traditional Prairie-influenced efforts by the partners, this home is one of the earliest examples of Gill's emerging modernism. Remove

the overhanging roof and you have the spare, carefully orchestrated cubistic forms of Gill's mature style.

5 / Katherine Teats Residence #1 (1906)

3560 Seventh Ave.
HEBBARD & GILL

Thin-wall construction, strong massing, and vine-covered walls are Gill's signature contributions to one of his final collaborations with Hebbard.

6 / Frederick R. Burnham Residence (1907)

3565 Seventh Ave.
HEBBARD & GILL

At heart, Gill was an artist and modernist, but unlike Wright, he didn't have an ego so huge that he would refuse the occasional request for something Old School—in this case a New England-style half-timber-and-

brick residence for George Marston's brother-in-law.

BANKERS HILL

7 / **Arthur H. Marston Residence** (1906)
3575 Seventh Ave.
HEBBARD & GILL

Brick is more Midwestern than West Coast, but this brick veneer home for department store magnate George Marston's brother is a quirky example of how Gill's strong sense of massing could work well within a variety of stylistic contexts.

---

8 / **Alice Lee Residence #1** (1906)
3574 Seventh Ave.
HEBBARD & GILL

As much Prairie as it is modern, this second of three homes around a common garden was designed for real estate entrepreneur Lee as her own residence..

---

9 / **Alice Lee Residence #2** (1905)
3578 Seventh Ave.
IRVING GILL

Gill's architecture was indigenous, so was his notion of designing homes in concert with gardens–like the three homes that included this one, which were organized around a shared garden. The vine-covered entry pergola is an example of Gill's merging of architecture and landscape. This home is also an early example of Gill's experimentation with cost-cutting thin-wall construction.

---

10 / **Solomon Apartments** (1959)
3200 Sixth Ave.
HENRY HESTER

These compact apartments with ingeniously varied plans are in a building that presents a carefully arranged front facade along busy Sixth Avenue. Projecting, private balconies become outdoor rooms with views of Balboa Park. Details such as louvered windows and punched vertical strip windows, together with changing shadows from adjacent trees, add a playful atomic-era aura.

11 / **Lightner & Hilmen** (1967)
3104 Fourth Ave.
MOSHER AND DREW

The vocabulary is different, but the idea of integrating architecture with site and landscape dates back to Gill. Though the style here is modern, the idea of a blank front facade that gives way to spectacular views is similar to the streetwall/courtyard concept used in countless Mediterranean plans.

12 / **LKR-Medical Building** (1967)
3260 Third Ave.
DEEMS-LEWIS-MARTIN

Designed by the firm that did several of San Diego's best modernist buildings, this structure has a modest scale and low-key street presence suited to its residential surroundings.

13 / **Gallagher Residence** (1912)
3315 Second Ave.
CLIVE JOHNSON

Prairie-style, with Craftsman and Italian Renaissance details, possibly designed by San Diego architect Clive Johnson, and built by the Schultheiss Brothers—who also built the San Diego Yacht Club, San Diego Congregational Church, and the Keating and Cole blocks in the Gaslamp Quarter.

14 / **A.F. Hunt Residence** (1910)
3255 Second Ave.
GUSTAVE HANSSEN

Iowa-born Hannsen arrived in San Diego in 1908. This is one of his more elaborate residential designs. Note the window through the chimney, and Tudor half-timbering. In 1924 and 1925, Hanssen partnered with architect Eugene Hoffman. Since many of Hanssen's buildings were downtown and bulldozed during redevelopment, the Hunt house is a rare remaining example of his work.

BANKERS HILL

15 / **Wood/Forney Residence** (1909)
3225 Second Ave.

Possibly designed by Dell Harris (a protégé in Pasadena of Craftsman patriarchs Greene and Greene), this two-story clapboard bungalow sports Craftsman/Greene details such as a brick fireplace and chimney, and a broad front porch with cobblestone piers, beneath a centered dormer.

---

16 / **Louis M. Arey Residence** (1902)
3200 Second Ave.
WILLIAM STERLING HEBBARD

Steep roof and narrow shiplap siding show an East Coast influence on a home with a double-height living room, huge stone fireplace, and acoustically designed music room.

---

17 / **Charles Martin Residence** (1911)
3147 Front St.
RICHARD REQUA

One of Requa's early Mediterranean designs also exhibits the clean-lined modernist tendencies of Requa's earlier partner Irving Gill.

---

18 / **Bishop's Day School** (1908)
3066 First Ave.
GILL AND MEAD

One of the few examples of the brief collaboration between Irving Gill and Frank Mead (who later partnered with Richard Requa), this first Bishop's School building is a jewelbox with arched front door and windows that set up a subtle asymmetry.

---

19 / **Rebecca Schiller Residence** (1913)
115 Redwood St.
EMMOR BROOKE WEAVER

An unsung hero of San Diego architecture who straddled the Craftsman and Modern eras, Weaver combined a love of fine woodworking and

beautiful landscapes with a good eye for simple massing and rhythmic window placement—the best qualities of the work he saw while employed by Hebbard & Gill.

20 / **White Residence** (1898)
136 Redwood St.
HEBBARD & GILL

Early example of the collaboration between leading turn-of-the-century San Diego architect William Hebbard and his then-protégé, Irving Gill. This design is modified Prairie style, with a landscape possibly done by Kate Sessions, and an interior awash in natural light.

21 / **Hortense Coulter Residence** (1916)
3162 Second Ave.
CARLETON WINSLOW

Mentored by Bertram Goodhue, Winslow developed his own eclectic style; a mix of modernistic massing and historical details including the arches, tile roofs, and towers that figured prominently in his and Goodhue's designs for the 1915 expo in Balboa Park.

22 / **Quince Street Bridge** (1905)
Quince Street between Third and Fourth Avenues
GEORGE D'HEMECOURT

Designed by city engineer George d'Hemecourt, this 236-foot-long wooden trestle footbridge (a style popular for 19th- and early-20th-century railroad bridges) is sited 10 feet below street level, making it almost invisible.

23 / **Palomar Apartments** (1914)
536 Maple St.
FRANK MEAD AND RICHARD REQUA

The Palomar, a Mission Revival building with Moorish and Islamic details, combines a Gill-like modernism with exotic decorative seasonings. Mead brought the influence of his North African travels to the partnership, as well as his five-year stint with Irving Gill and his fascination with Pueblo buildings of the Southwest. During his own travels through Europe, Requa assimilated Moorish details such as window grills and wrought iron.

BANKERS HILL

24 / **Park Laurel** (2003)
Bounded by Fifth, Sixth, Laurel, Maple
AUSTIN VEUM ROBBINS PARSHALLE

Tailoring their design to the neighborhood, the architects utilized such Balboa Park-like details as domes, grillwork, and stone, for these twin 14-story condominiums, plus street-level townhomes with pedestrian-friendly sidewalk entries.

25 / **Clayton Residence** (1907)
545 Laurel St.
HAZEL WATERMAN

Prime example from early San Diego modernist Irving Gill's protégé. Together with Lilian Rice in San Diego, and Julia Morgan in Berkeley, Waterman was part of a pioneering generation of female architects. Unlike Gill, she favored a more traditional approach, as in this simple, well-proportioned Prairie/Craftsman home.

26 / **E.F. Chase Residence** (1907)
205 Laurel St.
IRVING GILL

An early example of the cubistic approach that would become Gill's signature. Stark white walls are interrupted only by a few punched windows.

27 / **First Church of Christ Scientist** (1910)
2444 Second Ave.
IRVING GILL

All the Gill hallmarks, on a grand public scale: rhythmic series of arches, unadorned white stucco walls, and simple cubistic massing.

28 / **Tucker-Sadler-Noble-Castro Offices** (1965)
2411 Second Ave.
TUCKER-SADLER

Echoes of Los Angeles Case Study houses and the post-and-beam style espoused in the 1960s at USC, with floor-to-ceiling glass, an open plan, and Neutra-like wooden outriggers.

29 / **George Keating Residence** (1888)
2331-2335 Second Ave.
GEORGE H. SPOHR

Queen Anne Victorian with fish-scale shingles, triangular gables, and an octagonal turret.

30 / **Barcelona Apartments** (1923)
326 E. Juniper St.
EUGENE HOFFMAN

Four-story Spanish Colonial Revival structure, with decorative parapets, parabolic and arched openings, and romantic cantilevered balconies. German-born Hoffman came to San Diego from New York in 1910 and designed many large buildings, including power plants and boiler rooms for the local utility.

31 / **Laurel Bay Apartments** (2003)
2359 Fourth Ave.
RODRIGUEZ & SIMON

Four-story mixed-use development, including 150 apartments as well as office and retail space, at a height more compatible with the neighborhood than other taller new buildings nearby.

32 / **The Rees-Stealy Clinic** (1926)
Fourth and Grape
LOUIS GILL

Gill's modern medical building was touted in its time as the state of design and technology.

33 / **H.E. Watts Residence** (1896)
1767 Second Ave.

Hexagonal bay window, scrolled brackets, dentil mouldings, and arched windows are among elaborate design details of this Stick-style Victorian.

34 / **Sherman-Doig Residence** (1887)
136 W. Fir St.
JOHN SHERMAN

Stick-style Victorian by the same builder responsible for the Sherman-Gilbert house in Old Town. Check out the rhythm of those gables!

BANKERS HILL

35 / **Joseph Mumford Residence** (1887)
1929 Front St.

Victorian in the Eastlake style, sited to maximize its view of San Diego Bay.

---

36 / **Redwood Cottages** (1920)
2104 Front St. and 212 W. Hawthorn St.

Flat-roofed cottages with rare thin-wall construction, near experimental cottages by Irving Gill that use similar construction methods.

---

37 / **Major Miles Moylan House** (1894)
2214-2224 Second Ave.

FALKENHAN + GILL

Major Moylan was a cavalry officer who fought under Custer at Little Big Horn. This is Gill's first San Diego design, after he moved west from Chicago in 1893, and was probably a collaboration with his first San Diego partner, Joseph Falkenhan. Details include one of Gill's earliest uses of the arch that would become a hallmark of his spare, modern style.

---

38 / **Grove Residence** (1901)
2243 Front St.

WILLIAM HEBBARD &
IRVING GILL

Gill partnered with Hebbard from 1896 to 1906, and the older, more traditional Hebbard served as a mentor before Gill ventured into his experiment with spare, unadorned modernism beginning around 1906. Under Hebbard, Gill gained a working knowledge of neoclassical and Mediterranean styles, as well as practical elements such as skylights and cross ventilation.

---

39 / **Elisha Swift Torrance Residence** (1887)
136 Juniper St.

Grand Queen Anne Victorian, restored in the 1970s as offices for a prominent law firm.

40 / **Long-Waterman Residence** (1889)
2408 First Ave.
BENSON & REIF

John Long's eclectic Victorian, with its grand tower outlook, utilized wood veneers from his own factory in Coronado. It was bought in 1893 by former California Governor Robert Waterman.

41 / **Campbell Residence/Elnisa Tea Room** (1911)
312 & 314 W. Laurel St.
EMMOR BROOKE WEAVER

Early Italian Renaissance dwelling that foreshadows the huge popularity of various Mediterranean revival styles in San Diego. Weaver remains an under-appreciated master of his time, combining solid Craftsman details with hints of Gill's modernism.

42 / **Henry H. Timken Residence** (1887)
2508 First Ave.
COMSTOCK & TROTSCHE

It's a cruel twist of history that this elaborate Victorian by San Diego's lead practitioners of that style still stands, but the modernist Timken residence designed later by Irving Gill was torn down years ago.

43 / **Wegeforth Residence** (1914)
210 Maple St.
LOUS GILL

Irving Gill's nephew Louis was a prolific architect in his own right, and this example shows how he combined his uncle's spare modernism with his own historical leanings. Louis Gill led the all-star team of Richard Requa, Sam Hamill, and William Templeton Johnson who designed the County Administration Center.

44 / **First Avenue Bridge** (1931)
First between Nutmeg and Palm Streets
ALLEN & ROWE, ENGINEERS.

This 463-foot-long span across a 104-foot-deep canyon is a prime example of WPA-era public works—durable marriages of creative engineering and eye-pleasing design. The structure consists of a concrete deck over a steel truss three-hinged arch, with wrought- and cast-iron rails. A lone San Diego example of this style of bridge, this span also offers fantastic views of the harbor, Coronado, the Pacific, and Pt. Loma.

BANKERS HILL

45 / **Spruce Street Bridge** (1912)
Spruce Street between Front and Brant
EDWIN M. CAPPS, ENGINEER

Looking at some of San Diego's contemporary bridges and overpasses, one wonders what happened to the old tradition of creative public works. This 375-foot span was originally constructed to give residents access to the Fourth Avenue trolley that connected downtown and uptown.

---

46 / **Charles W. Fox Residence** (1908)
3100 Brant St.
WILLIAM HEBBARD

Prime example of Hebbard's take on the deep-eaved Prairie style.

---

47 / **Low Residence** (1929)
407 W. Spruce St.
WILLIAM TEMPLETON JOHNSON

A prime example of Johnson's tasteful Mediterranean style, which had a major impact on the character of Mission Hills a few miles to the north.

---

48 / **Lacoe/Gist Residence** (1922)
430 W. Spruce St.
QUAYLE BROTHERS

Stately Italian Renaissance style home in a neighborhood known for grand mansions in a variety of styles.

---

49 / **Sweet Residence** (1913)
435 W. Spruce St.
MEAD & REQUA

This is perhaps San Diego's most elegant combination of Mediterranean mystery with modernistic massing. A Mediterranean-style entry, consisting

of a courtyard behind an arched opening in a garden wall, leads to a finely crafted home, with a dining room ringed by French doors that look out on the garden and city views.

50 / **Ackerman Residence** (1912)
3170 Curlew St.
HAZEL WATERMAN

Widowed at 37, Waterman became an architect through correspondence courses and hands-on training as a drafts-man for Hebbard & Gill. This design combines simple massing with classical revival detailing.

---

51 / **Park Manor Apartment Hotel** (1926)
525 Spruce St.
FRANK ALLEN.

Two romantic rounded balconies look down on the entry of this seven-story red brick landmark, with corner quoins and belt courses between floors. The original landscape was designed by Milton Sessions, son of pioneer horticulturist Kate Sessions.

---

52 / **Churchill Residence** (1918)
3264 Curlew St.
WILLIAM TEMPLETON JOHNSON

This prime example of Johnson's tasteful and romantic Spanish Colonial revival style shows why he was popular both with his peers and with the many clients who helped make him one of San Diego's most prolific architects.

---

53 / **Evangeline Caven bungalow** (1915)
410 W. Upas St.
CARLETON WINSLOW

Designer of buildings for the 1915 expo in Balboa Park, Winslow was best known for his wood-sided bungalows. Landscape architect Harriet Wimmer lived here; more recently it has been the home of city planner Mike Tudury.

BANKERS HILL

54 / **Alice Lee Residence #4** (1913)
3353 Albatross St.
IRVING GILL

Lee was a pioneering female real estate developer, and this was the first of eight hillside residences Gill designed for her as part of this mini-master-planned development.

---

55 / **Alice Lee Residence #3** (1912)
3367 Albatross St.
IRVING GILL

Of all the homes designed by Gill, this jewel box most perfectly sums up his genius, with its balanced assymetry, yin-yang tile-roofed tower and garage entry, and single palm tree that casts a moving shadow across white walls. It's a place purely of the region, or at least our romanticized version of it.

---

56 / **Katherine Teats Residence #3** (1912)
3407 Albatross St.
IRVING GILL

Thin-wall construction—an economical eye-pleasing method suited to a warm climate—makes this last of the eight canyon houses one of the most experimental.

---

57 / **Katherine Teats Residence #2** (1912)
3415 Albatross St.
IRVING GILL

One, two, three…the way this home steps back subtly from the street to its arched entry provides yet another example of Gill's ability to improvise infinite variations with basic stucco boxes.

58 / **Letitia Lovett Residence** (1892)
321 W. Walnut Ave.

Moved here in 1911 from Walnut and Fourth, this Victorian combines elaborate period details (too bad the wood siding was stucco'd over in the 1920s) with one of San Diego's coolest Queen Anne towers – look at that steep conical peak.

---

59 / **Rental Cottage** (1912)
3506 Albatross St.
IRVING GILL

A simple cube with a projecting arched entry – Gill's modern approach stripped to bare essentials.

University Heights

University Heights is a friendly neighborhood of modest middle-class Craftsman and Spanish Revival bungalows—as well a handful of contemporary experiments. Ringed by canyons, the area benefits from the lack of through-traffic. Residents have rallied around public art projects such as the decoration of the Vermont Street Bridge by artists from Paper Rock Scissors, and murals painted on utility boxes by top San Diego artists including Blair Thornley.

Mission Cliff Gardens at Park Boulevard and Adams Avenue marks the spot where a new electric cablecar line from downtown ended in 1890. At the time this was the city's finest public park. In the trolley barn nearby, cars turned around on a rotating platform and headed back downtown. The cablecar company went bust in 1892, but there are still traces of cobblestone walls that defined University Heights more than 100 years ago.

By the early 1900s, this early suburb was known for Harvey Bentley's Ostrich Farm next to Mission Cliff Gardens—feathers were the height of fashion. University Heights was an early hub of a growing city's aspirations for higher education. The community takes its name from early plans for a college campus here—before San Diego

State University was established several miles to the east. At Park and El Cajon Boulevards, one of the original Beaux Arts State Normal School buildings is still visible. Along a few blocks of Park Boulevard north of El Cajon Boulevard, University Heights by the beginning of the current century has become a desireable urban neighborhood, with a mix of homes ranging from apartments to Craftsman bungalows, and with a vital art scene that includes a neighborhood theater, excellent restaurants, nationally renowned live music (and excellent espresso) at Twiggs Coffee & Tea.

Unlike some mid-city neighborhoods, University Heights staved off the 1970s and 1980s onslaught of dingbat apartment buildings, retaining much of its historical charm and pedestrian-friendly scale. When developers proposed a 325-unit condo project on the site of Mission Cliff Gardens, the community instead rallied around the idea of a new Trolley Barn Park.

University Heights Locations

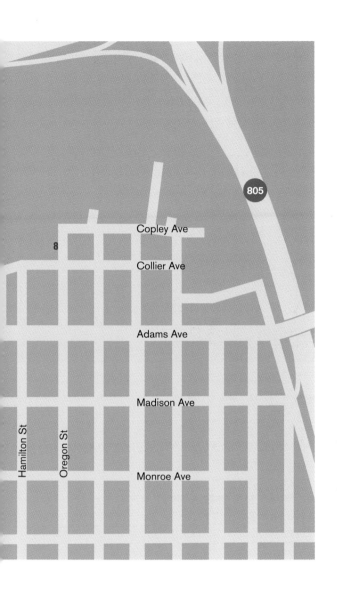

1 **Mission Cliff Gardens**

2 **State Normal School Annex**

3 **Grace Lutheran Church**

4 **Shirley Anne Place Historical District**

5 **Crook/Foster Residence**

6 **Dryden Bungalows**

7 **George Hawley Residence**

8 **Villa Montamar**
   Academy of Our Lady of Peace

UNIVERSITY HEIGHTS

1 / **Mission Cliff Gardens** (1890) /**Trolley Barn Park**

Adams Avenue near Park

The original elaborate gardens and adjacent trolley barn are gone, but stone walls, palm trees, and a fountain have been preserved. Trolley Barn Park is a monument to the sizeable cablecar garage that formerly stood here. Cablecars ran from 1890 to 1893, and again beginning in 1896 when they were converted from cable to electric.

2 / **State Normal School Annex** (1910)

Park Boulevard at El Cajon Boulevard

WILLIAM HEBBARD

Three Beaux Arts buildings designed by Hebbard + Gill between 1898 and 1904 are gone, but this neoclassical annex remains. Various plans have circulated for its re-use as as library or community center. Even though it wasn't designed by Hebbard & Gill, you can detect the influence of Gill's tenure with Chicago architect Louis Sullivan—the Windy City's Beaux Arts master.

3 / **Grace Lutheran Church** (1930)

3993 Park Blvd.

ALBERT SCHROEDER AND FREDERICK KENNEDY

With its red tile gable roofs, raised parapets, thick reinforced concrete walls, and wrought-iron grillwork, the church has been compared to a medieval Spanish monastery. It mixes Spanish Colonial and late Gothic elements, and it features stained glass windows by Frederic Wilson of the famed Judson Studios in Pasadena.

4 / **Shirley Anne Place Historical District** (1925-1927)

4500 block of Shirley Anne Place (between Madison and Monroe Avenues)

Collection of 24 small homes—predominantly Spanish Colonial Revival—and a grocery store. The architecture is important, but so is the pride of place that binds these homeowners together.

5 / **Crook/Foster Residence** (1914)

2242 Adams Ave.

One of 50 homes built north of Balboa Park by Craftsman master David Owen Dryden, this little jewel has a deep porch, exposed rafters, and patterned redwood siding.

6 / **Dryden Bungalows** (1913-1914)

4720-4724-4780 Panorama Dr.

DAVID OWEN DRYDEN

San Diego's master Craftsman, Dryden constructed dozens of Craftsman bungalows between 1911 and 1919 in various San Diego neighborhoods.

7 / **George Hawley Residence** (1907)

4744 Panorama Dr.

HEBBARD & GILL

From the tail-end of Gill's partnership with Hebbard, this half-timber Tudor-style home is simpler than the team's earlier efforts, pointing the way toward Gill's mature modern style.

8 / **Villa Montamar/**
Academy of Our Lady of Peace (1916)

4860 Oregon St.

FRANK MEAD

A modernistic take on Mediterranean Revival, in reinforced concrete. Originally an estate for the Vandruff family, the 20-acre property was acquired in 1924 by Our Lady of Peace.

Golden Hill Sherman Heights Logan Heights

Overlooking downtown, the waterfront, Coronado, and Mexico from its elevated perch, Golden Hill was a popular neighborhood where the upper crust built Victorian mansions at the end of the 19th century. Smitten with the glow on the hill at sunset, developers Daniel Schuyler and Erastus Bartlett gave the neighborhood its name.

Golden Hill and adjacent Sherman Heights have Victorian, Tudor, Classical Revival, Federal, Italianate, and Craftsman homes. The Sen. Leroy Wright residence on B Street in Golden Hill is particularly fine in its proportions and attention to detail. Leading Craftsman architect Emmor Brooke Weaver designed the English Cottage-style Strong residence.

Rueben Quartermass built the Queen of Queen Annes here in 1896. The Quartermass-Wilde residence (San Diego Mayor Louis Wilde lived in it from 1917 to 1921) anchors the corner of 24th and Broadway with three-stories of Classical Revival details including Doric columns and Greek pilasters, and an ornate tower that takes in the view through curved windows. Architect Irving Gill designed his first San Diego home in Golden Hill in 1893, a decade before his signature spare modern style emerged.

Matthew Sherman bought 160 acres and founded Sherman Heights in 1867. Just south of Golden Hill, Sherman Heights was originally pastoral, with grazing livestock, water wells, and sizeable vegetable gardens. Sherman's own home at 19th and J, completed in 1868, was the neighborhood's first residence. After a sabbatical in El Cajon, Sherman built another home in Sherman Heights in the 1880s. He served as San Diego's mayor in 1891 and 1892.

In 1869, the city set aside nearby acreage for a city park (eventually Balboa Park), plus 200 acres that became Mount Hope Cemetery, where luminaries including mystery author Raymond Chandler are buried.

Jesse Shepard's Villa Montezuma on K Street is an eclectic dessert of sherbet colors and whipped cream peaks, thought by many to embody Shepard's mystical beliefs. Today the Villa is a museum owned and operated by the San Diego Historical Society.

During the 1990s, the neighborhood banded together in landscape improvement programs that quickly restored several residential gardens. A landmark public building and symbol of pride, the Rob Quigley designed community center was built following several neighborhood design workshops..

As the current millenium began with plans for a new downtown ballpark and revitalization of downtown's East Village neighborhood, Sherman Heights and Golden Hill became increasingly desireable. Both neighborhoods are in the midst of transformation to a more diverse population, with gentrification promising to drastically alter this area's character. At the moment, older businesses exist alongside newer spots such as the Turf Club bar and restaurant in Golden Hill, where hip, young patrons swill good beer and wine and grill their own steaks and chicken.

Just to the south, Logan Heights was once San Diego's prestigious Mexican-American neighborhood. Turned over to military and industrial uses after WWII, split in the 1960s by I-5 and the Coronado Bridge onramp, the community was relegated to inferior status and has never quite recovered. Activists staked a claim with Chicano Park in the early 1970s, and the park's vibrant murals make a strong show of neighborhood pride and heritage, but Logan Heights is still waiting for full-blown support from political and business leaders.

Golden Hill/Barrio Logan Locations

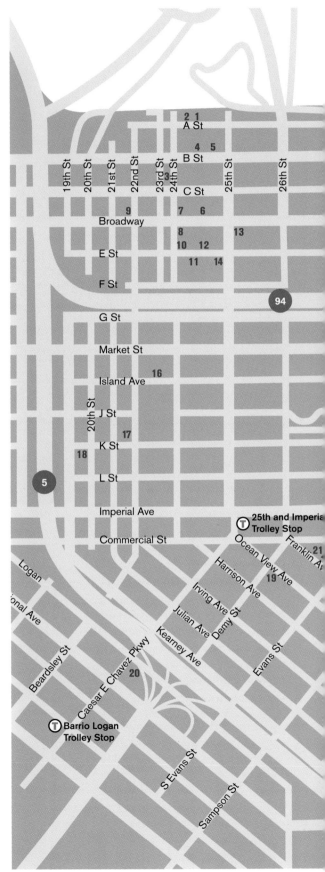

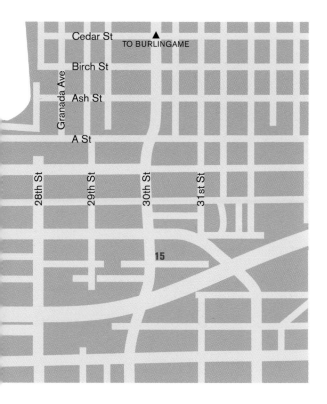

1 **Henry Fehlmann Residence**
2 **William Hugh Strong Residence**
3 **Naslund Residence**
4 **Clark McKee Residence**
5 **Senator Leroy Wright Residence**
6 **A.H. Frost Residence**
7 **Quartermass-Wilde Residence**
8 **Seventh Day Adventist Church**
9 **Haywood-Patterson Residence**
10 **Garrettson Residence**
11 **Samuel Rynearson Residence**
12 **Alfred Haines Residence**
13 **Fire Station #11**
14 **Daniel Schuyler Residence**
15 **Abraham Klauber Residence**
16 **Sherman Heights Community Center**
17 **Christensen Flats**
18 **Villa Montezuma**
19 **Mt. Carmel Baptist Church**
20 **Chicano Park Murals**
21 **James T. Weldon Residence**

GOLDEN HILL/BARRIO LOGAN

1 / **Henry Fehlmann Residence** (1911)
2470 A St.
DEL HARRIS

Harris, who may have apprenticed as a draftsman for Greene and Greene in Pasadena, designed this Prairie-inspired residence reminiscent of earlier San Diego homes by William Hebbard.

---

2 / **William Hugh Strong Residence** (1905)
2460 A St.
EMMOR BROOKE WEAVER

San Diego's answer to Greene and Greene, Weaver designed this English Cottage home, with its steep shingled roof and leaded glass.

---

3 / **Naslund Residence** (1993)
1154 24th St.
ERIC NASLUND

Built on a modest budget with architect and wife occasionally wielding hammers and saws, this house around a mock orange tree draws from a long California tradition of courtyard houses. Large dining and living room windows look down on the street, providing a sense of connection between public and private spaces, as well as a sense of security for neighbors who like knowing someone is home next door.

---

4 / **Clark McKee Residence** (1897)
2460 B St.
Intriguing asymmetrical pairing of a three-story circular tower with the adjacent pedimented main structure and sizeable wraparound porch.

5 / **Senator Leroy Wright Residence** (1898)
2470 B St.

This Classical Revival house for a California state senator looks more like something from the East Coast than turn-of-the-century California.

6 / **A.H. Frost Residence** (1897)
2456 Broadway

IRVING GILL

One of Gill's earliest San Diego designs (after arriving from Chicago) was for the bicycle manufacturer and founder of Frost Hardwood.

7 / **Quartermass-Wilde Residence** (1896)
2404 Broadway

One of San Diego's grandest Victorians features a four-story tower with distinctive detailing on each level, patterned shingles, and a neoclassical corner entrance with forms reminiscent of ancient Greek temples.

8 / **Seventh Day Adventist Church** (c. 1930)
SE corner Broadway and 24th St.

The neighborhood's lone Zigzag Moderne building, made of concrete.

GOLDEN HILL/BARRIO LOGAN

9 / Haywood-Patterson Residence (1887)
2148 Broadway

Italiante Victorian originally owned by carpen-
ter/developer/Yacht Club
Captain Albert Moses
Haywood, purchased in
1899 by photographer
Francis Patterson.

10 / Garrettson Residence (1896)
2410 E St.
IRVING GILL

Colonial Revival in
minimalist form.

11 / Samuel Rynearson Residence (1897)
2441 E St.

Classical revival meets
classic Victorian, with
unexpected touches
including the curved
Oriental dormer. A con-
tinuous frieze at the
roofline is an unusual
distinguishing feature.

12 / Alfred Haines Residence (1908)
2470 E St.
QUAYLE BROTHERS

Turn-of-the-century showplace by top San Diego architects.

13 / **Fire Station #11** (1997)
945 25TH ST.

ROBBINS JORGENSEN
CHRISTOPHER

Looking more like an inviting public building—say, a city hall—than a typical fire station, this building does double duty, fulfilling its public safety mission while providing a new landmark entry to Golden Hill. In another rarity among fire stations, this one even has its own site-specific artwork, "Signifire." This piece by Nina Karavasiles combines a coiled bronze fire hose and a concave dish containing glass mosaics that refect a flame pattern onto the hose's polished chrome nozzle. It's also a play on Victorian-era anamorphic lenses that decode cryptic images—a nod to the neighborhood's historical beginnings.

14 / **Daniel Schuyler Residence** (1893)
838 25th St.
IRVING GILL

Neoclassical variation on Victorian design, once the home of an early city parks commissioner.

15 / **Abraham Klauber Residence** (1888)
3000 E St.
M.D. FALK

The Klaubers lived in this Victorian home for several years; their significant remodels included addition of a cocond otory.

16 / **Sherman Heights Community Center** (1994)
2258 Island Ave.
ROB QUIGLEY

In the spirit of Irving Gill, Rudolf Schindler, Bernard Maybeck and other earlier California architects who loved concrete, Quigley designed this durable building for a neighborhood in need of a grand community space and source of pride.

GOLDEN HILL/BARRIO LOGAN

17 / **Chirstensen flats** (1908)
312 22nd St.
IRVING GILL

One of many San Diego examples of modest rental properties designed by Gill; this is a two-story clapboard duplex with a square corner bay window.

18 / **Villa Montezuma** (1887)
1925 K St.
COMSTOCK AND TROTSCHE

San Diego's most elaborate Queen Anne was built for writer/musician/mystic Jesse Shepard. Restored to pristine condition, it includes stained glass windows, carved wood detailing, large fireplaces.

19 / **Mt. Carmel Baptist Church** (c. 1885)
2001 Ocean View
Carefully crafted place of worship from the Victorian era.

20 / Chicano Park Murals (1973-1990s)

Between Logan and National Avenues, beneath Coronado Bridge approach

SALVADOR TORRES, JOSE MONTOYA, MARIO TORERO, VICTOR OCHOA, AND OTHERS

After Interstate 5 and the Coronado Bridge divided a once-vital community, Barrio Logan was promised a community park. Instead, grading began for a California Highway Patrol office, but community activists halted construction by forming a human chain around bulldozers. Residents began planting the park, and a Chicano flag was raised on a telephone pole. Torres—inspired by earlier Mexican muralists Orozco, Siqueiros, and Rivera—conceived the public art murals program in 1969. The first murals were painted quickly in one day by artists and residents as a throng of 300 rolled and brushed concrete bridge pilings. A second batch was added in the spring of 1975 by the Royal Chicano Air Force arts collective. In 1977, a third group of murals was painted.

21 / James T. Weldon Residence (1885)

3139 Franklin St.

Designed in the formal East Coast Stick Style, this home nonetheless embraces the pioneering West Coast notion of gardens and outdoor spaces that connect with architecture.

GOLDEN HILL/BARRIO LOGAN

HIGHLIGHT

Barrio Logan

San Diego's focal point for the 1960s Chicano movement, Barrio Logan was once the second largest Mexican-American community on the West Coast, with a population of 20,000. Divided by Interstate 5 in 1963 and Coronado Bridge pillars in 1969, the community was promised land for a community park. Instead, bulldozers began grading the site for a California Highway Patrol office.

On Nov. 9, 1969, artists, residents, and activists staked their claim to the 1.8-acre parcel, forming a human chain to block the machines. Led by artist Salvatore Torres, the community worked with city officials to create Chicano Park, beginning with a desert garden, followed by murals in the tradition of Rivera and Orozco, depicting Chicano heroes and legends.

Logan Heights takes its name from a street that was part of a subdivision laid out here on railroad lands in 1886. Eventually the neighborhood became known as Logan Heights, or the "East

End". A speculative boom ended in 1889, when Santa Fe decided to make Los Angeles—not San Diego—its western railway terminus.

Mexican immigrants settled in the area between 1910 and 1920, some taking defense industry jobs during WWI. In 1919, San Diego deeded acreage to the Navy for its Pacific Fleet headquarters, and by 1922, 84 destroyers had arrived. During the 1920s, 500,000 Mexicans crossed the border on permanent visas, accounting for as much as two-thirds of San Diego's labor force. For what they contributed, the Mexican-American community didn't get much civic support in return.

Since the 1930s, Logan Heights has seen its waterfront—once the site of a community beach and pier—taken over by military and industrial uses that destroyed neighborhood houses and businesses. Meanwhile, of some 50,000 new jobs in the community, most were filled by outsiders. With rezoning from residential to industrial use in the 1950s, the waterfront was scarred by traffic, pollution, and chain link fence-enclosed lots and junkyards. By 1979, the population had declined to 5,000.

In the 1990s, a new San Diego Trolley station connected the Barrio to the greater region, and the Mercado mixed-use project was conceived as a centerpiece of redevelopment. Moderate-income residential units were constructed, but while other areas in San Diego boomed, Barrio Logan never attracted investment dollars to fund the retail/commercial portion of the Mercado.

"The lack of investment in the Mercado commercial project creates a cycle of negative stereotypes, debilitated services, and neglect from politicians," wrote Caroline Liening of San Diego State University's Inter-Varsity Christian Fellowship, in 1999. Also in the 1990s, Barrio Logan began cleaning up toxic waste deposited over the years by industry. With mitigation underway, sites became available for development—which was still slow to come.

Today, Barrio Logan is a mix of industrial/commercial buildings, with newer developments including The Mercado Apartments mixed with industrial uses, and historic buildings ranging from Victorian and Craftsman, to Spanish Colonial Revival and modern. Although the community has suffered many abuses, its undying spirit is still evident in the surviving neighborhood restaurants and shops—and especially in the murals of Chicano Park.

Kensington/ Talmadge/ Normal Heights

One of San Diego's first suburbs remains one of its finest. Kensington has homes designed by architects including Richard Requa and Cliff May, as well as newer commercial buildings by Tom Grondona (a dental office) and Allard Jansen (mixed-use anchored by Starbuck's). On former mission land on the southern rim of Mission Valley, at the eastern end (at Marlborough and Adams) of the electric trolley line connected to downtown, G. Aubrey Davidson founded a 66-acre subdivision he named Kensington Park in 1910. Lots were arranged around a small neighborhood park; ornamental lights and pepper trees lined the streets in this once-scrubby locale.

Initially, Kensington was restricted to residential single-family use—no apartments, no duplexes, no hotels. As in Mission Hills, only whites could own property in Kensington. Competing with Mission Hills as San Diego's high-end suburb, Kensington was slow to develop. But with a healthy economy and affordable labor and materials after World War I, the community boomed, and by the late 1920s, several new subdivisions had been added.

Today's Kensington combines five original subdivisions: Kensington Park, Kensington Park Annex, Kensington Park Extension, Kensington Talmadge, and Kensington Heights. Before Kensington Heights, the neighborhood had developed in haphazard fashion, with poorly orchestrated land uses and a potpourri of architecture.

Davis-Baker, the Pasadena-based developer of Kensington Heights, established architectural guidelines—with assistance from Requa, who advocated a "Southern California Style" inspired by his visits to Spain, Morocco, Algeria, and other Mediterranean regions. Requa's experience included planning and architecture for Ojai and Rancho Santa Fe. In Kensington, Davis-Baker's "architectural committee" consisted of Requa.

During his Mediterranean travels, according to historian Anne Bullard, "Requa was intrigued by the 'charming composition of lines, arches, and flat roofs,' and liked the feeling of little cottages 'nestled in rich green and bright foliage of the countryside.' He sought the 'delightful informality of design and satisfying harmony with its environment.' These characteristics were ideally suited to the environment Davis-Baker worked to create for Kensington Heights. As they stated in an advertisement: 'The developers of Kensington Heights believe that in furthering the true type of Spanish architecture they are in a measure perpetrating traditions of San Diego. Behind San Diego is a romance of love, chivalry and struggling pioneers.'

Prior to marketing lots, the developers built a few houses to seed the style. They also seeded the landscape palette with palms, bougainvillea, acacia, and oleander, to "provide the rich greens and bright colors prescribed by Requa," Bullard states in the *Journal of San Diego History*.

Because of Requa's first-hand knowledge of genuine historic architecture, Kensington feels much more authentic than newer San Diego subdivisions that adopt Mediterranean themes.

There was another motive behind Requa's designs. His travels and resulting books were financed by Portland Cement Co. as part of a campaign to promote a style of architecture that used Portland's stucco in place of traditional wood siding. Requa wrote a column on architecture and design for the San Diego Union. The developer took out an ad stating that an anonymous property owner would award $100 for the best amateur Spanish-style home design. Competitors were urged to visit the lot in

KENSINGTON/TALMADGE/NORMAL HEIGHTS

Kensington. Next to Davis-Baker's ad was Requa's design column on the benefits of using stucco instead of wood siding.

Mrs. Margery Fickinsen won the contest, but the contest was a fix—in fact, the winning design came from Requa.

When deed restrictions in Kensington expired in 1926, developers seized the opportunity to create the current commercial district along Adams Avenue. Properties changed hands during the Depression, through foreclosures and sales at desperation prices. Kensington was annexed to the city of San Diego in 1936. World War II put a stop to new home construction; but steady demand has driven prices higher and higher since the post-war years.

Kensington's "main street" along Adams Avenue had an artsy appeal for many years, with the Ken Cinema the region's sole surviving art film house, and with the adjacent video store stocking rare films ranging from noir to sixties British. Architect Tom Grondona's dental office—spare, white, sculptural—made an exciting intervention on the conservative streetscape in the late 1980s. Allard Jansen's late 1990s mixed-use development near the Ken set a new neighborhood standard for contemporary commercial architecture.

Best known for their Hollywood roles, the three Talmadge sisters played a part in the development of Talmadge—they lent their name to the new community and turned up with Buster Keaton and other celebrities for the dedication of the new Talmadge Park subdivision in 1926. Its developer, Roy Lichty, viewed the Kensington-Talmadge area as "San Diego's Pasadena".

In addition to promoting quality planning and architecture, Lichty and company touted the benefits of living near a new state college to be built nearby. He envisioned an upscale community like the neighborhood around UCLA in Westwood.

Kensington-Talmadge has an exemplary range of school architecture, from the spare WPA-era St. Didacus on 34th Street, to Benjamin Franklin Elementary on Copeland—one of San Diego's few Streamline Modern buildings. Unfortunately, the original classical revival-style Hoover High School building on El Cajon Boulevard was demolished in the 1970s.

Head west on Adams Avenue from Kensington/Talmadge and you will find yourself in Normal Heights, one of San Diego's most resilient pedestrian-friendly retail districts. Businesses have come and gone, and there have been vacancies in recent years. Many buildings from the 1920s through 1950s have seen various uses; today, this jacaranda-lined strip of Adams has carved out its niche as the place for antiques, used books, records (especially at Lou Curtiss's Folk Arts Rare Records, occupying part of his own house), vintage fashion, and neighborhood spots ranging from restaurants, bakeries, and coffeehouses to beauty salons and markets (Pepe's Produce) and Smitty's Garage and a couple of Irish bars.

Architecturally, Normal Heights runs the gamut, from tradi-tional all-American main street styles along Adams, to pris-tine Craftsman bungalows, and some very contemporary places designed as replacements for 76 houses lost in 1985 to a wind-stoked brush fire that swept up from Mission Valley.

Led by San Diego's AIA chapter, the city drafted replace-ment guidelines that emphasized sensible planning and scale, but did not dictate architectural style. As a result, newer homes range from a cool modern place designed by RNP, to architect Lee Platt's revival of vintage Irving Gill, and Condia-Ornelas's fresh update of historic mission and Spanish elements. As the tragedy of the fire recedes into the distance, Normal Heights stands as a fine exam-ple of how old and new can gracefully co-exist in a neigh-borhood that retains all of its original charm.

Kensington/Talmadge/ Normal Heights Locations

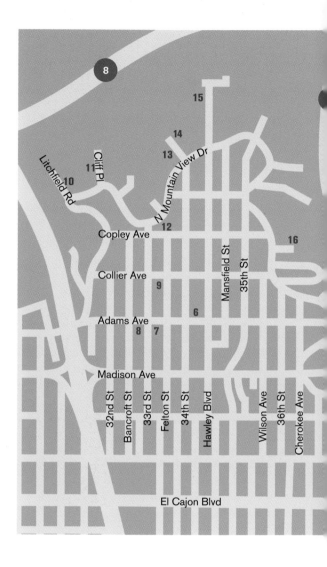

1 **Lindstrom/Roper Residence**

2 **Barstow Dental Building**

3 **Kensington Park Plaza**

4 **George H. Prudden House**

5 **Brenkert/Thorpe Residence**

6 **Wilkinson Block**

7 **Carteri Theatre/Discount Fabrics**

8 **Variety Hardware Building**

9 **St. Didacus Roman Catholic Church**

10 **Patterson Residence**

11 **Meisel Residence**

12 **Anderson Residence**

13 **Miller Residence**

14 **Sale Residence**

15 **Carmelite Monastery**

16 **Treat Artist Studio**

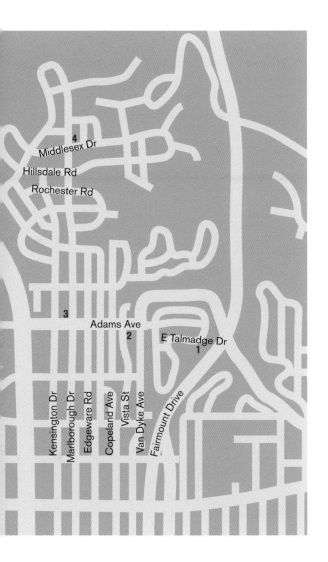

Middlesex Dr
4

Hillsdale Rd

Rochester Rd

3

Adams Ave
2

E Talmadge Dr
1

Kensington Dr

Marlborough Dr

Edgeware Rd

Copeland Ave

Vista St

Van Dyke Ave

Fairmount Drive

KENSINGTON

1 / Lindstrom/Roper Residence (1933)
4669 E. Talmadge Dr.
CLIFF MAY

Classic Cliff May hacienda, right down to the hefty wooden doors and colorful tile doorbell surround, developed as a spec house by O.U. Miracle and partners.

2 / Barstow Dental Building (1987)
4685 Vista St.
TOM GRONDONA

San Diego's leading artist/architect adds a healthy splash of fantasy (including a cylindrical tower) to Kensington's otherwise conservative main street. In the waiting room a giant periscope lets you scope the neighborhood; as you recline in the dentist's chair, mirrors provide views of the garden. If you've got to visit the dentist, Grondona's building almost makes the experience tolerable.

3 / Kensington Park Plaza (1999)
Adams Avenue and Marlborough Drive
ALLARD JANSEN

Borrowing columns, archways, and tile roofs from the neighborhood's predominant Mediterranean styles, the mixed-use building (including that well-known coffee chain) combines storefronts and townhomes in a pedestrian-friendly scheme.

4 / George H. Prudden House (1926)
5159 Marlborough Dr.
RICHARD REQUA

Instrumental in popularizing Mediterranean styles in San Diego, Requa inaugurated a neighborhood full of them with this model home for a new development. Originally owned by aviation engineer George Prudden (who helped site San Diego's airport), the home in recent years has been owned by

historian and Requa devotee Parker Jackson.

5 / **Brenkert/Thorpe Residence** (1914)
3805 Merivale Ave.

Simple but idiosyncratic example of Arts and Crafts ideals, built of cobblestones; featuring exposed rafter tails, stained glass, and a dramatic arched entry. Property includes a primary residence, a board-and-batten cottage, and garage.

6 / **Wilkinson Block** (1926)
3402-3408 Adams Ave.

Notable as an uncommon brick-veneer variation on the period's popular Mission Revival style, built by Adams Avenue developer Bertram Carteri, this was a central piece of the neighborhood's original commercial district.

7 / **Carteri Theatre/Discount Fabrics** (1925)
3325 Adams Ave.
LOUIS GILL

Centerpiece of Normal Heights' original commercial district, the building retains some of its original historical detailing.

8 / **Variety Hardware Building** (1925)
3285-87 Adams Ave.
LOUIS GILL

Early example of mixed-use (apartments over retail) by famous San Diego architect Irving Gill's under-appreciated nephew. The ground floor originally had folding glass doors that could create an open-air market. Weaned on his uncle's spare modernist style, Louis Gill preferred more traditional styles.

9 / St. Didacus Roman Catholic Church (1927)
4772 Felton St.

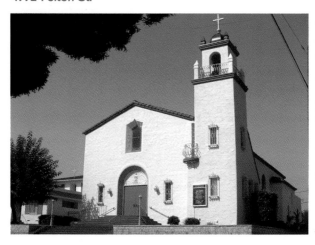

In honor of the patron saint for whom Mission San Diego de Alcala is named, this romantic structure features a corner bell tower, wrought-iron railings, and a small circular balcony over the entrance.

10 / Patterson Residence (1986)
5015 Litchfield Rd.
LEE PLATT

Platt died prematurely, this house is one of his best designs, a modernist place inspired by Irving Gill and San Diego's missions.

11 / Meisel Residence (1988)
5066 Cliff Place
ROESLING NAKAMURA

Well proportioned minimalist design combining concrete block, stucco, and stainless steel. Indoor hot tub takes in bird's eye views of Mission Valley; this fire-resistant home was designed to replace one of several homes destroyed in the June 3, 1985 Normal Heights canyon fire.

12 / Anderson Residence (1920s)
3348 Copley Ave.
Small Egyptian Revival-style home, featuring rolled cornice and door-frame shaped like a cartouche.

13 / **Miller Residence** (1987)
5128 34th St.
MARC TARASUCK

In another fire-replacement house, Tarasuck updates San Diego's popular Mediterranean revival mode with clean modern lines and an entry courtyard.

14 / **Sale Residence** (1986)
5163 34th St.
CONDIA-ORNELAS

The front echoes the original Spanish bungalow lost to a canyon fire, three other sides comprise a more modern aesthetic.

15 / **Carmelite Monastery** (1931)
5158 Hawley Blvd.
FRANK J. HOPE, SR.

Stately period revival building with details including plaster rosettes, and an amazing rose garden.

16 / **Treat Artist Studio** (1995)
3650 Copley Ave.
JEANNE MCCALLUM

Situated behind a Mission Revival bungalow, this artist's studio is made of simple, utilitarian materials, with details such as exposed studs and framing brackets.

North Park
South Park
Burlingame

Passionate about preservation and particularly the
Craftsman era, residents of North Park, South Park,
and Burlingame are the keepers of San Diego's finest collection of homes from the 1910s, 1920s, and 1930s. Built
in neighborhoods surrounding Balboa Park following the
1915 international expo there, these places range from
dozens built by Craftsman master David Owen Dryden, to

modest generic designs
probably inspired by plans
that appeared in The
Craftsman magazine, sea-
soned with a few wild contemporary designs by Randy
Dalrymple, Davids-Killory, and
others.

The ongoing success of downtown redevelopment has
made all three of these neighborhoods desireable, as evidenced by home prices that rival some beach areas. Along
30th Street at the edge of pink-sidewalked Burlingame,
there's been a business renaissance—without a peep from
that prolific Seattle coffee chain. Neighborhood bars and
coffeehouses, galleries, and even an Asian-American theatre company are among new establishments restoring and
occupying attractive older buildings. In 2002, preservationists gained city approval for a Burlingame Historical District
that will help protect dozens of prime period specimens.

In North Park, the old movie theatre appears destined for
renovation as a performing arts complex and will make a
valuable addition to the lively scene along University
Avenue, where the street-spanning "North Park" sign has
been restored. Neighborhood activists have rallied around

sprucing-up campaigns, including the recent addition of artistic paint jobs to camouflage streetside utility boxes. The landmark green metallic water tower has not been declared a historical site, but it should be.

South Park has a similar concentration of Craftsman-era designs. As Balboa Park has been restored and new museums have opened, South Park has become an extremely popular place to live within walking distance of the park.

Drive through North Park, South Park, and Burlingame, and you'll detect the rare spirit of these neighborhoods, in the painstaking preservation of historic architecture, and in the many colorful and personal touches residents have added to their homes and public places.

North Park/South Park/ Burlingame Locations

1 Hotel Lafayette/ InnSuites Hotel

2 North Park Water Tower

3 North Park Elementary School

4 Odd Fellows Building

5 North Park Theatre

6 Silvergate Lodge of the Masonic Order

7 Kenney House

8 George and Anna Carr Residence

9 Dryden Family Home

10 David Dryden Residence

11 John Thurston Residence

12 Bungalow courts

13 Beers Residence

14 Stake/Schilling Residence

15 Springer Residence

16 Fletcher/ Halley Residence

17 Edward Quayle House

18 Mitchell Residence

19 Mitchell Studio/ Residence

20 Burlingame Historical District

21 House

22 William A. McIntyre House

23 House

24 McIntyre spec House

25 Benbough/ Adams House

26 House

27 Casita Blanca

28 Louis Brandt House

29 Edgar Hendee Residence

30 Henry Sparks Residence

31 Library Tower

32 Bungalow

33 Bungalow

34 Wegeforth Residence

35 Mausoleum House

36 Edward and Blanche Gibson House

37 Cottee/McCorkle House

38 Pig With A Purple Eye Patch

39 Whitsitt Residence

40 Whiteman Residence

41 Mission Revival House

42 Fulford bungalows

43 Bungalow

44 Erwin D. Norris House

45 Bungalow

46 Leonard Lyons House

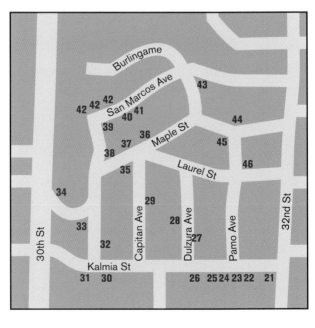

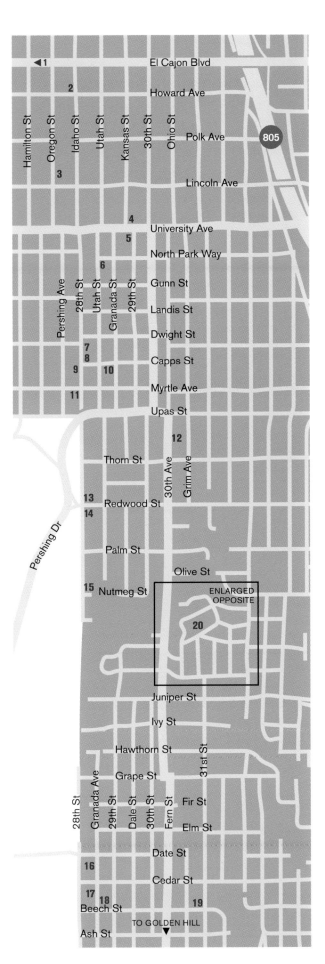

NORTH PARK/SOUTH PARK/BURLINGAME

1 / Hotel Lafayette/InnSuites Hotel (1946)
2223 El Cajon Blvd.

Built by playboy home-
builder Larry Imig, this
Colonial-style landmark
was a getaway destination
for stars like Betty Grable,
Harry James, and Ava
Gardner, who partied to
the sound of live big bands in the Mississippi Ballroom, and went for a dip
in a terrazzo Olympic-size swimming pool designed by Olympic swim-
mer/Tarzan actor Johnny Weissmuller.

2 / North Park Water Tower (1923)
Howard Avenue and Idaho Street

In the days when the neighborhood was a fledgling suburb, this
1.2-million-gallon reservoir was its
prime source of water. Built by
the Pittsburgh-Des Moines Steel
Corp. for $73,000, it was the
largest municipal tank in the country. Although drained of water for
good in the early 1990s, the 127-
foot-tall tower remains as North
Park's signature landmark.

3 / North Park Elementary School (1998)
4041 Oregon St.
MESQUITA AND ASSOCIATES

A grand river rock entry
solidifies this building's
connection with the sur-
rounding Craftsman-era
neighborhood. The
school's planning and design involved collaboration with residents,
teachers, and the school district.

4 / Odd Fellows Building (1929)
2906 University Ave.
EDWARD NEWMAN AND WILLIAM GIBB

Originally built in Spanish Revival style, with arched windows and a red
tile roof, the building was modernized in the 1950s. In the 1990s, its

restoration
was guided
by architects
Richard Bundy
and David
Thompson.

NORTH PARK/SOUTH PARK/BURLINGAME

5 / North Park Theatre (1929)
2895 University Ave.
QUAYLE BROTHERS

Stripped in recent years of its period ornamentation (including bulbous, pointy finials) and vertical marquee, the Spanish Renaissance Revival building embarks on a new future as of 2002, with developer Bud Fischer's plan to renovate it as performance space for San Diego Comic Opera and other groups.

6 / Silvergate Lodge of the Masonic Order (1933)
3795 Utah St.
CHARLES AND EDWARD QUAYLE

Inspired by King Soloman's Temple in Jerusalem, built of poured reinforced concrete, this fantastic Art Deco building has an interior featuring Egyptian details, glass light fixtures, and a decorative stenciled border. The main meeting room on the third floor is entirely Egyptian Revival, modeled after an Egyptian throne room, with three wooden "thrones," and pillars that meet the ceiling in a lotus-papyrus design.

7 / Kenney House (1915)
3571 28th St.
DAVID OWEN DRYDEN

Rare example of the Craftsman master's Swiss Chalet mode, featuring pitched, deep-eaved gable roof; cobblestone columns, big bay window, and beveled glass.

8 / George and Anna Carr Residence (1915)
3553 28th St.
DAVID OWEN DRYDEN

First of several Craftsman homes built by Dryden on 28th, this was his most elaborate design in the Oriental/ Craftsman mode more common in Pasadena: check out those curved roof peaks and beam ends. Mr. Carr worked for Independent Sash and Door Co., which supplied many of the custom doors, sashes, and art glass Dryden used in his homes.

9 / Dryden Family Home (1915)
3536 28th St.
DAVID OWEN DRYDEN

Dryden's later, larger family home, where he resided from 1915 to 1918.

NORTH PARK/SOUTH PARK/BURLINGAME

10 / David Dryden Residence (1913)
3548 Granada St.
DAVID OWEN DRYDEN

Craftsman bungalow where Dryden lived from 1913 to 1915.

11 / John Thurston Residence (1916)
3446 28th St.
DAVID OWEN DRYDEN

Prime example of Dryden's Craftsmen mastery, with a capacious veranda flanked by brick piers, shaded by a vine-covered gable.

12 / Bungalow courts (1905-1916)
3373-3379 and 3301-3315 30th St.

Classic early California courtyard apartments, in Mediterranean and Mission Revival styles.

13 / Beers Residence (1928)
3103 28th St.

The architect is unknown, but builder William Muehleisen did a good job in the California Spanish Revival genre popularized by architects such as George Washington Smith, Myron Hunt, and William Templeton Johnson.

14 / Stake/Schilling Residence (1935)
3037 28th St.
CHARLES SALYERS

In a neighborhood (and region) dominated during that time by Craftsman, Spanish Colonial, and styles imported from the East Coast, this boldly modern place blends the

sexy sweep of Streamline Moderne with simpler International Style forms.

NORTH PARK/SOUTH PARK/BURLINGAME

15 / Springer Residence (1925)
2737 28th St.

REQUA AND JACKSON

Excellent example of the
Mediterranean villa-inspired genre
popularized by these partners.

16 / Fletcher/Halley Residence (1906)
1612 Granada Ave.

One of the first homes built in this
neighborhood, this low-key neoclassical structure features Doric
columns, a hipped roof with
exposed rafter tails, beveled glass,
and upturned Japonesque eaves.

17 / Edward Quayle House (1915)
1528 Granada Ave.

EDWARD QUAYLE

Shingle style California
bungalow designed by
one half of the prominent
Quayle Brothers architec-
tural team. Restoration
utilized some non-authen-
tic materials, such as
machine-lathed shingles
that have a more orderly appearance than the originals.

18 / Mitchell Residence (1910)
1527 Granada Ave.

WILLIAM HEBBARD

The onetime home of
California impressionist
artist Alfred Mitchell is a
rare Colonial Revival-style
structure, in a neighborhood
best known for bungalows.

19 / Mitchell Studio/Residence (1937)
1506 31st St.

RICHARD REQUA, LLOYD RUOCCO

Designed by Requa, with
bronzework by artist James
Tank Porter from designs by
Ruocco, artist Alfred Mitchell's
later home consists of two
separate buildings, in a clean-
er, simpler California stucco
style than Requa's usual.

NORTH PARK/SOUTH PARK/BURLINGAME

20 / Burlingame Historical District (1912-1952)

Bounded by San Marcos Avenue, Kalmia Street, 32nd Street, 30th Street

Rose-colored sidewalks snake through curving streets that follow natural terrain. Isolated by limited street access, the neighborhood evolved its distinctive historical character under design guidelines administered by architect William H. Wheeler. More recently, organizations including Burlingame Women's Club (one of San Diego's oldest neighborhood organizations) have been protective of the neighborhood's character, and local activists got the historical district approved in 2002.

21 / House (1912)
3195 Kalmia St.

Flat-roofed variation on Prairie style, with stucco lower floor and wood-shingled second and third stories.

22 / William A. McIntyre House (1912)
3171 Kalmia St.
WILLIAM WHEELER

Three-story stucco Prairie-style home features arched entry and hipped roof.

23 / House (1912)
3163 Kalmia St.

Steep-gabled Craftsman, with an off-center entry anchoring a balanced but asymmetrical facade.

24 / McIntyre spec House (1913)
3155 Kalmia St.

One of ten bungalows built by contractors A.B. and William McIntyre, this cedar-shingled place, with its deep eaves and exposed rafter tails, rests on a concrete foundation—before they became standard.

NORTH PARK/SOUTH PARK/BURLINGAME

25 / **Benbough/Adams House** (1913)
3147 Kalmia St.

Restored in recent years to its original modernist appearance by former owner Malcolm Stallings, this three-story dwelling features a front defined by five square stucco columns interspersed with redwood panels, and Craftsman touches such as leaded glass windows.

26 / **House** (1912)
3127 Kalmia St.

Two story Craftsman combining brick with horizontal clapboard siding.

27 / **Casita Blanca** (1925)
2427 Dulzura Ave.

Spanish Colonial with Deco overtones such as the square, minimally decorated, pyramid-roofed entry.

28 / **Louis Brandt House** (1912)
2450 Dulzura Ave.

Rare (for San Diego) Dutch Colonial design distinguished by its steep, compound roof forms, brick chimney, and brick entry arch.

NORTH PARK/SOUTH PARK/BURLINGAME

29 / Edgar Hendee Residence (1912)
2457 Capitan Ave.
WILLIAM H. WHEELER

Craftsman design by
Burlingame's architectural czar.

30 / Henry Sparks Residence (1912)
3055 Kalmia St.
WILLIAM WHEELER

Craftsman style with Tudor details
such as steep gables and half-timbering.

31 / Library Tower (1988)
3031 Kalmia Street.
DAVIDS-KILLORY

Contemporary addition to a California bungalow prompted polarized local
opinions, and provided its owner/architects with a spectacular, well-lit
space for books and reading, with Balboa Park views.

32 / Bungalow (1920)
2415 San Marcos Ave.

Perfectly maintained stucco
Craftsman, with ultra-fine
woodwork.

33 / Bungalow (1932)
2432 San Marcos Ave.

Late Craftsman-era
home features neoclas-
sical columns that frame
the gable entry porch.

NORTH PARK/SOUTH PARK/BURLINGAME

34 / **Wegeforth Residence** (1912)
3004 Laurel St.
WILLIAM WHEELER

Early residence of the San Diego Zoo's founder was restored in the 1980s to its early California eclectic glory—modernist forms and crisp lines softened with traditional details such as shutters, awnings, and brick pilasters framing the arched entry.

---

35 / **Mausoleum House** (1924)
2484 Capitan Ave.

A rare Deco design featuring, with spare rectilinear forms off-set by curves—as on the divided front windows.

---

36 / **Edward and Blanche Gibson House** (1917)
3106 Maple St.

Craftsman-style with Japanese details including pointed gables and curved, exposed rafter tails.

---

37 / **Cottee/McCorkle House** (1912)
3048 Laurel St.

Fine example of early Mission Revival, the era that produced Bakewell & Brown's Santa Fe Depot downtown.

---

38 / **Pig With A Purple Eye Patch** (1983)
3030 Laurel Ave.
PAPA

Billboard architecture by the same dreamer (Dalrymple) responsible for Old Town's "Soldiers in Argyle" and Mission Hills' "Home Sweet Home".

NORTH PARK/SOUTH PARK/BURLINGAME

39 / Whitsitt Residence (1924)
2519 San Marcos Ave.

Prime example of Spanish Revival, from this neighborhood's prime growth years. Mabel Whitsitt was one of early San Diego's few female entrepreneurs. As proprietor of the Five Dollar Hat Shop at Fifth and Broadway, she outfitted generations of San Diego women.

40 / Whiteman Residence (1912)
2523 San Marcos Ave.
WILLIAM WHEELER

A two-story Craftsman with Swiss Chalet details, the design includes a sleeping porch, from a time when the nation was in a "health" phase and many people believed in natural foods and plenty of fresh air.

41 / Mission Revival House (1912)
2525 San Marcos Ave.

Mission Revival taken to its dreamy well-parapeted extreme.

42 / Fulford bungalows (1913)
2516-2518-2520 San Marcos Ave.
CARLETON WINSLOW

Contrasting with his Spanish Colonial buildings in Balboa Park, these three redwood bungalows show the architect's Craftsman side.

NORTH PARK/SOUTH PARK/BURLINGAME

43 / Bungalow (1920)
2605 San Marcos Ave.

Fine modest bungalow featuring stone chimney and porch piers.

44 / Erwin D. Norris House (1912)
3170 Maple St.

Eclectic Craftsman in brick and clapboard, with steep roof, and twin dormers featuring flared eaves.

45 / Bungalow (1912)
2526 Pamo Ave.

Modest Craftsman home from this subdivision's earliest years.

46 / Leonard Lyons House (1925)
3154 Laurel St.

Beautifully detailed, steep-roofed, brick-and-stucco Tudor Revival.

College
City Heights
East San Diego

Urban neighborhoods present their own challenges to planners and architects. San Diego State University has expanded from its original quaint Spanish Colonial cluster of buildings to include modern structures such as the main library, significant new housing, an underground San Diego Trolley station (opening in 2005), and plans by Los Angeles architect Jon Jerde for mixed-use development that would help make the college area a genuine community.

A few miles away, the older neighborhood of City Heights is in the midst of a parallel transformation. The advent of regional shopping malls beginning in the 1960s lured people away from neighborhood businesses, and City Heights was divided by demolition to make way for the extension of Interstate 15. But the freeway went unbuilt for many years, leaving a desolate strip through the center of the community. Meanwhile, basic public amenities such as a library, schools, and parks were neglected or completely lacking.

After former San Diego City Councilman William Jones earned his MBA at Harvard, he returned to San Diego, wanting to make a difference in his home town. Partnering with Price Club/Costco founder Sol Price, Jones developed City Heights Urban Village, a mixed-use development

that gave City Heights a new heart, including a new school, a new library/community center, shopping center, and an educational center for adults.

On Friday evenings now, City Heights residents turn out to enjoy the amphitheater that is part of the library, where musicians, dancers, and other performers animate a place that had been in danger of desertion.

Elsewhere in eastern San Diego is some of the region's most interesting public architecture—including the city's largest branch library (Malcolm X); a spare, modernist fire station (San Carlos); and a variety of period buildings and cool old neon signage along El Cajon Boulevard, San Diego's major east-west artery—a good place to take a Saturday cruise if you want to sample the true spirit of the city.

College/City Heights/ East San Diego Locations

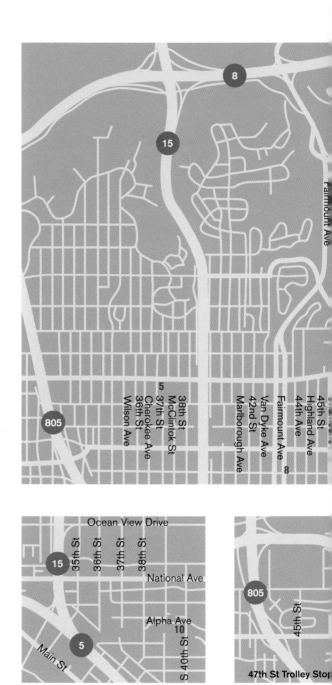

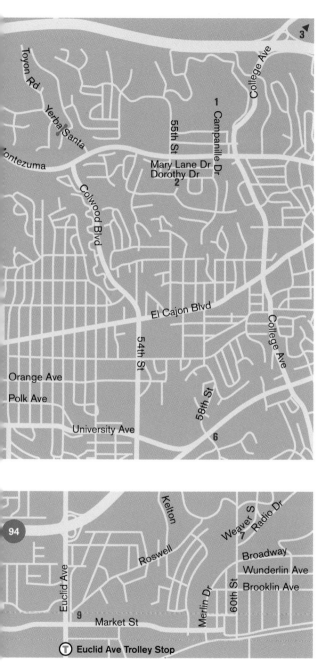

1. **San Diego State University**
2. **Bobertz Residence**
3. **San Carlos Fire Station**
4. **Bond House**
5. **Hille House**
6. **Sheng Haw Low neon sign**
7. **Weiss Churchill Residence**
8. **City Heights Urban Village**
9. **Malcolm X. Library**
10. **Cesar Chavez Elementary School**

COLLEGE/CITY HEIGHTS/EAST SAN DIEGO

1 / **San Diego State University** (1931-present)
5500 Campanile
DR. HOWARD SPENCER HAZEN, ORIGINAL CAMPUS BUILDINGS.

Although it has become one of California's largest university's, SDSU's original Mediterranean-style plaza (initially proposed by Palos Verdes urban planner Charles H. Cheney) and Mediteranean/Mission Revival architecture (approved by a committee including architect William Templeton Johnson) still provide the most beautiful places on campus. Originally, buildings were limited to two stories; gardens, plazas, and other spaces between buildings here are as thoughtfully designed as buildings that feature stone arches, red tile roofs, and wrought-iron window grates. At the campus's onetime main entrance, twin turrets stand like the towers of a Medieval fortress or California Mission compound. SDSU, like UCSD, lost control over its planning and architecture during rapid growth spurts beginning in the 1960s—even though a campus master plan was drafted by Frank L. Hope Associates in 1961. Today the campus ranges from newer Mediterranean revival buildings to

structures like the concrete-finned, partially underground Malcolm A. Love Library (1971, Albert Dennis, state architect), with rotunda entry added in 1996 by Mosher/Drew/ Watson/Ferguson, who also designed the light, soaring Aztec Center (1968). Blocks of new student housing range from kitschy, mediocre

revival designs to more elegant buildings by architects including Marc Steele and Joseph Wong. Other recent additions include the Aztec Athletic Center (2001, Carrier Johnson) and a new parking lot at 55th and Montezuma—one of the best of recent buildings, with its simple curve of concrete columns. Public art on campus includes Donal Hord's bronze "Montezuma" (1937) and Eve Andree Laramee's "100 Years, 100 Stones". A mass transit station connecting the San Diego Trolley to campus is scheduled to open in 2005.

2 / **Bobertz Residence** (1954)
5503 Dorothy Dr.
CRAIG ELLWOOD + ERNIE JACKS

Among a handful of San Diego houses associated with the L.A.-based Case Study Houses program organized by Arts + Architecture magazine editor John Entenza, this was one of six designs drawn by Jacks, Ellwood's draftsman, in the spirit of Ellwood's own Case Studies.

3 / **San Carlos Fire Station** (1963)
6565 Cowles Mountain Blvd.
HESTER-JONES

Soaring post-and-beam structure in the L.A./USC tradition, revealing Hester and Jones' died-in-the-wool modernist leanings.

4 / **Bond House** (1960)
4449 Yerba Santa Dr.
RICHARD NEUTRA

Designed by the prominent L.A. modernist, the only one of Neutra's five San Diego designs that remains in original condition. Neutra's Oxley residence in La Jolla, for instance, was moved to a different spot on its site. Neutra also designed the chapel at the former Miramar Naval Air Station (now a Marine Corps base).

COLLEGE/CITY HEIGHTS/EAST SAN DIEGO

5 / **Hille House** (1889)
3705 El Cajon Blvd.

Moved here from National City in 1893, this two-story, bay-windowed Queen Anne became one of the first, and remains one of the few, in this style in this part of the city. It predates the paving of the boulevard in the 1920s.

6 / **Sheng Haw Low neon sign** (1951)
5801 University Ave.

Restaurant owner Tom Sheng designed this classic roadside beacon, utilizing Chinese language characters, and depicting a woman soaring on the back of a bird.

7 / **Weiss Churchill Residence** (1993)
1271 Weaver St.
JEANNE MCCALLUM

A 1,200-square-foot addition provides flexible live-work space. A footbridge spans the slope from the street. Inside, one large wall serves as a "canvas" adorned by Linda Churchill's murals.

8 / **City Heights Urban Village** (2001)
10-block area surrounding intersection of Fairmount Avenue and University Avenue.
MARTINEZ + CUTRI

Providing a new heart for a neglected neighborhood, the village includes a new high-tech library, rec center, police station, community college classrooms, and townhomes (all by Martinez + Cutri), as well as a new shopping center (by Fehlman Labarre).

9 / **Malcolm X. Library** (1996)
5148 Market St.
MANUEL ONCINA

The city's largest branch library (27,000 square feet) is a colorful, kinetic example of contemporary libraries that also serve as comfy community centers for parents and children who come for events, recreational reading and video viewing, after-school study groups, internet access, and other options.

10 / **Cesar Chavez Elementary School** (1997)
1404 S. 40th St.
MARTINEZ + CUTRI

Glyphs and monuments tell students stories about their multi-cultural past; here is a commendable example of art and architecture working in harmony.

Mission Valley

When Junipero Serra founded Mission San Diego de Alcala at the head of Mission Valley in 1769, then moved it a few miles east up the valley, he couldn't have known he was launching development of what would become San Diego's biggest, most chaotic mish-mash of development, traffic, and architecture ranging from historical to glitzy collections of billboards that Venturi and Scott-Brown might admire.

One fringe benefit of the modern Mission Valley is a noteable piece of public art: the I-8/I-805 freeway interchange near the stadium, a soaring extravaganza of swooping concrete ramps and pillars that reeks of California Car Culture.

When architect William Templeton Johnson's Serra Museum (which many folks mistake for the Mission) opened in 1929 at the valley's west end, the view to the east was raw, rural riparian habitat. But change came quickly beginning in the late 1950s, with the arrival of Padres baseball at Westgate Park (1957) and the opening of Interstate 8 the following year (the historic Crosthwaite Adobe was a casualty).

Mission Valley's destiny as the region's most intensive hotbed of retailing began with the opening of Mission Valley Center in 1961, followed by the stadium in 1967, and Fashion Valley mall in 1969. After several expansions, the two centers together today offer nearly 3 million square feet of shopping. In the 1990s, MVC added a 20-plex cinema touted as the "largest west of the Rockies".

Newer retailing to the east includes Hazard Center and expanses of big-box discounters led by San Diego's first IKEA home furnishings warehouse.

Some of the newest retailing fronts Interstate 8 and has received mixed reviews for its low-budget buildings and high visibility graphics; but these newer projects seem well-suited to our car culture, and they provide eye-candy to steady streams of auto-shoppers.

Hotels from the 1950s and 1960s with names such as Stardust, as well as convention and meeting facilities, gave Mission Valley a 30-year run as the region's prime business and meeting center. That era came to a close when the new downtown convention center opened in the late 1980s, and business travelers gravitated to luxurious new hotels downtown and in University Towne Center. Mission Valley's own newer high-rise hotels are less dramatic.

Office space is a major land use in Mission Valley, including several reflective glass high-rises—architect Charles Slert's Rio Vista tower on Friars Road, with its slanted, eagle-winged top, is a public landmark on the order of his Pyramid building a few miles north on Miramar Road.

Much of the valley's newer growth has been guided by the First San Diego River Improvement Project. Planners are proud of the light-rail trolley that ferries passengers to stadium events, as well as to many shopping stops, and hundreds of new condominiums and apartments. Once seasonal, the re-aligned San Diego River now runs year-round—and without the catastrophic floods that formerly accompanied wet years.

River's edge, with restored marshes and wetlands, teems with wildlife, including fish and a variety of bird species. Portions of the riverfront are landscaped with natural materials and provide riparian views and pedestrian and bicycle paths. Compared with the University Towne Center area a few miles north, Mission Valley has better circulation between newer projects—for cars, pedestrians, and bus and trolley riders.

Look closely and you can still see a handful of old farmhouses, from a time when the valley was known for its Native American inhabitants, and later for its farms and its dairies. Today's valley offers an odd juxtaposition of the historical and the uabashed commercial: miles and miles of retailing, bookended by Johnson's romantic Serra Museum at the west, and at the east by Mission San Diego de Alcala.

Mission Valley Locations

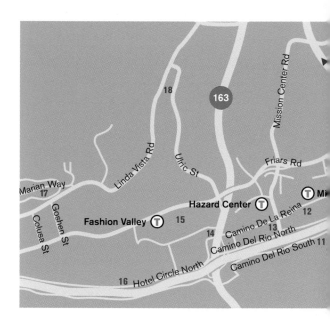

1 **Children's Hospital and Health Center**
2 **Mission San Diego de Alcala**
3 **Mission Trails Regional Park Visitors Center**
4 **Qualcomm Stadium**
5 **Industrial Indemnity/County Mental Health**
6 **Mission Valley Branch Library**
7 **I-8/I-805 Freeway Interchange**
8 **Rio Vista Tower**
9 **Rio Vista West**
10 **First United Methodist Church**
11 **Scottish Rite Center**
12 **Mission Valley Center**
13 **Gordon Biersch Brewery**
14 **Union-Tribune building**
15 **Fashion Valley Center**
16 **Mission Valley Christian Fellowship/
    Cinema 21 Theater**
17 **University of San Diego**
18 **Linda Vista Library**

1 / Children's Hospital and Health Center
(1993)

3020 Children's Way

NBBJ

A playful, castle-like confection
of forms and colors, the hospital
helps humanize the medical
experience for young patients. Inside are child-friendly rooms with
garden views, waiting rooms with play areas, and lively outdoor
spaces that include animal topiaries and a variety of landscapes
designed by Topher Delaney including a healing garden.

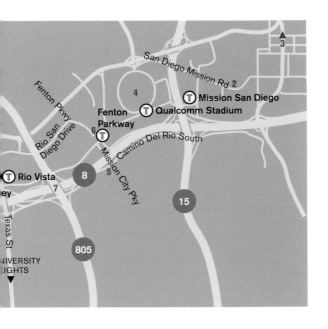

2 / **Mission San Diego de Alcala** (1813)
10818 San Diego Mission Rd.

Founded above Old Town in 1769, the first of California's 21 missions was moved to this permanent location a few years later. It was rebuilt several times over the years. As California's first church, it symbolizes the arrival of Catholicism in Southern California—to the detriment of Native Americans who had occupied the region for centuries. Fearing raids by the natives, the Franciscans eventually rebuilt this mission to fortress standards, with 5- to 7-foot-thick adobe brick walls. The courtyard plan is common in Spanish designs—including several of the ranchos built in San Diego County. Spurred by Charles Lummis's Mission Revival, reconstruction and stabilization efforts began early in the 20th century. By the time a thorough restoration began in 1930, only rubble remained. Complete restoration was finished the following year, including modern steel-reinforced concrete within walls. Replacement adobe bricks, floor tiles, and roof tiles were handmade in the original fashion. Today, this building that inspired generations of architects ranging from Irving Gill to Rob Quigley stands obscured by strip malls, condominiums, and traffic, but a visit reveals its primal power.

---

3 / **Mission Trails Regional Park Visitors Center** (1995)
Father Junipero Serra Trail off Mission Gorge Road
JOSEPH WONG

Mixing earth-toned materials with view-catching ceiling-height glass, the center utilizes a clean modern aesthetic and forms that fit the rugged terrain.

MISSION VALLEY

4 / Qualcomm Stadium (1967)
9449 Friars Rd.
FRANK HOPE (GARY ALLEN DESIGNER)

Previously known as San Diego Jack Murphy Stadium, Allen's sculptural natural-finish concrete stadium was considered one of the best in the west. Circulation is thoughtfully handled, with spiral ramps played up as an eye-catching forms. Following expansions and a bright paint job, it no

longer retains the purity of Allen's original vision. As smaller, urban baseball parks made a comeback in the 1990s, the San Diego Padres commissioned New Mexico architect Antoine Predock to design a new downtown ballpark. There has been discussion of a new football stadium for the San Diego Chargers—if they don't move to another city.

5 / Industrial Indemnity/County Mental Health (1970)
3255 Camino Del Rio South
DEEMS LEWIS

One of San Diego's first pre-stressed concrete structures uses concrete columns to supported a concrete waffle-slab floor beneath a clear span of more than 100 feet.

6 / Mission Valley Branch Library (2002)
2123 Fenton Parkway
WHEELER WIMER BLACKMAN

Referencing the valley's agrarian past, this 20,000-square-foot branch has a vaulted roof inspired by dairy farms and cow barns, with a curving floorplan that mimics and nearby San Diego River, and with curving stainless steel walls and banks of glass that bring the building into the present and future. Interior columns and supporting "branches" support a "sycamore tree canopy," and protective railings carry etchings of tall riparian grasses.

7 / I-8/I-805 Freeway Interchange (I-8: late 1950s/early 1960s, I-805: late 1960s/early 1970s)

Originally known as U.S. 80, the fledging east-west freeway was renamed Interstate 8 in 1964. With the addition of the soaring I-805 bridge across

Mission Valley, this interchange became one of Southern California's most spectacular swirling concrete monuments to 20th century car culture. Bridge pilings were retrofitted for earthquake safety in the 1990s.

8 / **Rio Vista Tower and Health Center** (1988)
8880 Rio Vista Dr. N.
CHARLES SLERT

Unlike buildings that only look cool from one or two directions, Slert's designs—often in high traffic areas—look great from every angle. This particular tower, with its slanted eagle-wing top, was intended as one of a pair, but when property changed hands, new owners developed a completely different project nearby. Slert has been San Diego's leader in doing interesting things with reflective glass towers.

9 / **Rio Vista West** (in progress 2003)
on 95 acres east of Fashion Valley Center
PETER CALTHORPE

Touted as San Diego's prototypical "TOD"—planner speak for "transit oriented development"—this mixed-use development is conveniently situated along the San Diego Trolley line, conceived as as pedestrian-friendly blend of homes and shops around a village-like town square, and with a K-Mart and other big stores purportedly designed in the spirit of early San Diego modernist Irving Gill. In light of failed plans for Riverwalk, another carefully planned mixed-use development in Mission Valley, it remains to be seen if people really want to live right where they shop.

10 / **First United Methodist Church** (1964)
2111 Camino Del Rio South
PERKINS & WILL/
REGINALD INWOOD

Take a gigantic piece of paper, fold it over, anchor each end to earth. In basic form you have this church, the most exotic, graceful structure in the area.

11 / **Scottish Rite Center** (1940s-1960s)
1895 Camino Del Rio South

An inverted flying V roof—in the spirit of 1950s "Googie" coffee shops—marks the entry to this popular spot for hobby shows and gatherings, formerly known as Bolero Lanes bowling alley.

MISSION VALLEY

12 / **Mission Valley Center** (1961)
1640 Camino del Rio North
FRANK L. HOPE WITH ALBERT C. MARTIN ASSOCIATES

San Diego's prototypical regional mall lured retailers and shoppers away from downtown with a mix of specialty stores and department store anchors (note the zig-zag roof and perforated precast walls). Since then, it's had makeovers and expansions by architects including Welton Becket, Homer Delawie, Salts Troutman, and the design division of current owner Westfield. A late-1990s expansion added a 20-plex cinema and glitzy new stores along the lines of Disney and Universal's theme part retailing centers. Westfield's newer mall to the west (including Borders and Old Navy) is an example of graphic freeway architecture, with its bright colors and bold forms hailing motorists on nearby I-8.

---

13 / **Gordon Biersch Brewery** (1999)
5010 Mission Center Rd.
ALLIED ARCHITECTURE/ARCHITECTURE AND LIGHT

Yes, America is being corporatized, but some of these capitalists have

good taste. This microbrewery/ restaurant is a kinetic study in steel-and-glass, with stainless steel brewing tanks visible from the street—think of them as functional public art.

---

14 / **Union-Tribune Building** (1974)
350 Camino de la Reina
FRANK L. HOPE

In his prime, Hope's office produced epic late-modernist buildings including this concrete-and-brick headquarters for the city's prime daily newspaper. When the building opened, the U-T made a controversial move away from downtown to the new location. More recently, publishers briefly considered moving back downtown.

---

15 / **Fashion Valley Center** (1969, 1981, 1997)
7007 Friars Rd.

San Diego's early Hahn mall gives a one-stop look at the recent history of shopping—from the original plan centered on an outdoor pedestrian promenade anchored at each end by department stores, through expansions that added a second floor, and in 1997, $120 million worth of new buildings (designed by Altoon & Porter) that grew the mall to 1.7 million square feet and transformed it into a contemporary "entertainment" experience with colorful signage, facades, and interiors. The most recent renovation

was conceived as a series of retail "precincts" within a garden city of terraces and trellised walkways, with the original Buffums department store transformed into an upscale Saks Fifth Avenue.

16 / **Mission Valley Christian Fellowship/ Cinema 21 Theater** (1963)
1440 Hotel Circle North

TUCKER SADLER & BENNETT

With its 60-foot screen and 32-speaker Dolby digital sound system, the Cinema 21 was once THE place to go when new movies premiered in San Diego. The original design calls to mind the 1950s "Googie" style of coffee shops and burger stands as practiced in Los Angeles by architects including John Lautner—-here, hallmarks from that era include the curved, vertical-finned entry facade, floating over Corbusian pilotis, and crowned by an angular parapet that contracts nicely with the curve. Perhaps it's a sign of the commercialization of both cinema and religion that the original 1,000-seat theater was put out of business by megaplexes—then adopted by a church in an era when religious organizations increasingly use commercial means to expand their congregations.

17 / **University of San Diego** (1952)
5998 Alcala Park
FRANK L. HOPE AND OTHERS

Modernists may cringe at San Diego's plethora of revivalist styles, but there's no denying this romantic, carefully planned university is the most inviting of San Diego's college campuses. Spanish Renaissance revival buildings are arranged along a central spine, some of them in the form of quadrangles surrounding open-air courtyards. The Immaculata church gives this student village the feel of an old Italian hill town. Tucker Sadler added a conference center and business school building (Olin Hall) in 1984, the same year Mosher Drew's two-story library addition was completed. Carrier Johnson's Donald Pearce Shiley Center for Science and Technology was finished in 2003 and includes aquariums, an astronomy deck, a greenhouse, and an aviary.

18 / **Linda Vista Library** (1987)
2160 Ulric St.
ROB QUIGLEY

Coming up the hill from Mission Valley into Linda Vista, you are greeted by this striking public building in a community that previously had no civic anchor. With its diagonal entrance from a prominent corner, the library connects with the community; a second entrance serves a parking lot that keeps cars out of sight in back. Inside is where this building really shines: natural light (ideal for reading) is uniformly strong, angled branch-like beams support the ceiling, and the floor combines diagonally scored concrete with tiles made from recycled tires. A footnote: Linda Vista Shopping Center was San Diego's first, opened in 1943 to coincide with completion of 1,000s of homes built almost overnight to house thousands who took defense-related jobs during World War II.

Beaches

Left Coast, California: the Pacific marks the end or the beginning of dreams. Westward moving pioneers wound up at the water because there was nowhere left to go. Explorers in search of a New World sailed thousands of miles and gazed with awe at our coastline. From Imperial Beach to La Jolla, San Diego's beaches have been distinguished by tall tales and surfing legends, as well as some of the region's most imaginative architecture.

Madame Tingley set the spirit for seekers at the turn of the century, with her compound on Pt. Loma, including several buildings of her own design. Odd towers, spiral stairs, glass domes—she captured the uplifting power of the place. Like Coney Island and San Francisco's Playland, Belmont Park in Mission Beach became San Diego's beachfront amusement zone, with its swoopy wooden roller coaster and gigantic pool called The Plunge. Years later, Sea World amusement park opened nearby.

A few miles up the coast, La Jolla was also one birthplace of the classic California beach bungalow: humble cottages like the redwood Red Rest and Red Roost. The beach vernacular also includes lifeguard towers (inspiration for Frank Gehry, Rob Quigley, and others), wave forms, surfboards, sea walls, public piers, sailboats, a lighthouse (Pt. Loma), and beachfront restaurants and surf shops.

Irving Gill produced some of California's most progressive architecture in La Jolla between 1906 and 1915: La Jolla Women's Club, the Ellen Browning Scripps residence, several buildings at Bishops School, the original concrete Scripps Laboratory. R.M. Schindler built El Pueblo Ribera apartments at Windansea Beach, using experimental poured-in-place concrete. One of Richard Neutra's few San Diego buildings is the Oxley residence near U.C. San Diego.

La Jolla has also produced progressive designs by Kendrick Bangs Kellogg, John Lautner, Gordon Drake, Rob Quigley, Wallace Cunningham, and Case Study architect Ed Killingsworth. U.C. San Diego and the surrounding business and brain trust have produced buildings by Louis Kahn, Edward Durell Stone, Venturi Scott Brown, and Antoine Predock.

In a new millenium, San Diego's beach communities face some difficult challenges: traffic and congestion (try to get in or out of La Jolla at rush hour), ocean pollution, overcrowded beaches, zoning changes to urge preservation and sensitive new development, and soaring real estate prices that are already transforming formerly middle class neighborhoods into the sole domain of the wealthy.

On warm, clear days, though, Mission Beach Boardwalk still drawns a youthful throng, the waves still send up white spray as surfers slice across them, visitors still flock to the top of Mt. Soledad in La Jolla to take in one of the world's most spectacular panoramas, rivaled only, perhaps, by the view at the feet of Christ the Redeemer atop Corcovado, above Copacabana Beach in Rio de Janeiro, Brazil.

Coronado Locations

1 **Lightner Residence**

2 **Crownview Condominiums**

3 **Wilde Flats**

4 **Village Elementary School**

5 **Coronado Library**

6 **Coronado Police Administration Building**

7 **First Church of Christ Scientist**

8 **Cuffaro Residence**

9 **Rew-Sharp House**

10 **Livingston/Mortensen Residence**

11 **Tutt House**

Imperial Beach

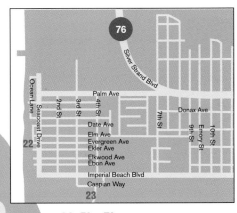

22 Pier Plaza

23 Tijuana Estuary Visitor Center

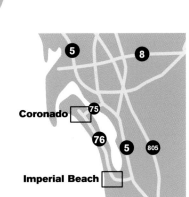

12 Richards House

13 Bank of Coronado/Spreckels Building

14 Bank of Commerce/Coronado Historical Association

15 Graham Memorial Presbyterian Church

16 Stephens House

17 Robert House

18 Drummer House

19 Pratt House

20 Glorietta Bay Inn/Spreckels Residence

21 Hotel del Coronado

CORONADO

1 / Lightner Residence (1989)
1322 Second Ave.

KATHLEEN MCCORMICK/SMITH & OTHERS.

With a landscape by Spurlock/ Poirier, this multi-layered design—built as a spec home—makes a fresh statement in a traditional neighborhood.

2 / Crownview Condominiums (2001)
1118-1130 First St.

GALVIN & CRISTILLI

A local favorite, this urban mixed-use project combines retail and residential, in a design drawn from Craftsman, modern, and contemporary forms.

3 / Wilde Flats (1919)
544 D St. and 545 Palm Ave.

IRVING GILL

Duplex apartments show Gill's commitment to providing fresh air and natural light even on modest projects—here he used a large kitchen window, movable glass panel in the front door, and a small window that admits light and air to an upstairs closet.

4 / Village Elementary School (1991)
600 Sixth St.

MOSHER DREW WATSON FERGUSON

Arches derived from missions-via-Irving Gill, but rendered in brick instead of adobe or stucco.

5 / **Coronado Library** (1909/1974/2004)
640 Orange Ave.
HARRISON ALBRIGHT/DELAWIE MACY HENDERSON/MARC STEELE

Albright's original neoclassical building was expanded by modernist Delawie to include a children's library and meeting rooms (wings added in the 1930s and 1950s were removed), and is undergoing a $7 million expansion designed by Steele that will incorporate a 47-foot mural by Alfredo Ramos Martinez that formerly adorned Coronado's popular La Avenida restaurant.

6 / **Coronado Police Administration Building** (1995)
700 Orange Ave.
MOSHER DREW WATSON FERGUSON

Well proportioned homage to the city's Irving Gill heritage, with arches and minimalist forms; unfortunately the station replaced one of the region's finest bungalow court apartment complexes.

7 / **First Church of Christ Scientist** (1927)
1123 Eighth St.
IRVING GILL

Third of Gill's Christian Science churches in San Diego, this is a minimal composition of cubes and arches—austere by comparison with his earlier Christian Science church at Second and Laurel near downtown San Diego.

8 / **Cuffaro Residence** (1988)
1034 G Ave.
GALVIN CRISTILLI.

Tasteful addition to one of Coronado's Craftsman houses.

9 / **Rew-Sharp House** (1918)
1124 F Ave.
ELMER GREY

Trained in Chicago, formerly Myron Hunt's partner in Pasadena, Grey was renowned both for his buildings and for his oil paintings.

CORONADO

10 / Livingston/Mortensen Residence
(1887/moved from Sherman Heights in 1983)

1144 Isabella Ave.
EDWARD BOOKER

Developer Chris Mortensen fell in love with this place. With cupolas removed, it was trucked, craned, and barged to its new location across the bay. An elaborate exterior with fish-scale shingles, octagonal tower, and widow's walk was methodically restored. Some interior rooms were brought back to original, while others—most notably the kitchen—were updated with contemporary materials and open spaces.

---

11 / Tutt House (1910)

1156 Isabella Ave.
IRVING GILL

Irving Gill pioneered his spare modernist style around 1906—but continued to work in the cozier Prairie style, as evidenced here with gently sloped roofs and brick first level.

---

12 / Richards House (1902)

1015 Ocean Blvd.
HEBBARD AND GILL

Known as Crown Manor, through the 1990s this was home to Hotel Del owner Larry Lawrence—who hosted Pres. Bill Clinton overnight here. This 27-room, 20,000-square-foot Tudor manse must be the largest Gill ever worked on, and is also Coronado's biggest home.

---

13 / Bank of Coronado/Spreckels Building (1917)

1190 Orange Ave.
HARRISON ALBRIGHT

Coronado's grandest revival-style building was commissioned by sugar magnate John Spreckels, designed by his favorite architect, built of reinforced concrete. Originally, the curving two-story structure contained a bank, movie theatre, stores, apartments, and offices. Exquisite details include Corinthian columns, floral medallions, and a belt course featuring plaster lion heads.

14 / Bank of Commerce/Coronado Historical Association (1910)

1100 Orange Ave.
MCDONALD & APPLEGARTH

This neoclassical former bank building helps anchor downtown's historical core.

15 / Graham Memorial Presbyterian Church (1891)

Tenth Avenue and C Street
REID BROTHERS

Hotel del architects rendered this spiritual beauty in redwood, with fish-scale shingles and stained glass windows.

16 / Stephens House (1898)

711 and 723 A Avenue
HEBBARD & GILL

English Tudor with half-timber gables, diamond-pane windows, and an upscale necessity from the pre-automobile era: a carriage house.

17 / Robert House (1917)

1000 Glorietta Blvd.
WILLIAM TEMPLETON JOHNSON

San Diego's revivalist master, here drawing on Pueblo traditions from the American southwest.

CORONADO

18 / **Drummer House** (1903)
1005 Adella Ave.
IRVING K. POND

Chicago architect's
take on English Tudor.

19 / **Pratt House** (1899)
1517 Ynez Pl.
HEBBARD AND GILL

Craftsman meets classical
revival.

20 / **Glorietta Bay Inn/Spreckels Residence** (1908)
1630 Glorietta Blvd.
HARRISON ALBRIGHT

Today a stylish period hotel, this building was originally Spreckels' mansion, designed by his favorite architect, built from the same reinforced concrete as other nearby Spreckels/Albright buildings.

21 / **Hotel del Coronado** (1888)
1701 Strand Way
REID BROTHERS

Advertised originally as
Mission style, the hotel—really
more of a Queen Anne
Victorian—was "the last of the
great 19th century resort
hotels," according to the late
architectural historian David

Gebhard. The Reids were prolific West Coast architects. After moving from San Diego to San Francisco in 1889, they designed that city's Fairmont Hotel (1906) and Cliff House restaurant (1908).

22 / **Pier Plaza** (1999)

Seacoast Drive at the foot of Evergreen

STUDIO E ARCHITECTS

Sculptor Malcolm Jones's "Surfhenge"–10 surfboard-like forms of colored acrylic–anchors the new public heart of this beachfront community. Artist Mary Lynn Dominguez's "Illuminations" consists of colorful glass tiles tucked beneath the lip of curving concrete walls just the right height for sitting. Artist Paul Hobson's waves of concrete cresting with glass mosaics occupies the nearby street median.

23 / **Tijuana Estuary Visitor Center** (1990)

301 Caspian Way

ROB QUIGLEY

Quigley's building peaks up from the marshy wetlands just enough to be distinguished as a man-made object, yet its pale gray and buff tones also blend with the scrubby coastal landscape.

Point Loma and Ocean Beach Locations

1 **Loma Theatre/ Bookstar**

2 **House**

3 **House**

4 **Prairie Houses**

5 **Delawie Residence**

6 **Price House**

7 **Deco Houses**

8 **Heller Residence**

9 **Goldman Residence**

10 **San Diego Yacht Club**

11 **St. Agnes Catholic Church**

12 **Hidden Fortress**

13 **Richards House #1**

14 **Castle**

15 **Reed House**

16 **Richards House #2**

17 **Mulliken Residence**

18 **Mann Residence**

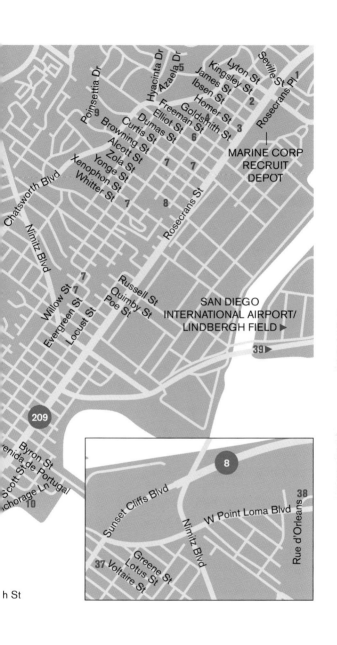

POINT LOMA/OCEAN BEACH

1/ **Loma Theatre/Bookstar** (1944)
3150 Rosecrans Pl.

One of the last old-school moviehouses built in San Diego, this was also one of the few that was preserved; adapted by Alamo Architects in 1990 for use as a bookstore, it still has its neon marquee. Murals were restored by artist Janet Lee Fenwick; new carpeting was milled to match the original.

2 / **House** (c. 1935)
2925 Locust St.

Zigzag Moderne and Streamline Moderne come together in one of San Diego's rare Deco diversions.

3 / **House** (c. 1939)
3026 Homer St.

Another Streamline Moderne rarity, with projecting bay window, and strip window that emphasizes horizontal form.

4 / **Prairie Houses** (c. 1914)
3220-3238-3252 Goldsmith Ave.

Two-story houses offer variations on the Midwestern Prairie Style.

5 / **Delawie Residence** (1972)
2749 Azalea Dr.

HOMER DELAWIE

Wood-and-glass home designed by one of San Diego's prime post-WW II modernists, with courtyards and outdoor spaces connected to interiors with sizeable windows and sliding glass doors.

6 / **Price House** (1915)
3202 Elliott St.
WILLIAM HEBBARD

Spare, two-story cubic design with flat overhanging roof, adorned by creeping vines, reminiscent of both Gill and his Viennese contemporary Adolf Loos.

7 / **Deco Houses** (c. 1935-1936)
3112 Curtis St./2505 Willow St./1925 Willow St. 1855 Willow St./3311Xenophon

More examples of Pt. Loma's monopoly on Streamline Moderne in San Diego.

8 / **Heller Residence** (1927)
3107 Zola St.
REQUA & JACKSON

Situated on a view lot overlooking San Diego Bay, the house is a prime example of authentic Mediterranean buildings and gardens by Requa, who had visited those regions sketching and photographing buildings.

9 / **Goldman Residence** (1971)
2451 Poinsettia Dr.
DON GOLDMAN

Subtle woody modern home merges into lush landscape on a sloping site.

POINT LOMA/OCEAN BEACH

10 / **San Diego Yacht Club** (1963)
1011 Anchorage Ln.

LIEBHARDT WESTON AND
MOSHER DREW

Landmark building in a
neighborhood with a long
boating tradition, by two of
San Diego's leading mod-
ernist firms.

11 / **St. Agnes Catholic Church** (1933)
1140 Evergreen St.

F.W. STEVENSON

Well-proportioned
Mediterranean Revival building
with a cute cupola and a trans-
verse gable roof

.

12 / **Hidden Fortress** (1986-present)
Canon Street at Akron Street

TOM GRONDONA

One of San Diego's
most inventive contem-
porary artist/architects,
Grondona designed
the original cinnamon
bun and french fry
stands in Horton Plaza
Shopping Center
downtown. The castle
is his handmade monu-

ment to the wonders of poured-in-place concrete, with many thoughtful
indoor-outdoor connections, terraces and rooms that maximize views of
the bay and downtown, and a landmark tower with a wine room in its
base. Grondona handled much construction himself; concrete was poured
in several stages; more recently he's experimented with new approaches
to structural steel and glazing.

13 / **Richards House #1** (1948)
977 Albion St.

SIM BRUCE RICHARDS

Rustic board-and-batten, shed-roofed home surrounding interior court.

14 / **Castle** (1983)
3425 Talbot St.
TOM GRONDONA

Another Grondona 'castle', this one resembles its roughly-sculpted beginnings as a clay model.

15 / **Reed House** (c. 1955)

946 Bangor St.
JOHN REED & SIM BRUCE RICHARDS

Masterful siting, subtle design by San Diego's under-appreciated organic architect.

16 / **Richards House #2** (1950)
3360 Harbor View
SIM BRUCE RICHARDS

Carefully sited on a steep slope, Richards' home combines his Frank Lloyd Wright leanings with various West Coast woodsy traditions.

17 / **Mulliken Residence** (1980s)
713 Rosecrans St.
RANDY DALRYMPLE

Asian/Mediterranean home designed by the same architect responsible for playful houses such as Soldiers in Argyle, and serious civic designs including Escondido City Hall (with Charles Slert and other partners at PAPA).

18 / **Mann Residence** (1990)
2921 Qualtrough St.
MCGRAW-BALDWIN

Spare white stucco-and-glass modernism, with subtle use of corner strips windows that wash interior walls with light.

19 / **Kellogg/Pt. Loma House** (1960)
596 San Elijo Dr.
KENDRICK BANGS KELLOGG

Built of redwood on a triangular grid plan, this home features tiles glazed by the architect himself.

POINT LOMA/OCEAN BEACH

20 / **Bowman-Cotton Residence** (1929)
2900 Nichols St.
REQUA & JACKSON

Richard Requa, who traveled through Morocco, Algeria, and other Mediterranean locales photographing and sketching vernacular buildings, here teams with his 15-year partner Herbert Jackson for an eclectic display of Spanish Colonial details.

21 / **Peckham Residence** (1928)
2905 Nichols St.
WILLIAM TEMPLETON JOHNSON

A two-story Mediterranean manse by one of San Diego's leading proponents of the style, also one of the first homes built in the La Playa neighborhood that would become one of the city's most exclusive—and most interesting architecturally. Details include a Turkish-rug fountain, and decorative exterior etchings in plaster, by artist S. Tomasello.

22 / **Houses** (1960s/1970s)
3250 McCall St./485 San Gorgonio St./ 305 San Antonio Ave.

Three modernist homes designed by Robert Mosher, showing his versatility in styles and materials.

23 / **Cabrillo National Monument** (1854)
Tip of Catalina Blvd.
AMI B. YOUNG

For decades, maritime travelers were guided into San Diego Bay by the lighthouse. In 1966 a Visitors Center was added by Frank L. Hope.

24 / **Reed Residence** (1989)
448 San Gorgonio St.
ROB QUIGLEY

 Sculptural and hard-edged, this home and studio contribute dynamic, contemporary forms to a traditional neighborhood. Courtyard plan is a variation on longstanding California (via the Mediterranean) tradition, but everything else about the design is turn-of-the-millenium hip.

25 / **House** (1953)
560 San Gorgonio St.
SIM BRUCE RICHARDS

Angular modernist wood-and-glass home, carefully tucked on a hillside site.

26 / **Strong Denison House** (1927)
373 San Gorgonio St.
HERBERT PALMER

A Mediterranean-style home on a steep site, built in a U-shape around a courtyard to maximize indoor/outdoor living. Details include arches, cast concrete Romanesque columns, decorative tiles in various colors, and ornate wrought iron gates leading to lush gardens.

27 / **Bungalow** (1914)
480 San Fernando St.
EMMOR BROOKE WEAVER

House, garden, walls, gates, pergolas, and walkways come together artfully in the best Craftsman tradition.

POINT LOMA/OCEAN BEACH

28 / **Residence** (1980s)
521 San Gorgonio St. S.
SCOTT EMSLEY

Finned concrete and fat glue lam beams, artfully combined in a home that embraces the site, views, and natural light.

---

29 / **Peterson Residence** (1976)
567 Gage St.
RUSSELL FORESTER

Modernist home of San Diego's former Mayor Maureen O'Connor and her then-husband, Jack-in-the-Box founder Robert O. Peterson— desgined by the same architect responsible for the first Jack-in-the-Box restaurant.

---

30 / **Theosophical Society/ Pt. Loma Nazarene College** (1897-1940)

Originally a yoga school, the complex founded by Madame Tingley features 10 of the original 50 buildings where Tingley practiced eastern yogic principles. Glass domes, arches, and a dreamy spiral staircase are among elements that evoke India and other exotic eastern locales.

BEACHES HIGHLIGHT

San Diego International Airport/Lindbergh Field

(1968/1998)
3225-3665-3707 N. Harbor Dr.
PADEREWSKI DEAN ('68)/GENSLER ASSOCIATES WITH SGPA ('98).

Subject to several decades of speculation that it should be moved (to Camp Pendleton? Miramar Naval Air Station? Brown Field on Otay Mesa? Tijuana, maybe?), San Diego's airport remains where it was dedicated in 1928, two years after Charles Lindbergh's historical solo flight across the Atlantic aboard his plane the *Spirit of St. Louis,* which was built in San Diego.

Paderewski Dean's Terminal #1 is a fine example of soaring 1960s optimism. Gensler/SGPA's Terminal #2 is a harder-edged design suited to San Diego's identity as an emerging tech-driven economy.

An exterior of slanted glass panels between bold concrete columns gives way to an interior rendered in golds, greens, and blues inspired by the waterfront locale.

31 / Beach Cottage Community Plan area

Collection of 42 vacation cottages built between 1887 and 1931, bounded on the west by the beach, on the north by West Point Loma Boulevard, on the east by Seaside and Froude, and on the south by Point Loma and Adair Avenues. Included are several fine early California bungalows in a variety of styles including Craftsman and Spanish Colonial.

POINT LOMA/OCEAN BEACH

32 / **Metal Jacket** (2002)
4767 Pescadero Ave.
STEVEN LOMBARDI

When a quirky 1950s redwood home was lost to an electrical fire, Lombardi rebuilt with metal on the original foundation, restoring the original serpentine corridor that widens from 30 to 48 inches to connect bedrooms with kitchen.

33 / **Residence** (1970s)
4551 Newport Ave.
HOMER DELAWIE

Another fine example of wood-and-stucco modernism, with desert gardens connected to interiors by garden paths and breezeways.

34 / **Lighthouse** (2001)
4510 Newport Ave.
STEVEN LOMBARDI

This energy-conserving addition to a California cottage combines space age polycarbonate with rock on the south (sun-facing) side, while east and west walls are primarily glass that lets in lots of natural light—but not heat. At night, the addition lights up in tribute to the lighthouse on the tip of Pt. Loma.

35 / **Dixon House** (1898)
3838 Dixon Place

Looking like a house out of a good Halloween story, this place was built in the Queen Anne/Free Classic style characterized steep, irregular roofs with a dominant gable; patterned exterior shingles; and an asymmetrical facade. The relatively simple style was easier to accomplish in terms of materials than more elaborate Victorian designs.

36 / **Sefton Campbell Residence** (1914)
3850 Narragansett St.
WILLIAM HEBBARD

A well-preserved and tasteful example of Hebbard's traditional preferences in home design. The original owner, Mrs. Harriett Sefton Campbell, was the widow of J.W. Sefton, who founded San Diego Trust & Savings in 1889.

BEACHES HIGHLIGHT

Marine Corps Recruit Depot

(1918)
Old Town Avenue exit from Interstate 5
(Base is on Barnett between Rosecrans and
Pacific Coast Highway)

BERTRAM GOODHUE.

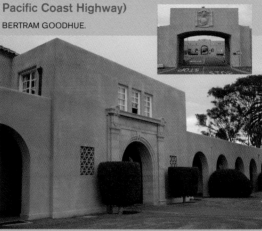

Designed in much more restrained Spanish Colonial style than
Goodhue's Balboa Park buildings, the military base is also a
prime example of clear, simple Beaux Arts planning. Enter Gate
#4 to visit the MCRD Museum.

37 / **O.B. Peoples Organic Food Market** (2002)

4765 Voltaire St.

HANNA GABRIEL WELLS

Cool green (i.e. energy
conserving) building
drawn from the steel-
and-wood, post-and-beam school. With its deep eaves and street-facing
wall of glass, this nutritional warehouse adds an inviting new architectural
presence to a street that needed one.

38 / **Carousel Apartments** (1969)

3050 Rue d'Orleans

TUCKER, SADLER & BENNETT

Landmark donut of a building enclosing a central courtyard and pool.

39 / **Pacific Rim Peace Park** (2000)

Shelter Island Drive at the tip of Shelter Island

JAMES HUBBELL

Students from four nations (U.S.,
China, Russia, Mexico) participated
in the construction of this public
space at the edge of San Diego Bay. Tile mosaics depict images from the
four nations. Concrete walls fan out along the rim of the park, which also
features a lacy wrought-iron gateway.

Mission Beach and
Pacific Beach Locations

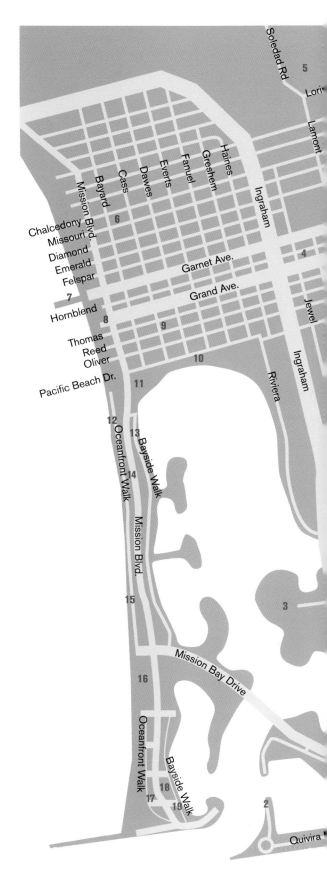

1 Sea World
2 Aquatic Control Center Building
3 Paradise Point/Vacation Village
4 Pacific Beach Women's Club
5 Kate Sessions Park
6 Tsunami P.B.
7 Crystal Pier
8 Penny Realty/Outryder Restaurant
9 Earl and Birdie Taylor Library
10 ZLAC Rowing Club
11 Catamaran Resort Hotel
12 Kellogg in concrete
13 Sayre Residence
14 Saska's Star of the Sidewalk
15 Beach House
16 Belmont Park/The Plunge
17 Tugboat House
18 Kellogg House & studio
19 Babcock House

MISSION BEACH/PACIFIC BEACH

1 / **Sea World** (1964-present)
500 Sea World Dr.
VICTOR GRUEN

Marked by its 320-foot tower, San Diego's main amusement park changed with the times—from 1950s marvel to millenial blockbuster. The main attractions evolved from sea animals seen up close, to whiz-bang rides designed to compete with Legoland, Disneyland, Magic Mountain, and Las Vegas. Contemporary designs include the Penguin Encounter and Shark Exhibit (1984/1980/Delawie Wilkes Rodriguez Barker), and Shipwreck Rapids, the park's most Disney-fied attraction. Early in the new millenium, debate raged about the size and scope of a proposed new expansion.

2 / **Aquatic Control Center Building** (1961)
2581 Quivira Ct.
SIM BRUCE RICHARDS

One of only a few buildings designed by San Diego's under-appreciated master of woody, organic architecture.

3 / **Paradise Point/Vacation Village** (1962)
1404 W. Vacation Rd.

Another Polynesian-themed resort, with wavy-roofed building supported by telephone poles, and guest rooms lining the shores of meandering lagoons. One of the first structures built on landfill as development claimed the edges of Mission Bay.

4 / **Pacific Beach Women's Club** (1911)
1721 Hornblend St.

Jewel of a Craftsman bungalow that has hosted many important community events and people over the years. Inauthentic additions include brick wainscoting on front wall and painting over of

wood siding that was originally left natural.

5 / **Kate Sessions Park** (1914)
Garnet Avenue and Soledad Mountain Road

San Diego's pioneering horticulturist bought land and moved here with her nursery. Her home still stands on Los Altos Road; many of Sessions' original plantings remain in the area today; the former nursery site is marked by a Tipuana tree.

6 / **Tsunami P.B.** (1995)
928 Missouri St.
EHM ARCHITECTURE

Added atop a traditional beach bungalow, this observation deck features a sculptural railing handmade by a German blacksmith, and a sail-like fabric awning.

7 / **Crystal Pier** (1927)
Oceanfront at the foot of Garnet Avenue

Originally a seaside resort complete with ballroom, the pier was closed for 10 years around the Depression, and closed again after 240 feet of wood was ripped away during 1983's wet, wavy winter. The Pier survives today as a collection of modest vacation cottages perched over the water.

8 / **Penny Realty/Outryder Restaurant** (1994)
4444 Mission Blvd.
KENDRICK BANGS KELLOGG

After successful designs for Charthouse restaurants, Kellogg here proved himself a better architect than restaurateur (his burger joint didn't survive). Compared with Kellogg's angular Frank Lloyd Wrightian designs in South Mission Beach, this later structure is more curvy and wavy— a fittingly playful approach for a fun-loving beach community.

MISSION BEACH/PACIFIC BEACH

9 / Earl and Birdie Taylor Library (1998)
4275 Cass St.
MANUEL ONCINA

Creator of an original organic modernism, Oncina has been particularly prolific designing libraries—including this free-flowing place that has become a community center as well as one of the county's leading art exhibitors.

10 / ZLAC Rowing Club (1932/1963)
1111 Pacific Beach Dr.
LILIAN RICE
SIM BRUCE RICHARDS

One of the first women to graduate in architecture from U.C. Berkeley, Rice (who laid out downtown Rancho Santa Fe) designed this low-key wood structure; Sim Bruce Richards made a modest addition in 1963.

11 / Catamaran Resort Hotel (1959)
3999 Mission Blvd.

Polynesian/Tiki kitsch enjoyed a brief run in San Diego, this hotel is a prime example, with A-frame roofs (modernized with copper), woven grass wall coverings, and cascading waterfall.

12 / Kellogg in Concrete (1990s)
3917 Ocean Front Walk
KENDRICK BANGS KELLOGG

Bold and angular concrete forms suggest a futuristic dinosaur about to invade the beach.

13 / Sayre Residence (1980)
3880 Bayside Walk
ROB QUIGLEY

Inspired by beach vernacular structures such as lifeguard towers and wood decks, this home utilizes industrial roll-up doors that open the living space to light, fresh air, and the parade of people on the bayside boardwalk.

14 / Saska's Star of the Sidewalk (1983)
3768 Mission Blvd.
TOM GRONDONA

Grondona's restaurant embraces the situation of a restaurant with a public sidewalk (and steady parade of beachgoers) running through it.

15 / **Beach House** (1962)
3361 Oceanfront Walk
TUCKER SADLER AND BENNETT

Prime example of Sadler's modernist talents, looks particularly stunning at night.

---

16 / **Belmont Park/The Plunge** (1925)
3146 Mission Blvd.
LINCOLN RODGERS/F.W. STEVENSON

San Diego's version of Coney Island, this was a romantic testament to an earlier time, with its wooden roller coaster and gigantic public pool, before 1980s renovation altered the original spirit of the place. Thankfully, the coaster was restored to working condition.

---

17 / **Tugboat House** (1992)
731 Balboa Court
SMITH & OTHERS

Drawing from Mission Beach's old-school beach culture, which includes the annual Over-the-Line softball tournament, this boat-like house is "moored" among more conventional neighbors a short walk from the beach.

---

18 / **Kellogg House & Studio** (1960)
836 Balboa Ct.
KENDRICK BANGS KELLOGG

Kellogg, a disciple of Frank Lloyd Wright, here deployed Wrightian detailing and Schindler-ish planning of walled, private spaces.

---

19 / **Babcock House** (1959)
2695 Bayside Walk
KENDRICK BANGS KELLOGG

This Wrightian architect's first major design stirred things up in its placid South Mission Beach neighborhood, and remains one of the area's most original buildings, distinguished by its gravity-defying stone chimney.

La Jolla Locations

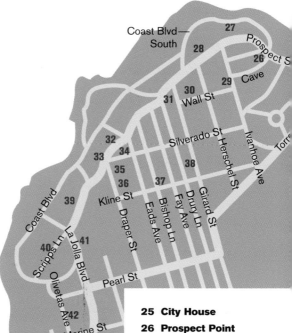

1   University of California
    San Diego

2   UCSD Stuart Collection

3   Shiley Eye Center

4   Neurosciences Institute

5   Scripps Green Hospital

6   Anderson Outpatient
    Pavilion

7   Torrey Pines Lodge
    at Golf Course

8   Torrey Pines
    Visitors Center

9   Salk Institute

10 Two organic Houses

11 Oxley Residence

12 Adat Yeshurun
    Synagogue

13 Scripps Crossing
    Pedestrian Bridge

14 Scripps Institution
    of Oceanography

15 Oxley Residence

16 Case Study
    Triad Houses

17 Palmer House/
    Taj Mahal

18 Forester Residence

19 Wheeler House

20 Judkins Residence

21 Robinson Residence

22 Easton House

23 Bluebird I & II

24 Youngson Residence

25 City House

26 Prospect Point

27 Red Roost & Red Rest

28 La Valencia Hotel

29 La Jolla Post Office

30 Old La Jolla Library/
    Athenaeum

31 Arcade Building

32 Wisteria Cottage

33 Museum of
    Contemporary Art
    San Diego

34 St. James-by-the-Sea
    in La Jolla

35 La Jolla Women's Club

36 Kautz Residence

37 Geranium Cottage

38 Cove Theatre

39 Original Scripps Hospital

40 Redwood Hollow

41 The Bishop's
    School

42 Darlington
    House

43 The Shack

44 El Pueblo Ribera

45 Ray

46 Trenchard House

47 Masek Residence

48 All Saints
    Lutheran Church

49 Mormon Temple

50 The Aventine/
    Hyatt Hotel

51 Miramar Pyramid

52 Jewish Community Center

53 Nissan Design Center

ENLARG
ABOVE

43

44C

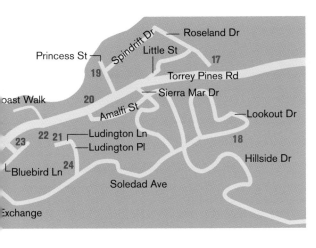

Roseland Dr
Princess St
Spindrift Dr
Little St
17
Torrey Pines Rd
19
Sierra Mar Dr
oast Walk
20
Lookout Dr
Amalfi St
22 21
Ludington Ln
23
Ludington Pl
18
Bluebird Ln
24
Hillside Dr
Soledad Ave
Exchange

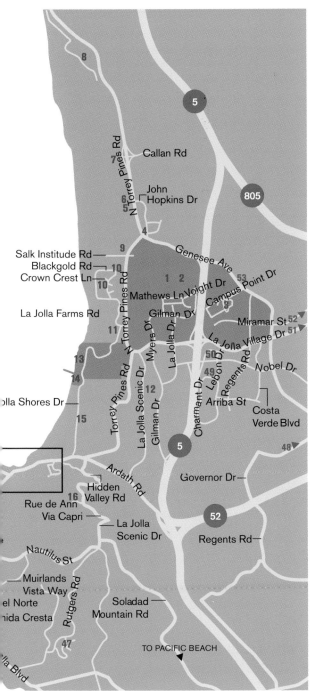

8

5

7
Callan Rd

N Torrey Pines Rd
John
Hopkins Dr
6
805
5
4
Salk Institude Rd
9
Genesee Ave
Blackgold Rd
10
Crown Crest Ln
53
10
1 2
Campus Point Dr
Voight Dr
Mathews Ln
La Jolla Farms Rd
Gilman Dr
Miramar St 52
51
11
La Jolla Village Dr
Myers Dr
La Jolla Dr
Regents Rd
Nobel Dr
13
50
14
49
Charmant Dr
Lebon Dr
olla Shores Dr
12
Arriba St
Costa
15
Verde Blvd
Gilman Dr
La Jolla Scenic Dr
48
5
Ardath Rd
Governor Dr
16
Hidden
Valley Rd
Rue de Ann
52
Via Capri
La Jolla
Scenic Dr
Regents Rd
Nautilus St
Muirlands
Vista Way
Rutgers Rd
el Norte
Soladad
nida Cresta
Mountain Rd
47
TO PACIFIC BEACH
lla Blvd

LA JOLLA

1 / **University of California San Diego**
(1965-present)
9500 Gilman Dr.

San Diego's leading university features buildings by leading architects, ranging from top locals to internationally renowned superstars. At 1,200 acres, this prime piece of real estate is roughly the size of Balboa Park, two or three times bigger than other U.C. campuses. And that has been its blessing and bain. Blessing: breathing room between people and buildings. Bain: difficult to implement planning that ties the place together. A 1989 Master Plan Study produced by SOM (Skidmore Owings Merrill) proposed solutions for various problems caused by inconsistent earlier planning. One result is Library Walk, which provides a much-needed public focal point to the south of the main library. On cool afternoons when ocean fog rolls in, the place puts on its strongest persona. As you wander through a eucalyptus grove discovering unexpected pieces from the Stuart Collection of public art, follow your reflection in the mirrored wall of Antoine Predock's theater building, or gaze down from a perch high up in William Pereira's otherworldly Geisel Library, your mind takes fanciful flights of the kind one imagines the minds of students and professors take, as they stretch the limits of learning. Allow at least a half day to explore UCSD's many buildings and spaces.

Geisel Library

Price Center Plaza (left),
Powell Structure, Laboratory (above)

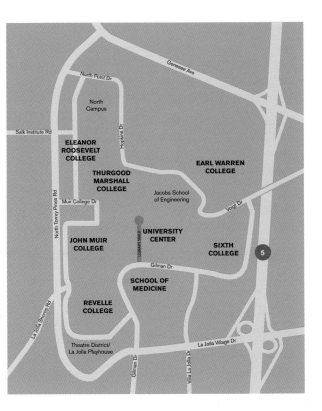

NORTH CAMPUS

- **San Diego Supercomputer Center** (1985).
  MOSHER DREW WATSON FERGUSON.

- **Torrey Pines Center North** (1979). HOWARD OXLEY.

- **Torrey Pines Center South** (1984). BRIAN PAUL.

ELEANOR ROOSEVELT COLLEGE

- **Gilman Parking Structure** (2002). ROB WELLINGTON QUIGLEY.

- **Eleanor Roosevelt College** (2003) + **Pangea Parking Structure** (2002). MOSHE SAFDIE.

- **Powell Focht Bioengineering Building** (2002). ANSHEN + ALLEN.

THURGOOD MARSHALL COLLEGE

- **Thurgood Marshall College Residence Halls and Commons** (1989). DELAWIE, BRETTON & WILKES.

- **Social Sciences Building** (1995). GWATHMEY/SIEGAL.

- **Preuss Charter School** (2001). HMC ARCHITECTS.

JOHN MUIR COLLEGE

- **Muir Commons/Tioga Hall/Tenaya Hall** (1969). DALE NAEGLE.

- **Biology Building** (1969). LIEBHARDT AND WESTON.

- **McGill Hall** (1969).
  FRANK L. HOPE.

- **Applied Physics and Mathematics Building** (1969). MOSHER DREW.

- **Humanities and Social Sciences Building** (1969).
  R.G. WHEELER.

- **Mandeville Center** (1974-1975). A. QUINCY JONES.
  A victim of last-minute budget cuts.

- **Ida and Cecil Green Faculty Club** (1987). MOSHER DREW.

- **Natatorium** (1967). LIEBHARDT AND WESTON.

LA JOLLA

REVELLE COLLEGE

- **Revelle Commons** (1964), **Revelle College Residence Halls** (1966). ROBERT ALEXANDER.
- **Galbraith Hall** (1965). DEEMS MARTIN.
- **Argo Hall, Blake Hall** (1967). TUCKER, SADLER & BENNETT.
- **Revelle College Provost Office** (1967). SIMPSON AND GERBER.
- **Natural Sciences Interdisciplinary Laboratory Building** (2002). BOHLIN CYWINSKI JACKSON and BUNDY/THOMPSON.
- **Pacific Hall** (1994). MITCHELL GIURGOLA and AUSTIN-HANSEN-FEHLMAN.

SCHOOL OF MEDICINE

- **Medical School Basic Science Building and Medical Library** (1968). ROBERT ALEXANDER.
- **Center for Molecular Genetics** (1984). LEONARD VEITZER.
- **Cellular and Molecular Medicine Building** (1991). MOORE RUBELL YUDELL.
- **Clinical Services Building** (1992). ARTHUR ERICKSON.

UNIVERSITY CENTER

- **York Hall** (1964). NEPTUNE AND THOMAS.
- **Geisel Library** (1970). WILLIAM PEREIRA, with underground addition (1993) by GUNNAR BIRKERTS/CARRIER JOHNSON.
- **International Center** (1971). JUDITH MUNK, LLOYD RUOCCO, ROBERT THORBURN.
- **Visual Arts Facility** (1993). REBECCA BINDER and NEPTUNE THOMAS DAVIS.
- **Price Center Plaza** (1990). KAPLAN MCLAUGHLIN DIAZ.
- **High Bay Physics Lab** (1986). LEONARD VEITZER.
- **Library Walk** pedestrian promenade (1996). PETER WALKER.

SIXTH COLLEGE

- **Pepper Canyon Aparments** (1991). ROSEN, JONES & ASSOCIATES

EARL WARREN COLLEGE

- **Warren College Residence Halls, Apartments, Canyon Vista Facility** (1994). DELAWIE, BRETTON & WILKES.
- **Warren College Residence Halls** (1985). LEONARD VEITZER.
- **Warren Lecture Halls and Literature Building** (1990). LIEBHARDT WESTON.

JACOBS SCHOOL OF ENGINEERING

- **Powell Structures Laboratory** (1986). LEONARD VEITZER.
- **Powell Structures Lab II** (1994). MBT ASSOCIATES.
- **Magnetic Recording Research Center** (1986). LEONARD VEITZER.
- **Engineering Building Unit I** (1990). BUSS SILVERS HUGHES.
- **Engineering Building Unit I Addition** (1998). CARRIER JOHNSON WU.
- **Engineering Building Unit II** (1994). ZIMMER GUNSUL FRASCA.

THEATRE DISTRICT/LA JOLLA PLAYHOUSE

- **Mandell Weiss Forum Theater** (1991). ANTOINE PREDOCK.

Applied Physics and Mathematics (left), Cellular and Molecular Medicine Building (top right), Mandell Weiss Forum Theatre (bottom right)

Institute of Geophysics (above), Library Walk pedestrian promenade (below left), Galbraith Hall (below right)

Engineering Building Unit II (above), Pacific Hall (below)

LA JOLLA

2 / UCSD Stuart Collection
(1983-present)

Initiated with the installation of Niki de Saint Phalle's "Sun God" near Mandeville Auditorium, the Stuart Collection, under the direction of Mary Beebe, has become San Diego's finest collection of public art. They select top artists and give them some

creative license. Highlights include Alexis Smith's "Snake Path," a metaphorical walk down the slope east from Geisel Library; Bruce Nauman's neon "Vice and Virtues" atop the Charles Lee Powell Structural Systems Laboratory, light-and-space artist Robert Irwin's "Twin Running Violet V Forms," and Terry Allen's talking "Trees," in the eucalyptus grove near the library.

---

3 / Shiley Eye Center (1991)
9415 Campus Point Dr.
ANSHEN + ALLEN

Disciples of Louis Kahn create a medical building in concrete, with hints of the master's visionary modernism, including an orderly hierarchy of spaces reminiscent of the orderly hierarchy of spaces at Kahn's Salk Institute a couple miles to the west.

---

4 / Neurosciences Institute (1996)
10640 John Jay Hopkins Dr.
TOD WILLIAMS-BILLIE TSIEN

By 2020, this building could evoke the sort of reverence reserved now only for the Salk Institute in San Diego. This sculptural concrete, limestone, stainless steel, and glass research facility snuggles into its slope in a way that makes outdoor spaces, courtyards, and landscaping as important as buildings. Standing in the courtyard as dusk becomes night and stars come out, one gets the same sort of cosmic vibes as can be had in Louis Kahn's Salk courtyard.

---

5 / Scripps Clinic/Scripps Green Hospital (1974)
10666 N. Torrey Pines Road
EDWARD DURELL STONE

San Diego's only building by this leading modernist, whose circle of friends included Walter Gropius, Marcel Breuer, the Saarinens, Alexander Calder, Buckminster Fuller, and Frank Lloyd Wright. This building is a collection of simple white masses, with texture added via patterned block used for the exterior.

6 / **Anderson Outpatient Pavilion** (1981)

10710 N. Torrey Pines Rd.
TUCKER SADLER

Next to Edward Durell Stone's earlier modernist structure, this later design by San Diego's own modernists is a tasteful addition.

---

7 / **The Lodge at Torrey Pines** (2002)
11480 N. Torrey Pines Rd.

WIMBERLY ALLISON TONG & GOO

Inspired by Greene and Greene's Blacker and Gamble houses in Pasadena, this latter-day Craftsman masterpiece has all of the Old School goodies: painstakingly crafted wood details, custom furniture, stone, tile, and a fine assortment of arts, crafts, and textiles.

---

8 / **Torrey Pines Visitors Center** (1923)
Torrey Pines State Reserve
RICHARD REQUA AND H.L. JACKSON

Built of adobe brick, this lodge was inspired by Hopi dwellings in the Arizona desert. Enter park along Coast Highway 101, one mile south of Carmel Valley Road.

---

9 / **Salk Institute** (1965)
10010 Torrey Pines Rd.
LOUIS KAHN

San Diego's most famous building is a testament to Kahn's spiritual modernism, also to the vision of his client, Jonas Salk, creator of the polio vaccine. Twin six-story laboratory buildings of cast-in-place concrete, with teak panels and windows, flank a minimalist courtyard split by a narrow channel of water. One story has it that Mexican modernist Luis Barragan visited the site with Kahn and advised him that the central space should be a stark plaza, not a formal garden. One of Kahn's innovations here is the ample "interstitial" space between floors, containing mechanical elements that can easily be altered as lab configurations change. Kahn's plan is a carefully ordered hierarchy of entry, open plaza, private study towers, and secluded laboratories.

LA JOLLA

10 / Two Organic Houses
Black Gold Road off La Jolla Scenic Drive
WALLACE CUNNINGHAM/KEN KELLOGG

On this side street near U.C. San Diego, houses from two generations of organic design stand a block apart from each other. Both inspired by Frank Lloyd Wright, Kellogg and Cunningham pursued different, personal variations. Kellogg's Turney house was built in the 1960s. A block to the south (9704 Blackgold Rd.) is Cunningham's 1995 Brush Stroke—with an inverted, curved roof inspired by forms found in nature.

11 / Oxley Residence (1958)
9302 La Jolla Farms Rd.
RICHARD NEUTRA

One of only two Neutra houses in San Diego, this place suffered various alterations (including removal of its original wooden outrigger spider legs) before it was moved to a subservient location on this site to serve as a guest house. Some of Neutra's homes in Los Angeles and Palm Springs had an International Style flavor, with white walls and exposed steel, but the Oxley home attains a more rustic modernism. It also typifies the indoor/outdoor connections that were key to the emerging California modernism of the 1940s and 1950s.

12 / Adat Yeshurun Synagogue (2001)
8625 La Jolla Scenic Dr.
M.W. STEELE GROUP

Organic site-conscious building with curved roof that mimics terrain (and nearby ocean swells), and a plan that thoughtfully wraps the building around a mature torrey pine tree that stands at the transition between outdoor and indoor sacred spaces.

13 / Scripps Crossing Pedestrian Bridge (1994)
La Jolla Shores Drive by Scripps Institution
FREIDER SEIBLE/BURKETT + WONG/SAFDIE-RABINES

Cable-stayed pedestrian bridge utilizes creatively engineered function to attain beautiful form.

14 / Scripps Institution of Oceanography
(1910-present)
8602 La Jolla Shores Dr.
IRVING GILL AND OTHERS

When completed in 1910, Gill's concrete Scripps Laboratory stood alone in La Jolla Shores. Since then, this research affiliate of UCSD has grown to include several other superb buildings: Lloyd Ruocco's Institute for Geophysics and Planetary Physics (1963); Frank L. Hope's Southwest Fishers Center (1963) and Hydraulics Laboratory (1964); Liebhardt, Weston & Goldman's Eckart Building (1975); Barton Myers' Ocean Atmospheric Research Facility (1998); Wheeler Wimer Blackman's Stephen Birch Aquarium (1992); and Hardy Holzman Pfeiffer's Ritter Hall Science Laboratory (1999).

15 / Oxley Residence (1983)
8319 La Jolla Shores Dr.
ROB QUIGLEY

With this modest, finely detailed gray stucco building, Quigley conjures dream-like images of American houses past, present, and future.

16 / Case Study Triad Houses (1960)
2329, 2342, 2343 Rue de Anne
KILLINGSWORTH BRADY & SMITH

San Diego's only official example of the post-WWII L.A.-based experiment that produced dozens of open-plan, post-and-beam houses. Two homes remain authentic, one was unfortunately remodeled with a mansard roof.

17 / Palmer House/Taj Mahal (1929)
2040 Torrey Pines Rd.
HERBERT PALMER

For a time Palmer worked with Frank Lloyd Wright, but clearly FLW's modernist ideas didn't stick. Instead, Palmer became a hopeless romantic, as evidenced by this dreamy, domed homage to Islam and historic designs in the Mediterranean.
Accessible from Roseland Drive.

LA JOLLA

18 / Forester Residence (1970)
2025 Soledad Ave.
RUSSELL FORESTER

Designed in collaboration with his wife Christine—trained as an architect in Switzerland—this is one of La Jolla's under-appreciated modern buildings, an impressive display of creative range from the designer of San Diego's original Jack-in-the-Box drive-in, who gave up architecture to become a successful painter.

19 / Wheeler House (1907)
7964 Princess St.
IRVING GILL

Pueblo-meets-modern, with sliding barn door connecting indoors and outdoors.

20 / Judkins Residence (1947)
1700 Torrey Pines Rd.
JOHN LLOYD WRIGHT

Designed by one of FLW's sons, this is typical of places designed by J.L. in the 1950s and 1960s, nestled into its hillside, with the upper  level supported by the lower level's poured concrete foundation, walls, and beam/cantilever system. Two-story glass curtain wall provides sweeping ocean views; rough textured brick ties the exterior to adjacent sandstone bluffs. Modifications made in the 1950s were reasonably sensitive to Wright's original intentions.

21 / **Robinson Residence** (1929)

1600 Ludington Ln.

LILIAN RICE

Rustic ranch house by San Diego's pioneering female architect—better known for her town planning and Spanish Colonial designs in Rancho Santa Fe.

22 / **Easton House** (1910)

1525 Torrey Pines Rd.

EMMOR BROOKE WEAVER

Another early 20th century redwood Craftsman classic by Weaver, thoughtfully wedded to its site and coastal locale. Jane Easton founded the Christian Science movement in La Jolla and hosted meetings in her home. Park on Coastwalk and look up and across North Torrey Pines Rd. to view house.

23 / **Bluebird I & II** (1980s)

1540 & 1550 Bluebird Ln.

BATTER-KAY

In their signature white modernist mode, the architects sculpt space and light, providing spectacular living spaces within buildings that double as public art for the miles and miles worth of motorists who pass here each day.

LA JOLLA

24 / **Youngson Residence** (1967)
7722 Ludington Pl.
ROD YOUNGSON

Modernist stucco boxes thoughtfully perched on a hillside site.

25 / **City House** (1990)
7902 Prospect St.
WALLACE CUNNINGHAM

Three telescoping pavilions provide provoca-
tive exterior and interior spaces—testament to
Cunningham's rigorous and inventive logic.
Designed for the son of one of Mies van der
Rohe's Chicago clients, the rectilinear house
was conceived with Miesian clarity and order.

26 / **Prospect Point** (1985)
Prospect Street at Ivanhoe Avenue
ROBERT A.M. STERN

At the peak of postmodernism and its eclectic collaging of classical forms,
Stern designed this highly visible corner building, updating the region's
Spanish Colonial heritage.

27 / **Red Roost & Red Rest** (1894)
1100 Block of Coast Blvd.

Vacant for 25 years as
preservationists lobbied to
save them, these are possibly the earliest examples of
the classic California redwood beach house.

28 / **La Valencia Hotel** (1926)
1132 Prospect St.
W.T. JOHNSON/HERBERT MANN

Downtown La Jolla's "pink lady" commands the village's center with romantic Mediterranean revival style, and details that include tile mosaics and hand-painted murals.

29 / **La Jolla Post Office** (1935)
1140 Wall St.

WPA-era Mission Revival-style building featuring Chicago-born La Jolla artist Belle Baranceanu's mural "Scenic View of the Village".

30 / **Old La Jolla Library/Athenaeum** (1921)
1008 Wall St.
WILLIAM TEMPLETON JOHNSON

One of San Diego's most prolific architects, Johnson here combined Spanish Colonial and Italian Renaissance elements. Concrete walls are covered by a low pitched tile roof; classical columns frame the entry. Despite additions over the years, the library retains its strong bone structure.

31 / **Arcade Building** (1926)
7910 Girard Ave.
HERBERT PALMER

In indoor/outdoor shopping experience in a Mission Revival-style pedestrian mall.

LA JOLLA

32 / **Wisteria Cottage** (1904)
780 Prospect St.

Remodeled under Irving Gill's supervision in 1907 (some evidence says he was also the original architect), the cottage is an early Craftsman bungalow, with the broad, horizontal profile of midwestern Prairie style. Pleasing combination of symmetry and asymmetry. This cottage—today home to John Cole's Books—is the last building left from the original Scripps family complex that also included Ellen Browning Scripps' landmark 1915 home designed by Gill—and later recreated by architects Robert Venturi and Denise Scott Brown as part of their Museum of Contemporary Art remodel in the 1990s.

33 / **Museum of Contemporary Art San Diego**
(1916/1960/1996)
700 Prospect St.
IRVING GILL/MOSHER DREW/VENTURI SCOTT BROWN

When the museum opened here in 1915, it occupied the Ellen Browning Scripps residence designed by Irving Gill. Over the years, the home was swallowed by additions. By the time Venturi Scott Brown was hired in the 1980s for major renovation, the community had a longing for the old Gill building. The architects recreated its facade as the centerpiece of the makeover, and elsewhere translated Gill's columns and arches into contemporary forms of their own. Unfortunately, the Gill facade is misleading—it beckons visitors, but the real entrance is hidden off to one side. Venturi Scott Brown's most dramatic and effective detail here is the interior rotunda beneath a dome ringed with curvy fins—a prime example of the architects' Vegas-inspired graphics.

34 / **St. James-by-the-Sea in La Jolla** (1929)
743 Prospect St.
LOUIS J. GILL

Gill modeled his tower on the tower of a church at Campo Florida outside Mexico City; he often favored a more traditional approach than his modernist uncle Irving. This complex mixes arches and smooth stucco walls reminiscent of Irving, with Louis's richly decorated tower and an interior that features a rugged beamed ceiling.

35 / La Jolla Women's Club (1912)
715 Silverado St.
IRVING GILL

Walls were poured in forms on site, tilted into place, fastened together into a durable and beautiful building. This structure combines Gill's minimalist Mission vocabulary of arches and unadorned surfaces, with his love of landscapes that intertwined with buildings, and his fascination with new construction techniques and materials.

36 / Kautz Residence (1913)
7753 Draper St.
IRVING GILL

John Philip Sousa rented the place for seven years and wrote about the experience in "My Family Right or Wrong". The house is one of the best examples of Gill's mature cubist style, made from tilt-up concrete slabs with arches and window openings cast in the concrete. Kate Sessions worked with Gill on a landscape that features creeping fig vines climbing walls to soften the building's hard edges. Today the building is used as a hotel—which means you can spend the night in a Gill building.

37 / Geranium Cottage (1904)
830 Kline St.

One of only two 1 1/2-story, side-gable bungalows built in La Jolla, this home makes a transition between 19th century board-and-batten beach cottages and modern Craftsman dwellings. Steep, curving roofs like this one are more common on the East Coast.

38 / Cove Theatre (1948)
7730 Girard Ave.

One of the region's few remaining single-screen movie theaters, it looks more like a modernist brick department store.

LA JOLLA

39 / **Scripps Hospital and Nurses Home** (1924)
483 Prospect St.
IRVING GILL

The expanding Scripps
medical group eventually
outgrew its original La Jolla
building, moving most oper-
ations up the hill to a more
accessible location near Interstate 5. In late 2002 the 15,000-square-foot,
tile-roofed building designed by Gill for La Jolla benefactor Ellen Browning
Scripps was on the market for $14.7 million, for a possible combination of
office and residential uses.

40 / **Redwood Hollow** (1915-1940s)
244-254 Prospect St.

Four cottages remain
from the original 20 sea-
side bungalows devel-
oped here by Walter
Scott Weaver, believed
by some to have been
designed by early 20th
century Craftsman-style
master Emmor Brooke Weaver. One bungalow has redwood siding, the
other three are shingled.

41 / **The Bishop's School** (1910-1934)
7607 La Jolla Blvd.
IRVING GILL, LOUIS GILL, CARLETON WINSLOW

Irving Gill designed the first buildings: Scripps Hall and Bentham Hall,
both utilizing reinforced concrete. Gill collaborated with his nephew Louis
on the 1916 Gilman Hall, a stark structure flanked by one of Gill's signature arcades. Winslow—who also designed buildings for the 1915 expo in
Balboa Park, added Bishop's chapel in 1916, a bit of Spanish Colonial
romance that contrasts with Irving Gill's minimalist vision. Winslow also
designed a second story addition for Bentham Hall, as well as adding a
tower to his chapel in 1930. In 1934, Winslow designed the Wheeler
Bailey Library. Gill intended
for his buildings to interact
with the landscape, and to
be softened by plant materials such as creeping vines.
Horticulturist Kate Sessions
consulted on the original
landscape. Decades later,
modern buildings were
added to the campus by
Mosher & Drew.

42 / **Darlington House** (1925)

7441 Olivetas Ave.

HERBERT PALMER, RICHARD REQUA, THOMAS SHEPERD

Following Palmer's original design of identical cottages joined by a central ocean-view living room, Requa added a library, kitchen, garage, and Andalusian courtyard in 1931, followed by Sheperd's 1940 modification of the front facade and addition of a second story. Over the years, hundreds of San Diego couples have been married in the garden.

43 / **The Shack** (1946)

6800 Block of Neptune Pl. (Beach Side)

Legend has it that GI/surfers returning from World War II built this tiki hut on the beach from local materials such as sugar gum eucalyptus (found near UCSD) and Canary Island palm fronds. Windansea Beach, the shack, the legendary waves, and the motley crew of local surfers known in the late 1960s as Mac Meeda Destruction Co. were made famous through Tom Wolfe's book *The Pumphouse Gang*.

44 / **El Pueblo Ribera** (1923)

230-248 Gravilla St.

RUDOLPH SCHINDLER

Considered a masterpiece of early California modernism, Schindler's 12-unit complex utilizes an inventive plan that gives each apartment its own private patio. Experimental board-formed concrete proved difficult to finance at a time when the material was not commonly used for homes. In recent years some units were restored and/or remodeled with additions. As the size of new homes as steadily grown, Schindler's modest bungalows illustrate that it is possible to live comfortably in a small space.

LA JOLLA

45 / **Ray** (2002)
724 Muirlands Vista Way
WALLACE CUNNINGHAM

Sun rays, manta rays, and other radiating patterns found in nature inspired this courtyard home with a patterned copper roof and ocean-facing wall of glass.

46 / **Trenchard House** (c. 1936)
6126 Avenida Cresta
CLIFF MAY

Understated, romantic Mediterranean ranch house, wrapped around a central court—one of several Mays in this neighborhood.

47 / **Masek Residence** (1967)
1439 Calle Altura
SIMPSON & GERBER

Angular modernism rendered in wood.

48 / **All Saints Lutheran Church** (1969)
6355 Radcliffe Dr.
SIM BRUCE RICHARDS

Courtyard entry leads under a high pitched metal roof supported by rugged wood beams, with abundant glass enhancing indoor/outdoor connections.

49 / **Mormon Temple** (1992)
7474 Charmant Dr.
DEEMS/LEWIS

Words fail. What can you say about San Diego's most fantastic building, engineered to last at least a millenium, all white and glorious like a gigantic wedding cake, crowned by the gold-leaf angel Moroni who serenades motorists on nearby I-5.

50 / **The Aventine/Hyatt Hotel** (1990)
3777 La Jolla Village Dr.
MICHAEL GRAVES

Many San Diegans (including most practicing architects) dislike this postmodern office-hotel-health club, designed during the architect's 1980s prime of popularity, before he graduated to doing kitchenware for Target. Compared to most of what's nearby, though, in fact compared with most buildings in San Diego, the Aventine is elegant and eye-catching, with its rich colors and strong neoclassical forms. It's kitschier than Graves's San Juan Capistrano Library north of San Diego, but it seems to be aging gracefully. Ever the control freak, Graves also designed most of the furniture and fabrics inside the hotel.

51 / **Miramar Pyramid** (1990)
7310 Miramar Rd.
CHARLES SLERT

A visionary on a grand scale, Slert gave this commercial/industrial wasteland an I.M. Pei-like icon visible from miles around. Countless San Diegans have since used the pyramid when giving directions, a testament to its civic value—even if the plan and interior layout make the building difficult to configure for retailing use.

52 / **Jewish Community Center** (1985/2001)
4126 Executive Dr.
DELAWIE WILKES RODRIGUES BARKER

Organized around a vaulted skylit gallery are tributary interior "streets and alleys", inspired by old European villages, that encourage mingling and catching up with friends. The complex includes a 500-seat theater, Olympic pool, tennis courts, and gym.

53 / **Nissan Design Center** (1983)
9800 Campus Point Dr.
RONCHETTI DESIGN

Nissan's in-house designers drafted the initial design; instead, the car company's Japanese administration selected a scheme by Ken Ronchetti, who had been hired to design interior spaces. Ronchetti's design utilizes pour-in-place, tilt-up, and precast concrete. In 2002, Ronchetti added a new digital design studio for this place where Nissan's hot "Z" car was reborn for the 2003 model year.

North Coast

Strung along San Diego's northern coast are postcard beach towns that have clung to the aura of the 1920s and 1930s, when Coast Highway was the main road connecting San Diego with the rest of California. Cruise the highway today and you still pass through modest downtowns that range from Del Mar's Tudor Revival, to the Edward Hopper-like look of Olde Encinitas, and born-again Oceanside—redeveloping with re-purposed older buildings as well as newer developments including a multiplex cinema and Charles Moore-designed Civic Center.

Coastal height restrictions keep the scale of construction compatible with historical buildings. Rising real estate prices have pushed residential and commercial development east of Interstate 5—which became the region's defining line when it opened in the 1960s.

Tucked among traditional style buildings in all of these coastal towns are some of the region's most interesting 20th century buildings.

John Lloyd Wright (Frank's son) designed homes in Del Mar, where in the 1980s architect Ted Smith developed his "Go Home" projects that combined individual living spaces on a single family lot, with a shared kitchen. Nearby in Del Mar, Sim Bruce Richards, James Hubbell, and Herb Turner are among architects of low-key buildings tailored to the terrain. In the village, Del Mar Plaza is a Jon Jerde design, from a time before the architect's vivacious mixed-use projects caught on around the world.

Published often in the 1980s and 1990s, some of Rob Quigley's most interesting buildings can be found along North County's coast: houses in Del Mar and the transit station at one end of Solana Beach's Cedros Design District.

East of Del Mar, the village of Rancho Santa Fe is a "must see"—for Lilian Rice's town plan and her design of several humble Spanish Colonial revival buildings. Tucked among the eucalyptus trees in this community are sprawling estates owned by corporate moguls and celebrities.

Encinitas is known for the golden lotus blossoms in front of Self Realization Fellowship, the ashram founded on a coastal bluff in 1937 by guru Paramahansa Yogananda. The ashram's meticulously manicured meditation garden on K Street is among of the region's prime horticultural attractions.

Other unconventional personalities built Egyptian Revival homes in Encinitas—among only a handful of buildings in San Diego inspired by this 1920s design trend. On oceanview hillsides in Cardiff-by-the-Sea, Encinitas, and Leucadia are some of the area's most interesting homes.

Just north, Carlsbad is known for its progressive public art program and its turn-of-the-century hot spring spa—many buildings remain from the city's early years.

In Oceanside is one of Southern California's longest piers, jutting out from a beach where vacationers still stay in pink cottages dating from a time when the town was primarily a summer escape. Also in Oceanside are some of the last buildings from the careers of two leading architects: Charles Moore and Irving Gill. Fifty years apart, the tail ends of their careers cross in Oceanside.

Del Mar Locations

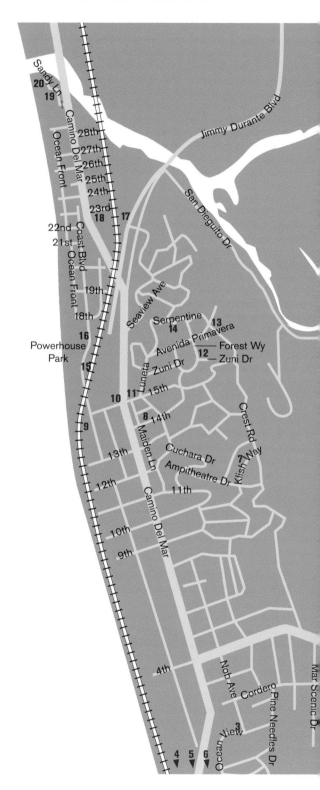

Sandy Ln
20
19

Camino Del Mar
Ocean Front

28th
27th
26th
25th
24th
23rd
18 — 17
22nd
21st
Coast Blvd
Ocean Front
19th
18th

Jimmy Durante Blvd

San Dieguito Dr

Seaview Ave

Serpentine
14
13

Avenida Primavera
12 — Forest Wy
— Zuni Dr

16
Powerhouse
Park
15

Lineta
Zuni Dr

10 11
15th

9

8 14th

Maiden Ln

13th

Cuchara Dr
Ampitheatre Dr

12th

11th

Camino Del Mar

10th

9th

Crest Rd

Klish Wy

4th

Nob Ave

Cordero

Ocean View

3

Pine Needles Dr

Mar Scenic Dr

4 5 6

1 **Torrey Reserve Offices**
2 **Torrey Pines High School**
3 **McPherson House**
4 **Go Homes**
5 **Squire Residence**
6 **North Torrey Pines Bridge**
7 **Heller Residence**
8 **St. Peter's Episcopal Church**
9 **Wave Crest**
10 **L'Auberge Del Mar**
11 **Del Mar Plaza**
12 **Turner House & Studio**
13 **Del Mar Castle**
14 **Gerber House**
15 **Del Mar Train Station**
16 **Powerhouse Community Center**
17 **Southfair**
18 **Triangle House**
19 **Jaeger House**
20 **Warren Beach House**
21 **Jenny Craig Building**

DEL MAR

1 / **Torrey Reserve Offices** (1998)
11452-11752 El Camino Real
BRIAN PAUL

Gracefully detailed four-building complex with metallic awnings and delicately posed steel sculpture by Jeffrey Laudenslager. Visible from I-5, a vast improvement over earlier office buildings in the area.

2 / **Torrey Pines High School** (1976, expanded 1989)
3710 Del Mar Heights Road
DEEMS/LEWIS

Natural light—imported by skylights, clerestories, and carefully placed windows—is a high priority in this site-hugging, energy-efficient (note sun-shading overhangs) building of steel, concrete, and fat glue lam beams. North side of Del Mar Heights road, opposite Torrey Ridge Drive.

3 / **McPherson House** (1947)
100 Block of Nob Ave.
JOHN LLOYD WRIGHT

Angular beachhouse variation on the ideas of Wright's famous father.

4 / **Go Homes** (1981-1988)
12712 Via Donada/12704 Via Esperia/12704 Via Felino
SMITH & OTHERS

Creatively interpreting building codes, the architect designed a dwelling for creative types who share one kitchen—thus qualifying the structure as a single-family home—but who each have their own living space. The concrete-block bunker of one building is a sound-proof room for electric blues-rock jams.

5 / **Squire Residence** (1979)
2402 Carmel Valley Rd.
ROB QUIGLEY

One of the architect's earliest adventures in narrative design—drawing from site, client, and fantasy to invent the story of a building—in this case for a professor. Also one of Quigley's first experiments in collaging forms and materials found nearby, in this case wood, concrete block, and red asphalt roofing, so that a new structure immediately connects with its context.

6 / **North Torrey Pines Bridge** (1933)
Coast Highway south of Carmel Valley Road

Elegant concrete bridge harks back to the time of artist-designed WPA projects across the country. After replacement with a new structure was threatened, preservationists advocated saving and upgrading the original bridge.

7 / **Heller Residence** (1953/1988)
1119 Klish Way
SIM BRUCE RICHARDS/J. SPENCER LAKE

Designed during Richards' "shinto" period, this home has both Japanese and Wrightian influences. After unfortunate remodels to Richards' design, Lake supervised restoration and addition.

8 / **St. Peter's Episcopal Church** (c. 1930)
334 14th St.
CARLETON M. WINSLOW

Rustic wood church by the architect known for redwood bungalows and various Balboa Park buildings; also popular wedding spot.

9 / **Wave Crest** (1984)
1400 Ocean Ave.
KLOCK ALLEN

Understated, organic approach makes this vacation enclave of shingled bungalows a good neighbor in a predominantly single-family neighborhood. View from Camino Del Mar Bridge

10 / **L'Auberge Del Mar** (1989)
1540 Camino del Mar
GALVIN CRISTILLI

Designed more like a seaside mansion with guest cottages than a resort hotel, this 120-room retreat (on the site of earlier historical hotels) frequented by celebrities in town for the horse-racing season defers to its ocean-view site on a prominent corner in a village where locals have fought for years to preserve Del Mar's quaint, homey character.

DEL MAR

11 / Del Mar Plaza (1989)
1555 Camino Del Mar
JERDE PARTNERSHIP WITH
TOM MCCABE

After engaging the community in
a lengthy planning and approval process, developers created a multi-level
retailing experience that draws from adjacent styles and materials so that
it fits the neighborhood fabric. Outdoor terraces and walkways take advantage of views and temperate weather.

12 / Turner House & Studio (1953-1970s)
606 Zuni Dr.
HERB TURNER

Modernist wood home designed
by the architect/owner—a former
apprentice to John Lloyd Wright.

13 / Del Mar Castle (1927)
544 Avenida Primavera
REQUA & JACKSON

Visible on its hilltop from Interstate 5,
the white-stucco, red tile-roofed castle
is probably Requa's grandest Spanish
Colonial Revival home, with a cylindrical
tower that commands attention.

14 / Gerber House
(1970)
421 Serpentine Dr.
JOSEPH GERBER

Woody modernism from
a time after modernism's
prime, but before whimsical postmodernism began popping up in
San Diego's beach neighborhoods in the late 1970s.

15 / Del Mar Train Station (1910)
1565 Coast Blvd.

Built to the railroad company's
standard #2A plan the year after
the now-displaced Stratford Inn
opened nearby, this was the only such California station using brick instead
of wood siding. After welcoming train-riding tourists and horse racing fans
for years, the station closed in 1995; it's future was in limbo as of 2002.

16 / Powerhouse Community Center
(early 1900s, refurbished 1999)
1658 Coast Blvd.

Originally a power plant supplying the
Stratford Inn with electricity and hot
water, the powerhouse today serves
as a multi-purpose community building.

17 / **Southfair** (1981)
2010 Jimmy Durante Blvd.
HERB TURNER

Redwood structures work in harmony with a landscape plan that includes a sculpture garden.

---

18 / **Triangle House** (1998)
203 23rd St.
LEW DOMINY

Snagging an "unbuildable" triangle lot on a busy street for $50,000, the architect/owner designed a 688-square-foot home that he says is like living on a boat.

---

19 / **Jaeger House** (1983)
2998 Sandy Lane
ROB QUIGLEY

Grouping of towers and bungalows connected by bridges, derived from a fantasy in which these objects were scattered on the sand by a tsunami. View from bridge.

---

20 / **Warren Beach House** (1982)
End of Sandy Lane
BATTER-KAY

Adjacent to Quigley's "tsunami"-derived design is this contrasting study in stark white modernism by the architects also responsible for the row of more recent white modern homes on Via de la Valle overlooking the Del Mar Fairgrounds. View from sand.

---

21 / **Jenny Craig Building** (1979)
445 Marine View Ave.
DEEMS/LEWIS

Formerly occupied by the diet maven's empire, this commercial building employs a vocabulary similar to the post-and-beam techniques used by the same architect for Torrey Pines High School in Del Mar, and the Motorola Building in Scripps Ranch. Features include massive laminated beams, and energy-efficient combination of overhangs and glazing. Visible from the 5 north of Via De La Valle.

Rancho Santa Fe Locations

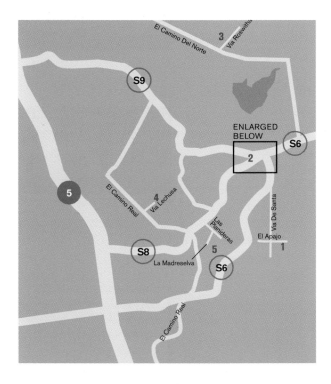

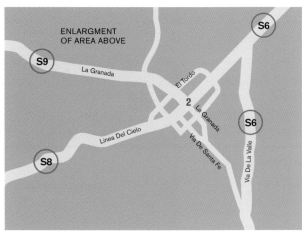

1 **Nativity Catholic Church**

2 **Rancho Santa Fe Village Plan and Buildings**

3 **Harmony**

4 **Winghouse**

5 **Brickwood**

1 / **Nativity Catholic Church** (1990)
6309 El Apajo

MOORE RUBLE YUDELL
WITH AUSTIN HANSEN FEHLMAN

One of Charles Moore's final projects before he
passed away in 1993, this contemporary abstraction
of historical Spanish and Mission forms provides an
uplifting experience, from a vertical strip window that washes the altar with
light, to the delicate wood lattice ceiling, and a seating arrangement that
connects the congregation with its minister.

2 / **Rancho Santa Fe Village Plan and Buildings**
(1920s)

LILIAN RICE

Dispatched by employers
Requa & Jackson to plan a
secluded village in what was
then the region's hinterlands,
Rice created a modest Mediterranean village of tile roofs, courtyards, and
grillwork, along a narrow landscaped main street. Today, Rice's town center
plan continues to set the community's understated style. One of the first

women to earn an architecture degree at U.C. Berkeley, Rice
also designed La Morada (now the Inn at Rancho Santa Fe),
Valencia Apartments on La Granda, and four townhomes on
Paseo Delicias between La Randa and El Tordo.

3 / **Harmony** (2002)
18128 Via Roswitha (off Camino del Norte)

WALLACE CUNNINGHAM

Cubistic stucco-over-steel
structure, set in a minimalist zen garden, with a roof twice the area of
enclosed space—outdoor "rooms" are as important as indoors.

4 / **Winghouse** (1980)
4624 Via Lechusa

WALLACE CUNNINGHAM

Cunningham's first design
utilizes gracefully nesting
arcs that unfold like a flower
or sea creature.

5 / **Brickwood** (1965)
15611 La Madreselva

JOHN LLOYD WRIGHT

Gorgeous brick home with
lines and decorative details
very reminiscent of Wright's
famous father's designs.

Cardiff By The Sea and Solana Beach Locations

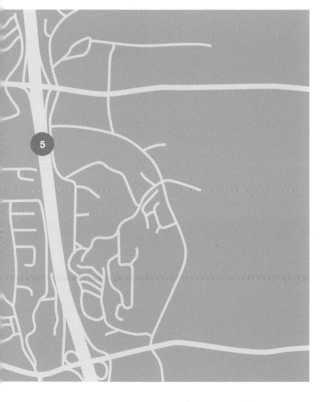

CARDIFF-BY-THE-SEA

1 / **Cardiff Towne Centre remodel** (2000)
Birmingham Avenue and San Elijo Avenue
TOM MCCABE

Built in the sixties as a supermarket/drug store strip mall, the complex was updated Cape Cod style in the 1980s, and madeover again by coastal mall maven McCabe. Some locals complained about the more massive scale of the remodel (and the arrival of that notorious Seattle coffee chain), but the concentration of people gathered in the main courtyard attests to the fact that the architect has effectively created a new village square.

---

2 / **Cardiff County Library** (2003)
2081 Newcastle Ave.
MANUEL ONCINA

The only new county branch library built from recycled materials, Oncina's building mixes clean modern lines with curvy organic forms appropriately inspired by waves, shells, and other forms seen at the seaside.

---

3 / **Farrell Residence** (1993)
2211 Cambridge Ave.
KEVIN FARRELL

Exploding Gehry-like with stucco and copper forms, this major addition to a modest bungalow with an ocean view captures the power of the sea. Florida.

---

4 / **Aperture** (1984)
2598 Montgomery
WALLACE CUNNINGHAM

Triangular roof panels and clerestories function like an eye or camera lens to admit views and natural light to this home visible from miles around, and to motorists on nearby I-5—making it the area's most visible piece of public sculpture. Visible on the hill north of Manchester, west of I-5.

SOLANA BEACH

5 / Roberto's Taco Shop (1991)

445 N. Highway 101

TOM MCCABE

With its curvy tortilla of a roofline, this roadside stand continues a SoCal tradition of food-as-function.

6 / Solana Beach Transit Station (1995)

105 N. Cedros Ave.

ROB QUIGLEY

Extrapolating from the area's history of military quonset huts and humble farm buildings, the transit center is a strong yin-yang composition of vault-roofed station and tower. Extra credit goes to public officials for lowering rails below grade, maximizing the pedestrian experience, minimizing noise and hazards. Residents battled the architect over whether or not to have a clock on the tower. He won. No clock up high, although there is one on the station's glass wall.

7 / Beachwalk Center (1992)

437 Highway 101

TOM MCCABE

Stand back at the edge of the street and take a good look. On the left, a Mexican restaurant's front facade becomes a woman's face with an eyebrow raised (over the upper right window) in flirtation. To the right rear is the object of her affections: a man with a 5 o'clock shadow rendered in olive stucco. This playful mall has helped revitalize this strip of Coast Highway with a pedestrian-friendly experience.

8 / Solana Beach City Hall (1993)

635 S. Highway 101

As the eighties era of conspicuous comsumption and disco ball pickup joints faded, Diego's night club in Solana Beach fizzled. In an unusually creative move for a public entity, Solana Beach officials acquired the club—a barely used reflective glass building—and renovated it into a city hall that looks and functions better than the original night club.

Encinitas/Leucadia Locations

1 **Crescent**

2 **Wave Roof House**

3 **La Paloma Theatre**

4 **Encinitas Hotel**

5 **Encinitas One-room Schoolhouse**

6 **Sidney Chaplin building**

7 **Derby House**

8 **Boathouses**

9 **Petrie Residence**

Mays Hollow

Quail Gardens Dr

15

Encinitas Blvd

La Via San Juan

16   17

La Via Guadalupe   Oakcrest Park Rd

18 ▶

El Camino Real

Balour Dr

Santa Fe Dr

ENCINITAS/LEUCADIA

1 / **Crescent** (2003)
532 Neptune Ave.
WALLACE CUNNINGHAM

After decades of living in the city, these clients wanted an oceanfront retreat that would embrace bluewater views while providing seclusion in a neighborhood of narrow lots. Wrapped around a reflecting pool enclosed by a spiral concrete ramp that connects three levels, this steel-frame structure has metal decks, cast-in-place concrete floors and shear walls, and an exterior of concrete, Portland cement plaster, flat-seamed zinc panels, and clear heat mirror insulated glazing. The roof is flat-seamed stainless steel with integrated gutters. Lift-and-slide stainless steel door panels open the house to views and breezes.

---

2 / **Wave Roof House** (1992)
208 Ocean View Ave.

At dusk, the saddle-like hyberbolic paraboloid roof seems to crest with curves of rafter tails, as surfers slice through the last waves of the day not far away. Owner Mark Whitley designed this dramatic remodel of a small beach bungalow, with the swooping roof topping a second story addition and first-floor remodel, both built from basic off-the-shelf parts. Whitley also owns the boathouse in Encinitas.

---

3 / **La Paloma Theatre** (1928)
471 S. Coast Highway 101

The Kilgen Wonder Organ played the "La Paloma Overture," vaudeville acts performed, and this Spanish Colonial revival theater opened with the film "The Cohens and Kelleys in Paris". It remains a landmark of this coastal commercial strip, as well as a historical venue known not only for screening Hollywood, indie, and surf films, but for concerts by Jerry Garcia, Ralph Stanley, and Eddie Vedder.

---

4 / **Encinitas Hotel** (1925)
511 S. Coast Highway 101

Bathing beauties helped W.B. Forbes open his new 21-room hotel in a mixed-use building that also featured ground-floor commercial uses. Today the upper floor is offices.

5 / **Encinitas One-room Schoolhouse** (1883)
560 Third Ave.

Built by E.G. Hammond and his son Ted, this Classical Revival schoolhouse utilizes redwood shiplap (later covered with stucco) and handmade square nails.

6 / **Sidney Chaplin Building** (1925)

656 S. Coast Highway 101

Charlie Chaplin's brother owned the building in the 1920s, when it contained a billiard parlor and barber shop. Charlie also owned property in downtown Encinitas.

7 / **Derby House** (1887)
649 Vulcan Ave.

Pie for breakfast? The native Vermonters who hosted train passengers here carried on their morning tradition in a large redwood home with several bedrooms,

a brick fireplace, a homey kitchen with a wood beam ceiling.

8 / **BoatHouses** (1925)
726-732 Third St.

Pioneering recycler Miles Kellogg moored these tugboats on a sloping lot and converted them for use as houses.

9 / **Petrie Residence** (1931)
842 Second St.

Tudor-Cotswold Revival gem of concrete blocks that were hand-cast by the original owner.

10 / **Self Realization Fellowship Temple** (1916)
939 Second St.

Formerly a schoolhouse overlooking downtown at Third Avenue and E Street, the mission-style building later served various school uses and as a recreation center before it was moved here in 1953, acquired by SRF, and restored to its original beauty for use as a temple.

ENCINITAS/LEUCADIA

11 / **Gresham's Service Station** (1933)
1205 S. Coast Highway 101

Quirky roadside classic, with a
pyramidal hipped roof and arches—
an eye-catching design aimed at
motorists entering or leaving Encinitas
from the south. Built in the midst of
a period when several downtown
Encinitas corners had a gas station.

12 / **Self Realization Fellowship Ashram and Meditation Garden** (beginning 1937)
215 K St.

Donated by one of Paramahansa
Yogananda's devotees, this sizeable
hunk of oceanfront acreage (on both
sides of Coast Highway) is the community's mystical and spiritual center.
Land east of the highway is still
farmed with pumpkins and vegetable,
preserved as valuable open space in
its increasingly dense neighborhood.
West of the highway, the ashram,
with its gold lotus towers and mod-
est roadside building that once served Yogananda's mushroom burgers,
adds an eastern Hindu flavor to this West Coast surf town. On the north-
west corner of the ashram grounds, a meditation garden meticulously maintained by monks is a cool, quiet retreat with lush vegetation and koi
ponds, the ruins of a seaside chapel long ago eroded over the edge, and
an empty blue swimming pool where the guru once swam. The popular
nearby surfing spot was long ago christened "Swami's".

13 / **Swami's Beach Steps** (1990)
Just south of Self Realization Fellowship
GLEN SCHMIDT

Simple, solid forms in wood and
concrete help stabilize the sandstone bluffs, while providing artful
access to the popular surfing spot
below—named for the guru who
founded the nearby ashram.

14 / **Egyptian Revival Houses** (1923)
959 Cornish Dr. and 1239 San Dieguito Dr.

Fascinated with the 1920s Egyptian Revival frenzy, developer O.L. Steel
built two homes in the style, featuring bas-reliefs, battered walls, symmetrical
temple-like plans, and other details inspired by the pyramids and the dis-

covery in 1922 of King Tut's tomb.
Steel intended these to serve as
models for future development,
but after the Stock Market Crash,
he sold the properties in 1932
and moved on.

15 / **Quail Botanical Gardens** (1943)
230 Quail Gardens Dr.

Architects consider this oasis a one-stop showcase for the range of exotic plant materials that can flourish in the San Diego region. Begun by Ruth Baird Larabee and Charles Larabee as a botanical farm for collecting exotic plant species, the 30-acre public garden (eventually donated to the county) remains true to its mission. Inside are cork oaks, palms, cycads, cacti, hibiscus, and the biggest bamboo collection in the country. In 2002, a rare Amorphophallus ("shapeless phallus") titanium on loan from a collector bloomed to 12 feet with a smell said to resemble rotting flesh. Tourists came from miles around to witness the plant's fetid three-day prime.

16 / **Encinitas Fire Station #5** (2001)
540 Balour Dr.
DOMINY & ASSOCIATES

Best North Coast fire station, with its standing-seam metal roof, 30-foot hose tower, and solid basic materials such as concrete block, wood, and steel.

17 / **Encinitas Senior and Community Center** (2001)
1140 Oakcrest Park Dr.
MARC STEELE

Impact of this sizeable building is minimized by intelligent siting. This modernist community center includes a community banquet hall and kitchen, gymnasium/auditorium, arts/crafts room, activity and meeting rooms, conference rooms, dance/activity room, senior game room, senior library/computer room, senior citizen outreach offices, a community information counter and administrative offices.

18 / **Tomascewski Residence** (2000)
513 Whisper Wind Dr.
GUILLERMO TOMASCEWSKI

Drawing from a context that includes the historical Olivenhain Meeting

Hall, the architect utilized simple materials including corrugated metal roofing in a simple, elegant way. The home follows the terrain, conserves energy, and was built for under $100 per square foot.

Carlsbad Locations

1 **Levy Residence**
2 **Army & Navy Academy/Red Apple Inn**
3 **Magee House**
4 **St. Michael Episcopal Church**
5 **Twin Inns/Neimans**
6 **Old Santa Fe Depot**

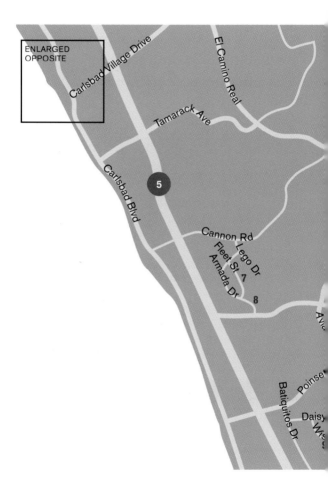

ENLARGED
OPPOSITE

1 / **Levy Residence** (1999)
2401 Mountain View Dr.
MCGEE-BEHUN

Imaginative, energetic
design by former staff
architects from Rob
Quigley's office. Best
seen off left side of
Carlsbad Blvd. north from
Carlsbad.

7 **Pacific Ridge Corporate Center**

8 **Gemological Institute of America**

9 **Habib Residence**

10 **Carlsbad City Library**

11 **Leo Carrillo Ranch/Rancho de Los Kiotes**

12 **St. Elizabeth Seton Church**

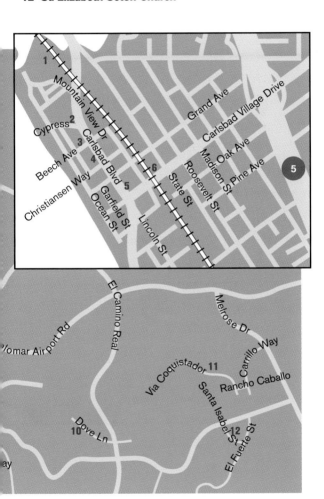

2 / **Army & Navy Academy/Red Apple Inn** (1925)
2605 Carlsbad Blvd.

ROBERT BAIRD

As a restaurant, the original white stucco, red tile-roofed building operated until 1936, when it was occupied by the school. The understated, Mediterranean-flavored structures are among the most tasteful along Coast Highway in Carlsbad, where some schlocko hotels and resorts have been served up over the years.

CARLSBAD

3 / **Magee House** (1887)
258 Beech Ave.

Single-story wood structure with a few Victorian frills.

4 / **St. Michael Episcopal Church** (1896)
2775 Carlsbad Blvd.

Little white chapel, like something out of Midwestern farm country.

5 / **Twin Inns/Neimans** (1887)
2978 Carlsbad Blvd.

Carlsbad's grandest Queen Anne Victorian was originally a mansion for Gerhard Schutte, proprietor of the nearby Mineral Springs Hotel (later Alt Karlsbad), which attracted health-seekers from across the country.

6 / **Old Santa Fe Depot** (1907)
400 Carlsbad Village Dr.

Now used as a Visitors Information Center, this rustic wood building gives the flavor of West Coast architecture prior to the Mission Revival boom.

7 / **Pacific Ridge Corporate Center** (1999)
5780-5790 Fleet St.
BRIAN PAUL

Portuguese limestone, Indian slate, pleasing proportions, elegant details such as colonnaded punched openings and a metal third floor with outriggers and sunshades.

8 / Gemological Institute of America (1997)
5345 Armada Dr.
LPA

World headquarters for the organization that oversees the precious stone industry, this modernist steel, glass, and masonry building is as precisely faceted as a valuable diamond.

9 / Habib Residence (1994)
7207 Wisteria Way
EHM ARCHITECTURE

Designed for two psychologists who profiled the architect's psyche before hiring him, this design began as a clay sculpture that grew into a quirky home with a round parapet and a landscape including crop circles visible to pilots landing at Palomar Airport.

10 / Carlsbad City Library (1999)
1775 Dove Lane
CALDWELL/THOMAS AND MCGRAW/BALDWIN

Stark white modern building in the spirit of Irving Gill, makes the adjacent peach stucco mall look like a silly cliché.

11 / Leo Carrillo Ranch/Rancho de Los Kiotes (1937)
6250 Flying LC Lane

Carrillo was a popular star of stage and television, best known for his TV role as Pancho— Cisco Kid's sidekick. In the 1930s, Carrillo decided he needed an Old California-style rancho. He bought this property, including an old adobe dating back to the 1800s. Carrillo constructed an authentic adobe brick, tile-roofed complex that today offers a glimpse of what life was like in Southern California more than 100 years ago. A new public park opened on this site in 2003.

12 / St. Elizabeth Seton Church (1995)
6628 Santa Isabel St.
DOMINY + ASSOCIATES

Clean-lined modern structure with Spanish Colonial details is a thoroughly solid design, from its architecture, pergola, and gardens, to an interior that welcomes the congregation.

Oceanside Locations

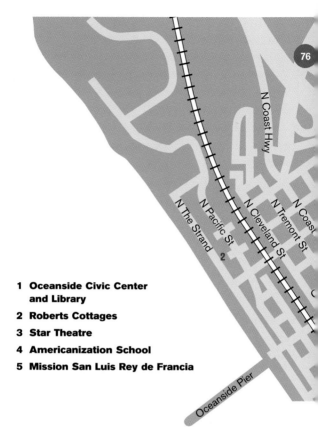

76

1 **Oceanside Civic Center and Library**

2 **Roberts Cottages**

3 **Star Theatre**

4 **Americanization School**

5 **Mission San Luis Rey de Francia**

1 / **Oceanside Civic Center and Library** (1990)

330 N. Coast Highway

CHARLES MOORE

Tapping the spirit of architect Irving Gill—who designed the nearby original City Hall (1934) and Fire Station (1929), now used by the Oceanside

Museum of Art and Historical Society—Moore created a white Deco-meets-Postmodern complex around a plaza featuring an "alluvial fan" of colorful tiles. By comparison, Moore Ruble Yudell's civic center in Escondido from this same period is a more contemporary design for a site where the historical context is not as significant.

2 / **Roberts Cottages** (1928)

704 N. The Strand

Twenty-four salmon-colored oceanfront bungalows offer a romantic counterpoint to some less beautiful newer housing nearby. For years these served as vacation retreats. In the 1950s individual units were first offered for sale—starting at $5,950.

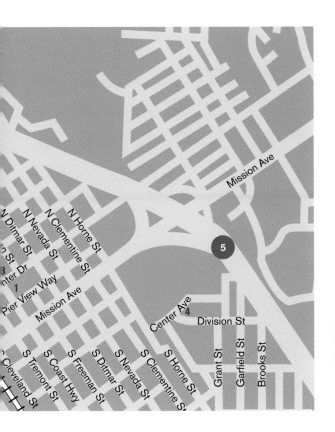

3 / **Star Theatre** (1956)
402 N. Coast Highway

In 2003, the Star was midway through a $4 million renovation that would reinstate the neon-marquee'd movie house to its original status as a downtown landmark, and add shops including a coffeehouse along the south wall. In the process, it was being converted from a film venue to a place for theatrical productions.

4 / **Americanization School** (1930)
1210 Division St.

IRVING GILL

Islamic influences appear in the octagonal-based dome. South-facing classroom doors open to a courtyard.

5 / **Mission San Luis Rey de Francia** (1798)
4050 Mission Ave.

Known as "King of the Missions," this was the 18th and largest of California's 21 missions. Built of adobe brick, original buildings were grouped in a 500-foot quadrangle that covered 6 acres. A pepper tree purported to be California's first, planted here in 1830, still stands here. The asymmetrical front facade, with its corner bell tower, is particularly beautiful, as is the long colonnade that stretches to one side.

Inland/ North County

Ranging east along Interstate 78 from Vista and San Marcos to Escondido, and south along Interstate 15 through Rancho Bernardo, Rancho Penasquitos, Poway, and Scripps Ranch, the Inland North zone contains some of the region's most important historical buildings. Inland North also exemplifies the growing pains inherent in suburban areas where buildings and services are spread out, where creating efficient transportation systems is challenging, and where smaller cities don't always have the political and economic clout to pull off beneficial new projects. Many of these former cowtowns were caught off guard by

the booms of the 1970s, 1980s, and 1990s. Historical buildings were torn down and new buildings went up with little comprehensive planning.

Take Vista, for instance. For decades Vista was a neighborhood where people moved to partake of suburban life: small town atmosphere, open spaces, comfortable single-level ranch houses on generous lots in an area where land is less costly than at the coast.

By the 1980s, however, with the advent of planned communities like Shadowridge, and with more San Diegans choosing to live outside the region's urban core, Vista began a troubled adolescence. Over the years the community preserved its grand 19th century estates: Rancho Guajome and Rancho Buena Vista. But plans to redevelop the town center encountered obstacles. Although big box retailers eventually came in, the hoped-for overhaul of downtown including a mega-plex cinema was slow to generate enough interest that it could be financed and built.

Meanwhile key streets such as Santa Fe Drive and Main Street are in transition between their small town past and a busier future. In this new millenium limbo, with cities eager to attract new business, recent development has sometimes occurred with an eye more toward economics than design. But the good news for architects is that Inland North communities like Vista, San Marcos, and Escondido offer a tabula raza where fresh designs aren't inhibited by the weight of historical precedent.

San Marcos and Escondido have grown up quickly. By landing a new California State University campus, San Marcos instantly established itself as a respectable nexus of academia, business, and culture. Under founding campus architect Al Amado, the first CSUSM buildings were designed in a spare, clean style that updates a Hispanic heritage dating back to the missions and the ranchos.

By simultaneously developing a civic center/business core just across I-78 from the campus, San Marcos, in one fell swoop, put a new "there" there. This brand new city center is destined to have a light-rail transit station, when the new North County trolley line opens late in the first decade of the 2000s.

Escondido has also made mass transit a priority. Architect Rob Quigley's transit center just east of I-15 is a grand civic plaza that points the way toward an efficient future, when buses, trolleys, and cars will come together here, taking a load off freeways.

While other cities in the San Diego region dream about grand new civic centers, Escondido actually built one in only a decade: first a new City Hall designed by PAPA (led by Chuck Slert and Randy Dalrymple), then the new California Center for the Arts, one of the last projects designed by the late Charles Moore.

If congested I-78 has relief in store in the form of a light-rail line, the north-south I-15 corridor has no similar mass transit stroke in its immediate future. There are car pool and commuter/bus lanes and widening plans, but nothing as dramatic as an efficient trolley.

Along I-15, Rancho Bernardo, Poway, and Scripps Ranch tend toward architectural conservatism.

Rancho Bernardo, one of the region's first master-planned communities, is a collection of red tile roofs and earth-toned stucco.

Rancho Penasquitos has conservative tracts that provide comfortable if uninspiring family homes. At a time when other San Diego neighborhoods opted for hip new branch libraries, Scripps Ranch selected a Mission Revival design.

Yet even if Inland North is predominantly a good old-fashioned American family zone, once in awhile architects create a building that rings both the traditional and contemporary bell. Exhibit A is St. Gregory the Great Catholic Church in Scripps Ranch, a gorgeous, finely detailed structure built of concrete—a timeless material with both historical and futuristic implications.

VISTA

1 / **Rancho Buena Vista Adobe** (1845)
651 E. Vista Dr.

One of San Diego's original indigenous buildings, this home in an L-shape around a courtyard has adobe brick walls and rests on a 2-foot-thick cobblestone foundation. It was built on a land grant of 1,184 acres from Gov. Pio Pico to Felipe Subria, a Luiseno Indian who converted to Christianity. Covered outdoor corridors connect rooms and channel cooling breezes. The building is only one room wide, which helps cross ventilation. Despite modernizations including plastering and hardwood and tile floors (the Dons covered dirt floors with Oriental rugs), this grand old home offers an authentic glimpse of life in the Old West. In 1886 Vista Land Company bought a sizeable hunk of the original 4,269-acre rancho and laid out the new town of Vista.

2 / **Rancho Guajome Adobe** (1853)
2210 N. Santa Fe Dr.

Vista's best-kept historic adobe, Rancho Guajome includes a 20-room adobe mansion, as well as out buildings ranging from a blacksmith shop to a chapel. The adobe house has been altered several times, but portions of it still offer an authentic example of original California Rancho design. Legend has it that author Helen Hunt Jackson stayed here while researching her famous novel "Ramona".

3 / **Avo Theater** (1948)
303 E. Vista Way

Modest building in Deco-revival style, re-purposed as the Avo Playhouse after moviegoers flocked to the multiplex. As of 2003, the city was hoping to build its own new megaplex as the centerpiece of downtown redevelopment.

4 / **Bonsall Bridge** (1925)
Old Hwy. 395 at San Luis Rey River

Replaced by higher-capacity, lower-beauty span in 2000, this original concrete bridge is a classic period concerto, with orderly rhythms set in motion by arches that gracefully span the San Luis Rey River. The new bridge nearby is a soulless ribbon of concrete passing through atop plain concrete columns.

5 / **Vista Depot/Chamber of Commerce** (1913)
201 Washington St.

Typical Santa Fe train depot from the period, this preceded the Mission Revival craze that soon dominated California depot design. Moved to this site in 1981, as home to Vista's Chamber of Commerce.

6 / **Lincoln Middle School** (1937)
151 Escondido Ave.

Harking back to the tail end of California's Mission Revival era, the school was one of the best until it was remodeled in the 1990s—without much empathy for the historic style.

7 / **American Legion Building** (1946)
321 S. Santa Fe Ave.
J.A. MURRAY

One of this old main street's few stately period buildings, this two-story flat-roofed white stucco Art Deco building has some unconventional touches, like its modest tower with four slanting sides.

8 / **McCurdy/Morton House** (1928)
1260 Alta Vista Dr.
GORDON B. KAUFMAN

Spanish Colonial Revival style home designed by the architect also responsible for the *Los Angeles Times* building (in L.A. of course), and Santa Anita Racetrack (near Los Angeles).

SAN MARCOS

9 / California State University San Marcos
(1992-present)
333 S. Twin Oaks Valley Rd.

San Diego's newest university campus was founded on a solid modernist base (under the direction of original campus architect Al Amado) from which it is exploring newer directions in architecture. Still young, it will be interesting to see what CSUSM looks like when it has been around as long as SDSU, UCSD, or USD.

* **Craven Hall** (1992). CRSS.
* **University Commons** (1992).
* **Arts Building + Science Hall II** (2002). ROSETTI ARCHITECTS.
* **M. Gordon Clarke Fieldhouse/Student Union** (2003). ROBBINS JORGENSEN CHRISTOPHER.
* **Residence Halls/Commons** (2003). ONYX ARCHITECTS
* **Kellogg Library** (2003). CARRIER JOHNSON and GUNNAR BIRKERTS

---

10 / San Marcos City Hall (1994)
1 Civic Center Dr.
LPA

This modernist edifice signaled the city's coming of age by establishing the new town center.

---

11 / Gateway Office Building (2002)
100 E. San Marcos Blvd.
CONWELL SHONKWILER

Sheathed in glass and reddish Mexican Adoquin stone, this building aims squarely for corporate tenants. Energy-efficient, it uti-

lizes sun-screening glass that admits light and maintains interior temperatures while keeping utility bills low.

---

12 / Old Richland Schoolhouse (1889)
134 Woodland Parkway

A grand Victorian without the usual frills, the community's landmark school has been used for social events in recent years.

13 / **Hollandia Dairy** (1950)
622 E. Mission Rd.

Nearly 100 dairies once operated in
North County, now only a handful
remain including Hollandia. Here you
can view a remnant of the city's
quaint agrarian past, as it moves toward the future with an expanding university campus and civic center. Although this dairy remains, most of its
milk cows were moved to Hanford in Central California in 1999. Historical
buildings here include a house that predates Hollandia.

14 / **The Williams Barn** (1950)
Sycamore Avenue at
Walnut Street

Moved here from its original location
at Mission Avenue and San Marcos
Boulevard, the barn was one of the
city's first commercial structures and
harks back to the region's agricultural past.

15 / **Vallecitos Water District Administrative and Operations Facility** (1998)
201 Vallecitos de Oro
DONALD GILLIS

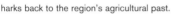

User-friendly building is residential in
character, contrary to the kinds of
buildings usually occupied by municipal utilities. Best of all, it doesn't fall
into the region's usual Mediterranean/Mission cliches.

16 / **Palomar College** (1949)
1140 W. Mission Rd.
C.J. PADEREWSKI & OTHERS

Leading San Diego architect C.J.
Paderewski was vacationing in Hawaii
when he spied his first Buckminster
Fuller dome. A decade later, Paderewski designed what some say was the
West Coast's first geodesic dome—145 feet across, 58 feet high at its peak,
constructed with 575, .081-inch thick, diamond-shaped panels. The durable
dome encloses a pillar-less space of 16,250 square feet, with a capacity of
3,000. Paderewski designed other campus builds, and he collaborated with
art professors Larry Bliss and Ted Kilman on the folksy clock tower: four 70-
foot telephone poles leaning together, crowned by a 4-foot clock with faces
on all four sides that plays music on the hour. More recently, the
Wellness/Fitness Center (1994), designed by Marlene Imirzian, added a
sleek, contemporary structure with a thin roof that curves over to shade a
floor-to-ceiling wall of glass. Imurzian's Student Union opened in 2003.

17 / **North County Corporate Center** (1999)
277 Rancheros Rd.
CONWELL SHONKWILER

An upscale addition to the
growing city's business center.

ESCONDIDO

18 / **Escondido Transit Center** (1990)
700 W. Valley Parkway
ROB QUIGLEY

Exploring his love of unadorned concrete surfaces, Quigley created a park-like collection of outdoor arrival and departure spaces. Landscape, buildings, and circulation combine to mini-mize the impact of big, noisy buses and maximize the pedestrian experience.

19 / **Escondido City Hall** (1988)
201 N. Broadway
PAPA

Conjuring influences that ranged from Balboa Park's Botanical Building to Irving Gill's spare, modernist designs, architects (led by Randy Dalrymple and Charles Slert) from the young San Diego firm PAPA gave the city a beautiful new public centerpiece in historic Grape Day Park. Oriented toward its prominent downtown corner, the diagonal entrance leads visitors through a charming sequence of spaces, from outdoor walk-way, to lathe-covered courtyard, to open-air courtyard with fountain, and finally through any of seven doors that offer Democratic, equal-opportunity access to the seat of city government. This modest building is more invit-ing than Moore Ruble Yudell's adjacent, more elaborate California Center for the Arts.

20 / **California Center for the Arts** (1994)
340 N. Escondido Blvd.
MOORE RUBLE YUDELL

One of the last buildings designed by Moore, CCA combines two per-forming arts spaces with a museum in a campus that is architecturally exciting and frustrating. The plaza in front of the 1,500 seat theater is Moore at his off-kilter best, but the architects never found a way to dis-guise the towering "fly space", which accommodates tall sets for theatri-cal performances. Also, Moore entirely ignored PAPA's original master plan for Grape Day Park, which would have linked the local firm's City Hall to the new arts complex with a diagonal pedestrian promenade across the site. As it turned out, these two public buildings don't relate to each other at all.

21 / **Escondido Medical Arts Center** (1993)
225 E. Second Ave.
RICHARD YEN

A few blocks east of Escondido's new civic center, this modernist courtyard building anchors the city's new medical district. It's a landmark building visible from blocks away, a reassuring symbol that health is as important as governance, arts, and commerce

22 / **San Diego Wild Animal Park** (1972)
15500 San Pasqual Valley Rd.
LIEBHARDT WESTON GOLDMAN AND OTHERS

Due to its expansive site and Liebhardt Weston's meandering plan, the park has a naturalistic aura. Structures including offices, gift shop, animal care center, and aviary defer to gardens, pathways, and outdoor spaces. The architects looked to African villages to create this Nairobi Village, with steep-roofed buildings including the Mombasa Cooker in village-like clusters.

23 / **Daybreak Grove** (1993)
1256 E. Washington Ave.
DAVIDS-KILLORY

The only California building to make *Time* magazine's 1994 list of 10 top American designs, Daybreak Grove has a dignity, grace, and finesse uncommon to low-income housing. In the manner of California bungalow courtyard apartments from the 1920s and 1930s, these modest family homes share a courtyard that provides useable outdoor space and encourages residents to mingle. Overcoming a petition against the project signed by 100 neighbors in this mostly single family neighborhood, this 13-unit project proves that NIMBY-ism, a low budget, and difficult financing don't necessarily have to kill affordable housing.

24 / **Sunrise Place** (1993)
1245 E. Grand Ave.
DAVIDS-KILLORY.

Like nearby Daybreak Grove by the same architects, these simple units for those of modest means are arranged around a common court. Shading trellises and a catchy color scheme add low-cost vitality.

ESCONDIDO

25 / Orange Place Townhomes (1997)
1500 Orange Pl.
STUDIO E

Expanding on their earlier supporting role with Davids/Killory on Sunrise Place and Daybreak Grove, Studio E with this 32-unit project continued the notion of modest, reasonably priced homes that retain a sense of individuality and privacy, and that make pedestrians a higher priority than automobiles.

---

26 / Emerald Garden Townhomes (2001)
425 W. 11th Ave.
STUDIO E

Drawing forms and materials from the surrounding neighborhood, this 16-unit in-fill project retains some of the neighborhood's character, while offering a fresh, thoughtful paradigm for moderately priced rental housing.

---

27 / Eucalyptus View Cooperative Housing (2002)
1805 S. Escondido Blvd.
STUDIO E

Yet another smartly designed low-cost housing project from the Studio E office, featuring a shared garden, and wood trellises and canopies that provide shade and create changing shadow patterns.

---

28 / Escondido Historical District (1890s-1910s)

Bounded by Escondido Boulevard, Fifth Avenue, Chestnut Street, and 13th Street.

The city's original neighborhood has homes ranging from Queen Anne Victorians to Craftsman and Modern dwellings. Sidewalks still bear original street names, such as the intersection of Broadway (formerly Lime) and Fifth (formerly Dakota). District highlight include:

- **The Beech House** (1896), 700 S. Juniper St. Large Victorian built by real estate and insurance agent Albert H. Beach, meticulously renovated during the 1990s.

- **John Lloyd Wright House** (1913), 455 E. Fifth Ave. John Lloyd Wright. Prairie-style residence inspired by Frank Lloyd Wright's 1906 Ladies Home Journal article, the first home designed by Wright's son John.

- **Hooper House** (1887), 1006 S. Juniper St. Italianate Victorian slightly flawed due to stuccoed over brick, and a kitchen addition in the back.

ESCONDIDO HISTORICAL DISTRICT CONTINUES NEXT PAGE

Escondido Historical District (continued)

- **Thomas-Turrentine House**
(1887), 208 E. Fifth Ave. Queen
Anne Victorian with a Classical
Revival addition on the east side,
originally the home of G.V.
Thomas, founder of Escondido
Land & Town Company and origi-
nal developer of the city.
Occupied today by the family's
fourth generation.

29 / Plymouth Hall (1925)
240 S. Maple St.
LOUIS J. GILL
Mediterranean Revival design by
Irving Gill's nephew.

30 / Schnack-Trenton Apartments (1912)

200 E. Second Ave.
Escondido first apartments, built
for photographer Peter Schnack,
arranged in a circle around a
courtyard.

31 / Wohlford-Ting House (1910)
209 E. Fourth Ave.
Craftsman home built for Alvin W.
Wohlford, namesake of the
Escondido lake.

32 / Laundromat (c. 1940)
1214 S. Escondido Blvd.

Sleek Streamline Moderne building
with rounded corners and flat roof.

33 / Heritage Walk Museum (1890s)
in Grape Day Park, 321 N. Broadway

This collection of eight historical
structures moved to the park at the
civic center includes the city's original library (1895); a steep-roofed
Victorian country home (1890)

designed by architect Jesse Pomeroy; a restored barn (1901) and blacksmith shop (1908); and the Santa Fe Depot (1888), in the Stick style with
fishscale shingles and shiplap siding.

ESCONDIDO/1-15 CORRIDOR

34 / Harrah's Rincon Casino & Resort (2002)
777 Harrah's Rincon Way, Valley Center
PAUL STEELMAN

Gaming industry veteran Steelman brings his profit-making design abilities to San Diego with this pink stucco gambling mecca, which includes four themed restaurants. The architect's goal is to make buildings that make money for their own- ers. That means creating a "theme experience", carried out in a way that "stimulates and delights the mind while generating a mood." Presumably a gambling mood. "A theme has to promote comfort, security, and optimism while being stylish".

35 / Pala Mission (1816) and Casino (2001)
11154 Highway 76, Pala

KLAI::JUBA (CASINO)

From the sacred to the—well, to the profitable. The mission here offers anoth- er design variation among 21 California missions. Designed by architects who also worked on Mandalay Bay, Excalibur, Luxor, and the MGM Grand in Las Vegas, Pala's casino is among several on San Diego reservations, giving locals a miniature taste of Vegas.

36 / Los Penasquitos Adobe (1823)
12020 Black Mountain Rd.
At the eastern end of Penasquitos Canyon, another historical remnant from California's rancho era, when 4,243 acres here were occupied by a cattle ranch.

37 / Canyonside Recreation Center (1993)
12350 Black Mountain Rd.
LEE PLATT/MATT WELLS WITH SPURLOCK POIRIER
(LANDSCAPE ARCHITECTS) AND CHRISTINE OATMAN (ARTIST).

Experimental and successful collab- oration between architect, land- scape architect, and artist, wherein the "art" became an integral part of the planning and design.

38 / Carmel Mountain Ranch Community Library (1999)
12095 World Trade Center Dr.
M.W. STEELE GROUP

This planned community's only major public building also serves as its community center and "town square".

1-15 CORRIDOR

39 / Scripps Ranch Community Recreation Center (2000)
11454 Blue Cypress Dr.
RNP

Steel, masonry, and glass come together in a modernist structure that pro-
vides a much-needed jolt of newness in this conservative community.
Horizontal banks of windows provide good natural light inside, and provide transparency that lessens this building's impact.

40 / St. Gregory the Great Catholic Church (2000)
11451 Blue Cypress Dr.
HYNDMAN & HYNDMAN.

You don't think of them as being progressive, but in the late 1990s those
Catholics began commissioning some
cool new West Coast buildings. This copper-domed beauty is a lesson in
creative use of concrete—not only for walls, but for a floors and other surfaces, in a variety of colors and textures that provide the richness that
used to come from fabrics, carpets, and delicate decoration, but with the
added durability of concrete. Combining modern lines with neo-classical
details, this church captures the 100-year-old spirit of the Bay Area's
Bernard Maybeck, known for his beautiful and eclectic designs.

41 / Scripps/Miramar Ranch Library (1993)
10301 Scripps Lake Dr.
BUNDY & THOMPSON

The Scripps name goes back to the
founders of the newspaper chain and
the La Jolla matron of the arts who
launched an art museum in a home designed for her by Irving Gill. In
Scripps Ranch, artifacts from the historical Meanley (connected by marriage to the Scripps family) residence were incorporated into this Mission
Revival style building.

42 / Fire Station #37 (2001)
11640 Spring Canyon Rd.
JEFF KATZ

The front is detailed with Carolina
stone, and firefighters enjoy cedar-lined closets, a home theater, and a
gym. The only thing old fashioned about this fire station praised by residents for its sensitivity to surroundings is its good old fire pole.

43 / Miramar College Aquatic Center (1999)
10440 Black Mountain Rd.
BUNDY & THOMPSON

Designed for both public and college
use, the pool complex is enclosed by
concrete and concrete block wall topped by an awning supported by orange
steel beams. Carefully detailed, elegantly proportioned, the project proves
that a public building can give something both to its users and to the greater
community outside.

East County

Lasso a few small midwestern towns and plunk them down in San Diego's expansive eastern reaches, and you'll have a semblance of East County, an area least effected by the greater region's contemporary boom. From Lakeside to La Mesa, Santee to Spring Valley and Lemon Grove, there's a slower pace to life. Even in El Cajon, largest of East County's cities, the main street looks much the same as it has for decades: a mix of buildings from the 1890s through 1930s, many of them in transition, awaiting whatever comes next.

Beyond East County, California's wide open desert stretches to the Arizona border; there's a raw Old West aura: the sweeping panorama of sky and green valleys, mountains that rise up quickly to the east, dark storms that blow in suddenly from the great beyond. Out here, it is still possible to see livestock grazing, and Lakeside still holds a popular annual rodeo. Western artist Olaf Wieghorst lived and worked in El Cajon and captured the essence of the place in his paintings.

Because East County has grown gradually, many fine older buildings remain: Victorians in downtown La Mesa, a theater in Lakeside reborn as a theatrical playhouse, the Santee Drive-In, last of a dying breed. In the Old West, vast tracts of East County were part of Mission San Diego de Alcala's holdings. Santee's Old Mission Dam stands as a monument where Father Junipero Serra tapped a water supply for the mission.

History remains, but the future arrives. Thanks to an existing railroad right-of-way that had gone unused, East
County was connected to downtown a decade ago by a
light-rail trolley line. Mt. Helix in La Mesa provides homeowners with twinkling night views of the downtown skyline
and Coronado Bridge, as well as sweeping back-country
scenes. Residents can ride the rails to San Diego's urban
center in minutes,
for work, shop-
ping, or culture.
New mixed-use
centers like
Santee's Trolley
Square take
advantage of tran-
sit station traffic.

As San Diego has grown and coastal home prices have
gone through the roof, East County has remained more
affordable. Architecturally, homes here tend toward the traditional. Classic California ranch houses arranged around
courtyards can be seen in numerous variations, ranging
from wood-and-shingle to stucco and adobe brick. East
County's hillsides challenge architects to come up with
creative designs, and because East County has some of
San Diego's most extreme weather, it has also inspired
ingenious energy-conserving designs such as pioneering
straw bale houses.

In a new millenium, much of East County's economic
might is centered at Native American reservations
such as Barona, Campo, Viejas, and Sycuan, where
legalized gambling has transformed sleepy, depressed
communities into financial powerhouses. Big bright
buildings and neon signs have materialized like cher-
ries, bananas, and lemons from a slot machine dream.

LA MESA/SPRING VALLEY/LEMON GROVE

1 / La Mesa Community Center (1984)
4975 Memorial Dr.
BRADSHAW BUNDY

As usual these architects do a fine job suiting the design to the community and context. The adjacent historical Nan Couts Cottage is a cozy meeting space with bowed beams supporting the tall ceiling.

---

2 / Grossmont Hospital Women's Center (1990)
5555 Grossmont Center Dr.
THE DESIGN PARTNERSHIP

Aimed to meet women's needs at all stages of life, the center utilizes residential forms to personalize a variety of experiences including childbirth.

---

3 / La Mesa Village/Euro Theme (1970s)
GEORGE FELIX

After Felix led a Euro village makeover of downtown with new facades, sidewalks, and landscaping, the annual Oktoberfest and Old-Fashioned Christmas became the first of several new annual events that bring the community together.

---

4 / La Mesa Depot (1894)
4695 Nebo Dr.

Typical California train station, from a time before the Mission Revival style became popular for depots 20 years later.

5 / Methodist/ Episcopal Church (1921)
4690 Palm Ave.
ARTHUR G. LINDLEY

Spanish Colonial revival, in all its romantic glory.

6 / First National Trust & Savings/ County Records Center (1941)
4757 Palm Ave.
A.O. TREGANZA

Cool Deco building with a pre-cast concrete facade featuring bands of decorative foliage.

7 / Old La Mesa Store (1894)
8241-8249 La Mesa Blvd.

Major additions have changed this structure over the years, but the decorative dark wood eave and dentils reveal its Victorian heritage.

8 / La Mesa Drug Store (1921)
8301 La Mesa Blvd.

On a prime commercial corner, this two-story concrete building is a solid retail anchor that seduces shoppers with neon signage and merchandise displayed behind large ground-level windows.

9 / Bank of Southern California (1927)
8302 La Mesa Blvd.

Concrete and stucco, used to mimic rusticated stone. Red tile roof and arches add Spanish/ Neo-classical flavors.

10 / Farrell's Jewelry/Pretty and Plump (1928)
8333 La Mesa Blvd.

Parapeted entry, urn-like finials, and carved wood window frames make this one of the village's finest buildings from the days depicted by American artist Edward Hopper.

LA MESA/SPRING VALLEY/LEMON GROVE

11 / Erickson-Anderson Mortuary (1930)
8390 Allison Ave.
WILLIAM WHEELER

Elegant WPA-era building, mixes Mediterranean with modern.

12 / Rev. Henry A. McKinney House (1908)
8369 University Ave.

Grand, sleek two-story home from a time when California began moving away from frilly Victorian designs and styles imported from the East Coast and Europe.

13 / Owen Wister House (1910)
9499 El Granito Ave.
MEAD & REQUA

Finely detailed Craftsman home with dark wood siding, exposed rafter tails, and stone walls and steps, with wooden ladders incorporated as a fire safety feature.

14 / Schumann-Heink House (1913)
9951 El Granito Ave.
DEL HARRIS

Built on a base of granite boulders, the home features a blue granite Romanesque first floor with a stucco second story. Some additions have been made.

15 / Grossmont Cottages/Wray House (1909)
9772 Evans Pl.
EMMOR BROOKE WEAVER

Wood-shingled, hip- and gable-roofed Craftsman cottages from Weaver's prime, using fieldstone and dark-stained board-and-batten siding.

16 / Norman/Davis House (1927)
9840 Grosalia Ave.

French Country cottage constructed from hand-cut stone, with a steep shake shingle roof, multi-pane windows, and brick chimney.

17 / **Hill House** (1917)
5310 Valle Vista Dr.
WHEELER AND HALLEY

Craftsman home built of shiplap siding, with exposed beams and stone chimney, cozily snuggled into a boulder-strewn site.

18 / **Bunting House** (1930)
9217 Virginian Ln.

Broad-eaved stone cottage, as rustic as the homes of national park rangers.

19 / **Bancroft Ranch House** (1863)
9050 Memory Ln., Spring Valley

Judge Augustus S. Ensworth built the modest adobe, Rufus King Porter bought the home on 160 acres for $400 in 1865, Porter sold it to Hubert Howe Bancroft in 1885. Naming his place Helix Farms, Bancroft planted guavas, palms, olives, citrus, almonds, raspberries, blackberries, and currents, and later built a home on a nearby hill and a rock house near the spring. In the early 1900s Helix Farms was one of the state's largest olive ranches. Wood used for beams and doorways came from the ship *Clarissa Andrews,* which ran aground in San Diego Harbor.

20 / **Lemon Grove Senior Center** (1990)
8235 Mt. Vernon St.
VISIONS ARCHITECTS

Dynamic, energetic design by San Diego architect Richard Friedson, a refreshing arrival in the neighborhood, perhaps a bit beyond comprehension by its users.

EL CAJON

21 / Knox Hotel/Historical Museum (1876)
280 N. Magnolia Ave.

Simple wood-sided hotel was one of downtown's earliest buildings and now serves as a museum.

22 / Grossmont High School (1922)
1100 Murray Dr.
THEO C. KISTNER

Grand old ivy-covered structure, built with locally quarried granite, with flat roofs, a Gothic entry arch, and multi-paned casement windows topped by breeze-grabbing transom windows.

23 / Fire Station #8 (1958)
843 N. Third St.
ARTHUR DECKER

Catchy 1950s design with a folded-over roof resembling Los Angeles "Googie" coffee shops from that era.

24 / Olaf Wieghorst Museum and Studio (1945)
131 Rea Ave.

Rustic wood ranch-style home captures both the flavor of vernacular architecture here, and the spirit of this great western artist collected by history buffs including Pres. Ronald Reagan.

LAKESIDE/SANTEE

25 / Olde Community Church (1896)
9906 Maine St.

Lakeside's first church still stands; additions have been made over the years, but the original building, with its perpendicular gable roofs intersecting in a bell tower, is still the centerpiece, sporting its original stained glass windows and pews.

26 / Lakeside/Lindo Hotel (1887)
Sycamore Avenue and River Street

Moved here from its original location on the south side of Sycamore behind the Old Lakeside Store, the two-story building began as a boarding house for construction workers on the San Diego-Cuyamaca Eastern Railroad.

27 / Castle House (1887)
12747 Castle Court Dr.

Lakeside's first home was built from Oregon redwood, in the Queen Anne style with diamond-shaped shingles and colored glass window panes.

28 / Rancho Barona/Blessed Virgin Mary Church + Concrete Cottages (1932)
1000 Wildcat Canyon Rd.

IRVING GILL

To see this beautiful modest chapel and small low-cost homes (many of them substantially altered) is to step inside Gill's head and imagine his ideal of clean, modern living at a reasonable price.

29 / Santee Drive-In (1958)
10990 Woodside Ave.

When it opened at the peak of America's fascination with watching movies from cars, the drive-in was one of 5,000 across the country. By the 1990s, less than 1,000 remained, and Santee's was one of the last in San Diego.

30 / Desert Tower (1922-1928)
Interstate 8/In-Ko-Pah exit/Jacumba

Bert Vaughn, who owned the town of Jacumba, built this 70-foot stone tower by hand beginning in 1922—a tribute to pioneers who made the treacherous trek west through Arizona and California across sizzling deserts. Don't miss the boulder garden: huge hunks of granite chiseled into snakes, lizards, and human skulls, during the Depression.

OTHER EAST COUNTY

31 / **Jacumba** (1920s)
Old Highway 80

Yes, San Diego has a cool ghost town. The grand hotel at Jacumba Hot Springs burned down in 1942, but you can still take a dip in hot baths at a smaller hotel nearby—after you wander among the burned out ruins (including what remains of the 1919 train depot) of this once-popular place frequented by stars like Clark Gable.

32 / **Campo Store** (1885)
Highway 94 at Campo Creek

Built by Silas and Luman Gaskill, the store was part of a complex including a black-smith shop, hotel, and flour mill. Campo was a small railroad town; a railroad museum is nearby.

33 / **Anza-Borrego Visitors Center** (1979)
200 Palm Canyon Dr.
ROBERT FERRIS

Deferring to its spectacular locale, this wood and stone build-ing merges into the ground, with a landscaped roof that makes it virtually invisible from some angles.

34 / **Julian Hotel** (1897)
2032 Main St.

Opened as the Hotel Robinson by Margaret and Albert Robinson (a freed Missouri slave), the hotel is a rare artifact of African-American history in San Diego County, as well as a place where numerous celebrities and politicans signed the guest register over the years.

35 / **Julian Drug Store** (1886)
2134 Main St.

In the old days, horse-drawn car-riages pulled up and families went inside for a soda at the old fashion marble-topped bar. Today you can still sidle up to the counter for an ice cream or milk shake. Also see a dozen or so other historical public buildings and homes in the heart of downtown Julian.

36 / **Amy Strong Castle** (1921)
At Mt. Woodson Country Club/Ramona
JOHN VAWTER AND EMMOR BROOKE WEAVER

Spectacular 27-room, 12,000-square-foot granite manse built by the San Diego seamstress/entrepreneur.

37 / **Campo Mill** (1920s)
Highway 94 two miles east of Campo Creek

Felspar from Campo's mines was milled here by Sanitary Standard Manufacturing, for use in their popular lines of bathroom fixtures. Today, the building is occupied by the Motor Transport Museum: check out their collection of vintage trucks. Contemplating the ascending rhythm of three gables, and the contrast between the angular mill and adjacent cylindrical water tower, one understands why architects ranging from San Francisco's William Wurster to San Diego's own Rob Quigley and Ted Smith have found inspiration in humble vernacular buildings.

38 / **Spencer Valley School** (1876)
Highway 78 at Wynola

Still this district's lone schoolhouse, this East Coast-style shiplap structure doubles as the town's historical museum.

39 / **Witch Creek School/Julian Library** (1888)
Southwest corner of 4th Avenue and Washington Street (behind the town's museum)

In Witch Creek, this one-room schoolhouse opened at a time when there were at least 10 one-teacher schools in the Julian area. It served this ranching community until 1954, and was relocated to Julian in 1974 where it became a branch library.

40 / **Kidwell Residence/Straw Bale House** (1999)
3696 Alta Loma Dr. Jamul
DREW HUBBELL

Straw bale construction consists of 2-foot-thick walls of straw bales covered with plaster. To date, Drew Hubbell (James Hubbell's son and frequent collaborator) has built nine straw bale homes in the San Diego region. The cost is comparable to conventional construction—but the cost to the environment is far less. Straw bales are a renewable resource. Straw is also a great insulator, retaining interior heat during cold months, warding off exterior heat during summers. This pale gold mission-inspired design features arches, a tower, and a corrugated metal roof.

41 / **Hubbell House + Studio** (1958-present)
Santa Ysabel
JAMES HUBBELL

Designed and built by San Diego artist-architect, James Hubbell, this hilltop retreat on a secluded site has inspired its many visitors over the years. Built over several decades, the complex combines tile, stone, concrete, wood, shells, and other basic materials to achieve the organic, nature-inspired forms that have become Hubbell's trademark. There is usually a studio tour held each June. For more information and to join the mailing list, please visit the website: www.hubbellandhubbell.com

South Bay

Closest to the border among this region's communities, the South Bay has a diverse heritage that ranges from pioneer aviators on Otay Mesa, to National City's railroad boom, bayfront shipyards, and the steady stream of Mexican immigrants who settled here to provide the backbone of the region's labor force.

Volatile politics and a nearby border where thousands cross each day have forced South Bay to rise above the tensions and fears that plague anyplace where diverse cultures exist side by side. Cities such as Chula Vista have done an admirable job planning for the future. While South

Bay has been slow to attract new investment, Chula Vista has a very inviting downtown that mixes period buildings with newer businesses. Chula Vista also has the region's finest major outdoor entertainment venue: Coors Amphitheatre.

South Bay was the first San Diego region to benefit from a light-rail trolley line, which in the 1980s connected downtown San Diego to the border, with stops in National City, Chula Vista, and San Ysidro.

As land costs rose during the 1980s and buildable land became scarce, homebuilders looked to South Bay as a land of opportunity. Planners worked with them on two exemplary planned communities: EastLake and Otay Ranch. Unlike earlier San Diego tracts that sprang up overnight and lacked essential services, these two grew up gracefully, with parks, schools, and libraries accompanying the arrival of populous residential neighborhoods. Otay Ranch incorporated suggestions made by San Francisco-Bay Area architect and planning guru Peter Calthorpe, who helped create a user-friendly, pedestrian-oriented community.

UNBUILT

Architecturally, South Bay ranges from a cool contemporary nature interpretive center on the former site of a bayside gunpowder factory, to Mexican architect Ricardo Legorreta's colorful South Chula Vista Library, and several fine Victorians in National City. National City long ago demolished a stately, turn-of-the-century Carnegie library, but other historical buildings including the original train station remain. Here, too, is the commercial glitz of the Miles of Cars auto row.

On both sides of the border, architects have experimented with plans drawn from the area's rich fabric: on a clear day Tijuana's brightly colored hillside colonias are visible. Newer South Bay designs range from spare modern structures in concrete and stucco, to miles and miles of malls in pseudo-Spanish or econo-stucco-box styles.

NATIONAL CITY

1 / **Granger Music Hall** (c. 1896)
1615 E. Fourth St.
HEBBARD & GILL

Ralph Granger struck silver in Colorado and built a family estate here, including a private recital hall with a ceiling mural depicting the muses Euterpe and Erato.

2 / **St. Matthews Episcopal Church** (c. 1887)
521 E. Eighth St.
WILLIAM HERMAN

Rare South Bay example of English Country style.

3 / **Brick Row on Heritage Square** (1887)
909 A Ave.
R.C. BALL

Designed by the same architect responsible for Folsom Prison (where Johnny Cash recorded one of his finest albums), these 10 rowhomes were built for Santa Fe Railroad executives, in the style of similar buildings on the East Coast.

4 / **Santa Fe Depot** (c. 1882)
922 W. 23rd St.
W.A. STRATTON

Original transcontinental railroad terminus, hub of National City's 1880s boom.

5 / **Coors Amphitheatre** (1998)
2050 Entertainment Circle

BILL BETHMANN/HNTB-JIM KIER

The region's finest large outdoor music venue (20,000 seats), and the first amphitheater in the U.S. designed to meet all ADA requirements for wheelchair and disabled access. It has excellent sight lines, plenty of legroom, smooth pedestrian circulation—and best of all, a design incorporating the latest big-screens and sound equipment that make catching Dylan or Eminem a prime live experience.

6 / **Melville Block** (1920s)
301-301 Third Ave.

A mainstay of the original downtown, this Asian-flavored building originally housed a bank/real estate office, bakery, millinery, and meat market.

7 / **Edward Gillette House** (1895)
44 N. Second Ave.

This Queen Anne, featuring a sizeable tower with widow walk, was one of Chula Vista's original Orchard Houses, at a time with Southern California was covered with citrus groves.

8 / **Chula Vista Women's Club** (1928)
357 G St.

EDGAR V. ULLRICH

Spanish Colonial design by the architect also responsible for St. Charles Borromeo Church in Pt. Loma, Casa de Manana Hotel in La Jolla, and an early building at San Diego State University.

CHULA VISTA/OTAY MESA

9 / **South Chula Vista Library** (1992)
389 Orange Ave.
RICARDO LEGORRETA

Colorful modernist design by the Mexican master, captures the border spirit while providing well-lit interiors that look out on courtyards and gardens.

---

10 / **Norman Park Senior Center** (1992)
270 F St.
VISIONS STUDIO

Old folks don't necessarily want stodgy buildings, especially at a time when folks in their sixties were actually a part of the sixties. Architect Richard Friedson's design features spare, powerful volumes dynamically connected to outdoor spaces.

---

11 / **Edmund Russ House** (c. 1930)
200 K St.

Wonderful wavy parapet distinguishes this small Mission Revival bungalow.

---

12 / **Fire Station #43** (1996)
1590 La Media Rd.
ROBBINS JORGENSEN CHRISTOPHER

Combining a hangar-like curved roof drawn from local aviation history, with

a home-like residence for firefighters, this 10,000-square-foot station serving Brown Field and the Otay industrial area proves that fire stations can become public landmarks as inviting as libraries, schools, and city halls.

---

13 / **Otay Mesa Branch Library** (1985)
3003 Coronado Ave.
DEEMS LEWIS

One of the region's few "green" branch libraries, this building has a distinctive sawtooth roof with clerestories that scoop in natural light and ocean breezes.

OTAY MESA/SAN YSIDRO

14 / El Toreador Motel (1920s)
631 E. San Ysidro Blvd.

Once a romantic Mission Revival motel immortalized in postcards (including one depicting the motel's "Traditional Good Luck Wishing Well"), only a portion of the historic building has been preserved, with the rest of the site now occupied by a strip mall.

15 / Casa Familiar/Living Rooms at the Border
(2000/UNBUILT)

ESTUDIO TEDDY CRUZ

Revitalization project for central San Ysidro. A three-stage, eight-year plan calls for renovating the heart of this border town by rezoning to promote higher density, mixed-use, and affordable housing. Phase One includes renovating a historical church into a community center, and a new public garden. Phase Two adds a concrete frame arbor in the garden. Phase Three adds affordable housing atop this concrete frame.

16 / Auxiliary Naval Air Station Brown Field
Historic District (1941-1945)
1424 Continental St.

Representative of San Diego's essential contribution to aviation during the war effort, this district surrounding the WWII-era fire station also includes the original control tower and four "nose end" hangars housing service bays and offices, with roofs resting on laminated wood piers and triangular laminated wood trusses. Otay Mesa's aviation history dates from its use as an airfield during WWI.

17 / San Ysidro Free Library (1924)
101-105 San Ysidro Blvd.

Jewel-like example of this era's popular Mission Revival style, from a time when community benefactor Frank Beyer built the Civic Center on Hall Avenue, as well as donating land for this library, for Our Lady of Mount Carmel Church, and for Sunset School.

Tijuana

In the days when Baja and Alta were one California, the village of Tia Juana (Aunt Juana) became part of the San Diego mission's holdings. Following the Mexican-American War, the Guadalupe Hidalgo Treaty of 1848 divided these lands between the two countries, with Tijuana on the south side of the border.

But Americans continued to spend time in Mexico. In the 1870s, they crossed the border in search of gold in the mines of Real del Castillo near Ensenada. The binational San Diego and Arizona Railroad line crossed through Tijuana and Tecate. In the early 20th century, Tijuana became a popular tourist destination known for the resort

of Agua Caliente Hot Springs. American Prohibition from 1920 to 1933 helped popularize Tijuana's casinos and bars.

The city's unusual street patterns began with a map made when Tia Juana Ranch was divided in 1889. The map proposed a city of "Zaragoza," with diagonal streets departing from plazas, surrounded by a rectilinear grid of streets and plazas more common in America. Only a small portion of the map was developed, but remnants remain, such as the diagonal street Arguello, renamed Santa Cecilia Plaza in 1980.

Avenida Revolucion—known originally as Olvera Street, and part of the grid pattern—became a tourist mecca of hotels, bars, restaurants, and souvenir shops within walking distance of the border. As San Diego's military population boomed during and after World War II, Tijuana found a whole new market for its night life. Some businesses thrived, but as the town grew into a major metropolis, it struggled to shed its reputation as an all-night, anything-goes party spot.

Tijuana was officially incorporated as a city in 1940. In 1948, the inauguration of the Sonora-Baja California railroad and the national highway strengthened the city's ties

with the rest of Mexico, and shifted economic and cultural relationships with San Diego. In the 1960s, American corporations began taking advantage of low-cost Mexican labor, and a border economy built on maquiladoras developed. The "maquilas" are "twin plants", where companies set up manufacturing in Tijuana, with distribution and administration on the San Diego  side. In recent decades, Tijuana became Mexico's fastest growing city.

Architecturally, the city is a mix of historical, modernist, and contemporary designs, as well as vernacular structures such as roadside fish taco stands, Euro-style public parks with bronze statues of heroes, and exotic folk art such as a multi-story artist's home in the form of a nude woman.

Tijuana's landmarks include two bullrings, remnants of Agua Caliente Casino, the modernist downtown cultural center with a spherical IMAX theater as its centerpiece, and splashes of fruit salad colors everywhere.

Over the past decade, through the American Institute of Architects San Diego, and its Tijuana counterpart, the Colegio de Arquitectos, and through connections made between various colleges and universities on both sides of the border, a new spirit of cooperation and collaboration has grown among planning and design professionals. People who devote their lives to creating homes, neighborhoods, and cities are beginning to realize that in a global cyber-connected economy, Tijuana and San Diego are essentially one metropolis, divided by a line.

Tijuana Locations

1 **Plaza Santa Cecilia**

2 **La Comercial**

3 **Old Municipal Palace/Woolworth Building**

4 **Jai Alai Palace**

5 **Torremol**

6 **Tijuana Cultural Center**

7 **Floreria Jardin**

8 **Bullring**

9 **Iglesia del Espiritu Santo – Holy Spirit Church**

10 **Agua Caliente Casino**

11 **Tijuana Tercer Milenio (La Mona)**

12 **Student Center/UABC-Tijuana**

13 **Plaza Mundo Divertido**

14 **Bujazan Movie Theatre**

15 **Playas de Tijuana Binational Area +
Border Monument**

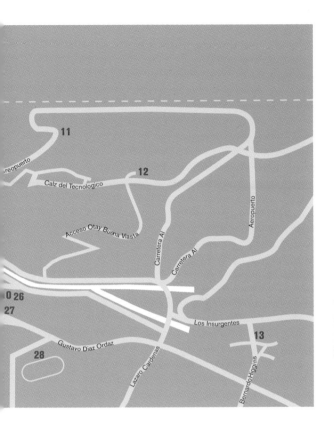

16 **Craftsman Bungalows**

17 **Cathedral**

18 **Cinco de Mayo Building**

19 **The Clock**

20 **Caesar's Hotel**

21 **Electrical Company Building**

22 **Francis Hotel**

23 **The Border Gate Building**

24 **Train Station**

25 **Medical Specialties, IMSS**

26 **Agua Caliente Bungalows**

27 **Lazaro Cardenas High School**

28 **Agua Caliente Racetrack**

1 / Plaza Santa Cecilia

One of the few diagonal streets remaining from the years following 1889, when Tia Juana Ranch was divided to resolve a legal dispute amongst the Argüello family, this boulevard departed from the rectilinear grid pattern of streets that characterizes most American cities and much of Tijuana. Completion of the "Reloj Monumental" arch (visible for miles around on both sides of the border) at the turn of the millenium signified the city's emerging identity as a binational metropolis involved in the global economy.

2 / La Comercial
(1887-1920s)

Eclectic with Italian renaissance details such as the floral relief sur-rounding the clock, this prime cor-ner building was inspired by the architecture of Mexico City. Destroyed by fire in 1925, it was rebuilt in 1928. This site was origi-nally home to the "Big Curious Store" owned by Mr. Jorge Ibs. Later, the building was headquarters for the producer of Mexicali Beer, followed in 1939 by Banco de Baja de Baja California, S.A. In 1963 the International Bank was installed there and now is the Banco Bital.

3 / Old Municipal Palace/Woolworth Building
(1921)

Calle Segunda (Second Street) and Avenida Constitucion (Constitution Avenue)
QUAYLE BROTHERS

Built in neoclassical style, at the request of North District of Baja Gov. Epigmeo Ibarra, remodeled in Mexican colonial style in the 1950s. Occupied since 2000 by the Instituto Municipal de Arte y Cultura (IMAC).

4 / **Jai Alai Palace** (1929-1947)
Avenida Revolucion & Calle Septima (7th Street)

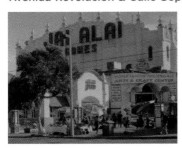

Built in the indigenous "mud jar" style, this was a prime tourist attraction in the 1930s and 1940s, before it burned down in 1959 and was reconstructed in only seven months. The statue of the athlete playing "El Pelotari" is by sculptor Eduardo Corrella.

5 / **Torremol** (1989)
Ave. Paseo de Los Heroes, and Francisco Javier Mina, Zona Del Rio
LUIS LICEAGA CAMPOS

One of the first mid-rise buildings in Tijuana, designed in a contemporary/modernist style, it includes a multi-floor atrium that would make Donald Trump proud.

6 / **Tijuana Cultural Center** (1982)
Avenida de Los Heroes, and Francisco Javier Mina. Zona del Rio
MANUEL ROSEN AND PEDRO RAMIREZ VASQUEZ

Bold, modernist design with a globe-shaped IMAX theatre as its centerpiece, at the edge of a broad public plaza. It includes a multi-purpose theater, and both ecological and historical museums.

7 / **Floreria Jardin** (2001)
Josefa Ortiz de Dominguez #1302 Zona Del Rio
MIGUEL ROBLES DURAN

Representing a new wave of fresh architecture in Tijuana, this small flower shop harks back to the simple, bold modernism of both Mexican architects and Californians such as R. M. Schindler in Los Angeles.

Floreria Jardin was one of the first buildings from this new generation to win an award from San Diego's American Institute of Architects chapter.

8 / **Bullring** (1938, 1957)

One of the world's most famous venues to enjoy the colorful and thrilling spectacle of the "Fiesta Brava", or bull fight. One of two bullrings in Tijuana (the other is "La Monumental", next to the Pacific Ocean), it was built in 1938 entirely of wood construction. Completely destroyed during a fire, it was re-built in 1957 with a metal structure.

9 / **Iglesia del Espiritu Santo – Holy Spirit Church** (1940s)

MARCO ANTONIO SANDOVAL
EDWARD CASTA (CO-DESIGNER AND
BUILDING DIRECTOR)

Nesting arches interspersed with colored-glass clerestories create a sculptural interior washed with bands of color that change throughout the day. When the cathedral opened, this was one of Tijuana's wealthiest neighborhoods.

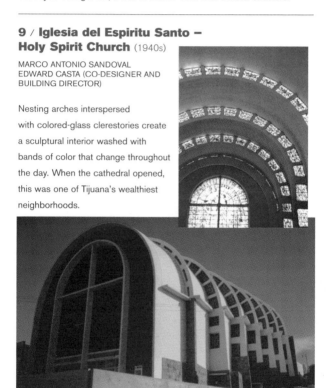

10 / **Agua Caliente Casino** (1920s)

WAYNE AND CORINNE MACALLISTER

Originally a hot springs resort, Agua Caliente became a popular Hollywood and celebrity hangout, when the Mediterranean Revival style hotel was added in the 1920s. Today the site is mostly ruins, but you can still view the remains of an Olympic-size pool with Alhambra-inspired decoration. In 1939, the site was acquired by the government for educational use, which continues today. Nearby, at the corner of Boulevard Agua Caliente and Avenida Fundadores, is a 22-meter replica (1988) of the resort's original tower. The "Monument to the Text Book" now stands nearby on the original tower's site, in front of a classic 1950s diner today occupied by El Potrero restaurant.

11 / Tijuana Tercer Milenio (La Mona) (1990)

In the colonia near the airport
ARMANDO MUNOZ GARCIA

This sexy, 50-foot-woman of a house was built over a two-year-period, using concrete and steel, covered with fiberglass and clay. Beneath her curves are a kitchen, bedroom, bathroom, living room, and dining room. Gov. Ernesto Ruffo Appel inaugurated this lady as a monument to the city's anniversary in 1990.

12 / Student Center/UABC-Tijuana (1998)

14418 Calzada Tecnologico
JAIME BRAMBILA WITH DEPARTMENT OF PROJECTS AND CONSTRUCTION/UABC

Contemporary showplace of this campus, this project marks a significant departure from the institutional guidelines imposed on all previous university/educational architecture. Outdoor corridors and plazas connect buildings and take advantage of temperate climate.

13 / Plaza Mundo Divertido (2000)

Via Rapida Poniente #1538 Fracc. San Jose
BEJAR ARQUITECTOS

Colorful neo-modernist strip shopping center, from Mexico's neo-modernist movement, utilizing bold textures, forms, and materials. In the spirit of its U.S. counterparts, this center combines retail uses with diversions such as interactive games, movie theaters, a bowling alley, and an elevated train that circles the complex.

14 / Bujazan Movie Theatre (1949-1951)
Art nouveau theater from the post-WWII boom years.

15 / Playas de Tijuana Binational Area + Border Monument (1959)
First came a seaside bullring and surrounding colonia. The marble monument marks the U.S./Mexico border agreed upon in the Guadalupe Treaty of 1849. There are also a lighthouse and park here. To the north is the U.S.'s own Borderfield Park and Natural Reserve.

16 / Craftsman Bungalows (1910s, 1920s)

Along First, Second, and Third Streets downtown; and around Teniente Guerrero Park
Craftsman-style dwellings similar to their peers north of the border.

17 / **Cathedral** (1902-1964)
Calle Segunda (Second Street) and Avenida Ninos Heroes
The original wood church hosted its first mass in 1902. It was remodeled and expanded in the early 1930s, and again beginning in 1949. It became a cathedral after the most recentphase of construction was completed in 1964.

18 / **Cinco de Mayo Building** (1918-1919)
Calle Segunda (Second Street), in front of the former Municipal Palace.
Tijuana's first mixed-commercial building was occupied by offices and retail stores.

19 / **The Clock** (1943)
Second Street next to former Municipal Palace
Built in Pennsylvania by Seth Thomas, originally located in front of La Placita jewelry store in downtown Los Angeles, the clock was acquired by Aztec Jewelry owner Ramon Madrueno for his T.J. shop in 1943.

20 / **Caesar's Hotel** (1930)
Avenida Revolucion and Calle Quinta
A house was remodeled as a hotel by Cesar Cardini—whose Italian chef (Libio Cardini) created the popular salad dressing that bears Cesar's name. In its heyday, the hotel was visited by many famous bullfighters, who had rooms named for them: Joselito Huerta, Manuel Capetillo, Eloy Cavazos, and Manuel Rodriguez ("Manolete").

21 / **Electrical Company Building** (1934)
One-story Art Deco building, featuring a decorative lightening bolt.

22 / **Francis Hotel** (1906, moved here in 1920)
Calle Segunda (Second Street) and Avenida Revolucion
This Spanish Colonial/Neoclassical hotel was built north of the border in Imperial Beach, moved to Tijuana in 1920, and shifted to its current site north of Second Street in 1928. It was one of city's first two-story buildings.

23 / **The Border Gate Building** (1960s)
Near the border
The current design—following a shell form that features several vaults—replaced the original gate from the 1930s. Curio shops and federal offices occupy the building.

24 / **Train Station** (c. 1919)
Built by John D. Spreckels as part of the Tijuana-Tecate line of his San Diego and Arizona Railroad, the depot utilizes a modest bungalow style common to railroad depots of the era.

25 / **Medical Specialties, IMSS** (2002)
Via Rapida Poniente #3A, Canal de Tijuana
DEPARTMENT OF PROJECTS/IMSS.

26 / Agua Caliente Bungalows (1930s)

Built in Craftsman, Mission, and Mediterranean styles, these 52 cottages—originally for casino visitors—are now occupied by retired instructors from Lazaro Cardenas high school.

27 / Lazaro Cardenas High School (1940s)
Agua Caliente School Center

This modernist/Art Deco building was added when the high school opened, after the former Agua Caliente casino site had been acquired by the government in 1937 for educational use.

28 / Agua Caliente Racetrack (1929)
Boulevard Agua Caliente, near the bullring

This track is the successor to the original, which opened in 1916 near the border.

Other Places of Interest

Carl's Jr. Restaurante (2001)
Calle Tecnologico and Parque Industrial
OCTAVIO SERRANO AUTRIQUE

Perhaps liberated by the city's freer attitudes toward colors, the corporate chain built a drive-through that is much more exciting than its U.S. outlets.

Plaza Andrea (2001)
Blvd. Las Americas #3706, Col. 20 de Noviembre
FIDEL PEREZ SAUCEDO

Contemporary retail mall, part of the city's revitalization effort.

Conjunto Real Del Mar (1980)
Km 19.5 Carretera Escenica Tijuana-Ensenada
JOSE LUIS MARTINEZ BLANCO

Alvaro Obregon School/Tijuana House of Culture (1930)
Colonia Alta Mira, at the edge of downtown
GUERRERO

This two-story red brick elementary school was modeled after a school in Yuma, Arizona. It became home to TJ's Casa de la Cultura in 1977.

SAN DIEGO ARCHITECTUAL FAMILY TREE

Irving Gill Branch

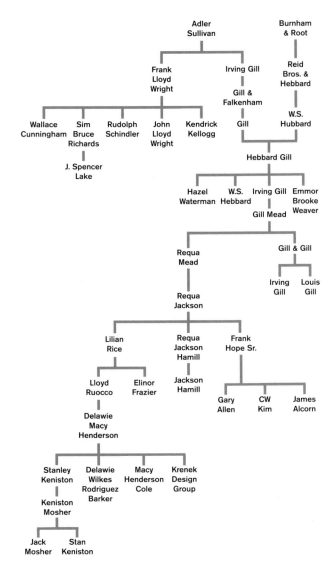

William Wheeler Branch

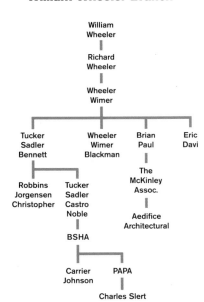

Johnson/Mosher Drew Branches

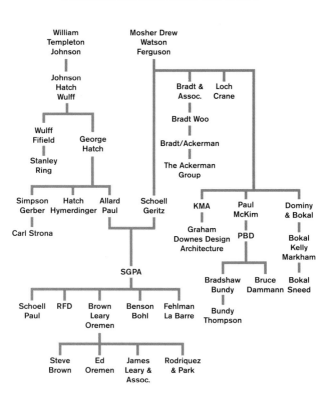

- William Templeton Johnson
  - Johnson Hatch Wulff
    - Wulff Fifield
      - Stanley Ring
        - Simpson Gerber
          - Carl Strona
    - George Hatch
      - Hatch Hymerdinger
      - Allard Paul

- Mosher Drew Watson Ferguson
  - Bradt & Assoc.
    - Bradt Woo
      - Bradt/Ackerman
        - The Ackerman Group
  - Loch Crane
  - Schoell Geritz
  - KMA
    - Graham Downes Design Architecture
  - Paul McKim
    - PBD
      - Bradshaw Bundy
        - Bundy Thompson
      - Bruce Dammann
  - Dominy & Bokal
    - Bokal Kelly Markham
    - Bokal Sneed

- SGPA
  - Schoell Paul
  - RFD
  - Brown Leary Oremen
    - Steve Brown
    - Ed Oremen
    - James Leary & Assoc.
    - Rodriquez & Park
  - Benson Bohl
  - Fehlman La Barre

Deems Martin Branch

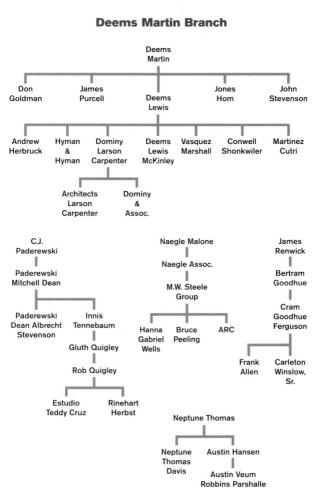

- Deems Martin
  - Don Goldman
  - James Purcell
  - Deems Lewis
    - Andrew Herbruck
    - Hyman & Hyman
    - Dominy Larson Carpenter
      - Architects Larson Carpenter
      - Dominy & Assoc.
    - Deems Lewis McKinley
    - Vasquez Marshall
    - Conwell Shonkwiler
    - Martinez Cutri
  - Jones Hom
  - John Stevenson

- C.J. Paderewski
  - Paderewski Mitchell Dean
    - Paderewski Dean Albrecht Stevenson
    - Innis Tennebaum
      - Gluth Quigley
        - Rob Quigley
          - Estudio Teddy Cruz
          - Rinehart Herbst

- Naegle Malone
  - Naegle Assoc.
    - M.W. Steele Group
      - Hanna Gabriel Wells
      - Bruce Peeling
      - ARC

- James Renwick
  - Bertram Goodhue
    - Cram Goodhue Ferguson
      - Frank Allen
      - Carleton Winslow, Sr.

- Neptune Thomas
  - Neptune Thomas Davis
  - Austin Hansen
    - Austin Veum Robbins Parshalle

DOWNTOWN TRANSIT MAP

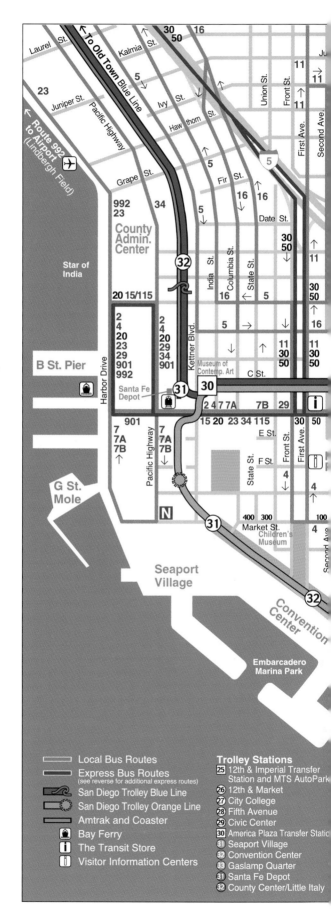

Local Bus Routes

Express Bus Routes
(see reverse for additional express routes)

San Diego Trolley Blue Line

San Diego Trolley Orange Line

Amtrak and Coaster

Bay Ferry

The Transit Store

Visitor Information Centers

Trolley Stations

25 12th & Imperial Transfer
   Station and MTS AutoPark
26 12th & Market
27 City College
28 Fifth Avenue
29 Civic Center
30 America Plaza Transfer Station
31 Seaport Village
32 Convention Center
33 Gaslamp Quarter
31 Santa Fe Depot
32 County Center/Little Italy

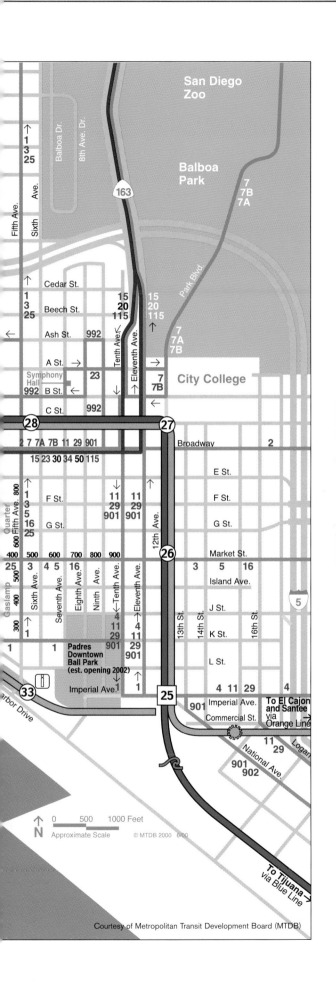

REGIONAL TRANSIT MAP

Solana Beach

Fairbanks Ranch

Ran
Peñ

Del Mar

Carmel
Valley

Sorrento
Valley

Mira
Mesa

University
City

La Jolla

Clairemont

Pacific
Beach

Serra
Mesa

Mission
Beach

Mission
Bay

North
Park

Ocean
Beach

San Diego
Bay

Coronado

Point
Loma

Im
Be

Transportation:

This map provides a
general overview of public
transportation in San Diego.
For a more detailed map
please call 1-800-COMMUTE
or visit www.sdcommute.com

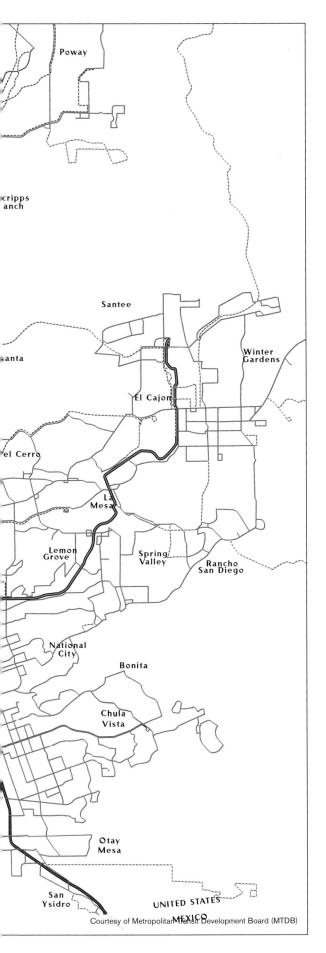

Poway

cripps
anch

Santee

santa

Winter
Gardens

El Cajon

el Cerro

La
Mesa

Lemon
Grove

Spring
Valley

Rancho
San Diego

National
City

Bonita

Chula
Vista

Otay
Mesa

San
Ysidro

UNITED STATES

MEXICO

Courtesy of Metropolitan Transit Development Board (MTDB)

SPONSORS

Corinthian ($15,000)

Centre City Development Corporation

Ionic ($10,000)

Architects Delawie Wilkes Rodriugues Barker

Carrier Johnson Architects

Highland Partnership

HMC Group

McGraw-Hill Construction

Reno Contracting

Doric ($5,000+)

Metropolitan Transportation Development Board

Architects Larson Carpenter

Tuscan ($2,500)

Tucker Sadler Noble Castro

Mosher Drew Watson Ferguson

GUIDEBOOK PROJECT TEAM

Photography Team

Neil Larson, AIA Chair

Zachary Adams

Tom Anglewicz, AIA

Gerardo Arroyo

J. Paulino Caballero

Mike Campos

Kevin Carpenter

Todd Carpenter

Wallace Cunningham

Alex Doherty

Erin Gettis, Assoc. AIA

John Henderson, FAIA

Romero Hernandez

Anne Hewitt and
David Garrison

Paul Joelson, AIA

Bethany Johnson,
Assoc. AIA

Mario Lara

Jeanne McCallum, AIA

Gregory Mellberg, AIA

Ben Meza, AIA

Robert Mosher, FAIA

Eric Naslund, AIA

Patrick O'Donnell,
Assoc. AIA

Hector Reyes, AIA

Phillip Scholtz Rittermann

San Diego Historical Society
Photograph Collection

Ernesto Santos, Assoc. AIA

Diana Scheffler

Jerry Shonkwiler, AIA

James Skovmand:
San Diego Union-Tribune

Tom Stepat

Dirk Sutro

El Colegio de Arquitectos
de Tijuana

University of California
San Diego

Xan Waldron

Brian Washburn

Reviewing Team

Harold Sadler FAIA

John Henderson FAIA

Michael Stepner FAIA

Members of SOHO

Catharine Herbst. AIA

Dr. Ray Brandeis

Research Team

John Henderson, FAIA

Brian Washburn

Monique Parsons

Christine Alexander

Students of The New School
of Architecture

Maria E. Castillo Curry

Mapping Team

Kevin Carpenter,
AIA Assoc. Chair

Todd Carpenter

Kurt Wittkow

Omneya Salem

Ernesto Santos, Assoc. AIA

Monica Lopez

George Campos

ACKNOWLEDGEMENTS

Transit Maps

Courtesy of
Metropolitan Transit
Development Board (MTDB)

Distribution

Distributed by
Sunbelt Publications

Printing

Printed by Rush Press

INDEX

INDEX

INDEX